GETTING THROUGH TO YOU

Communication is necessary because *communion* is rare

Truth

*The Truth may set us free
But if you try to slaughter me with truth
Then you, and I, and it
Will all remain . . . in chains!*

I truly believe that most of the pain, problems, ugliness in life – even wars – are the result of someone's low self-esteem, which he can't even talk straight about! I have met so many people who have never shared their insides – probably because they don't know how to, or they are scared to.

Virginia Satir

GETTING THROUGH TO YOU

Success and Failure in Communicating
. . . at home
. . . at work
. . . with friends

Alex Howard

Gateway Books, Bath

First published in 1991
by GATEWAY BOOKS
The Hollies, Wellow,
Bath, BA2 8QJ

© 1991 Alex Howard.

Cover cartoon by David Austin

Set in Palatino by Character Graphics, Taunton.

Printed and bound by
Billings of Worcester.

British Library Cataloguing in Publication Data:

Howard, Alex
    Getting through to you: success and failure in communicating
    1. Communication skills
I. Title
302.2

ISBN 0-946551-60-X

Contents

Acknowledgements

The author would like to thank the following for permission to reproduce extracts from copyright material:

Jonathan Cape Ltd. and Roger McGough for his poem 'You and I'; Random Century Group for Ram Dass and Paul Gorman's *How Can I Help?*; Souvenir Press Ltd. for Virginia Satir's *Peoplemaking*; Routledge, for Erich Fromm's *The Sane Society;* David Brandon for *Zen in the Art of Helping* (now available in Penguin); Andre Deutsch Ltd. for *The Selling of the President,* by Joe McGinniss; Abacus Press, for Christopher Lasch's *The Culture of Narcissism*; Unwin Hyman Ltd. for Erich Fromm's *The Art of Loving*; BBC Books, for Anthony Clare & Sally Thompson's *Let's Talk about ME* & for Jonathan Lynn and Anthony Jay's *Yes Minister* Vol. 2; Random Century for Fisher & Ury's *Getting to Yes*.

1. Introduction

You and I

I explain quietly. You
hear me shouting. You
try a new tack. I
feel old wounds reopen.

You see both sides. I
see your blinkers. I
am placatory. You
sense a new selfishness.

I am a dove. You
recognise the hawk. You
offer an olive branch. I
feel the thorns.

You bleed. I
see crocodile tears. I
withdraw. You
reel from the impact.

Roger McGough

Why are you reading this book? What has prompted you to open
these pages? Perhaps you are looking for some answers, ideas or
hints in relation to problems you have in communicating with
others? We all feel frustrated at times in our efforts to 'get through';
perhaps you are very clear indeed about the problems you have
in communicating and the people with whom you have the most

difficulty? Alternatively, you may feel uneasy yet uncertain about what the problems are. If so, the questions at the end of this chapter may help you to begin to focus on particular difficulties in communicating that may be bothering you.

So often and so easily, we can feel out of touch with other people whom we would dearly love to know and be known by. There may be (many) times when close friends, particularly of the opposite sex, seem incomprehensible and impossible in the extreme. We can even feel out of touch with *ourselves*; and cover up our own internal emptiness with distractions, masks and superficialities of many kinds!

This book, which is the product of courses I have taught on communication skills over many years, will explore some of the mundane and profound ways in which we fail to communicate at home, at work and with friends. We shall also consider what small steps we might take to 'get through' more effectively to others and to avoid misunderstanding and self-defeating behaviour. All this will, I hope, be of practical use and general interest to a wide variety of readers.

Of course, let's face it, we don't always want to get through to others! We may want (and need?) to defend ourselves; to disguise our intentions; to cover up our feelings; to deceive others about our real thoughts. We may want to prevent people from seeing us as we really are and from reaching into us too deeply. We may prefer to practise our style and polish our image rather than come to terms with our reality. We may want to get away from others or, at least, control the degree of contact there may be between us.

Moreover, even when we may think that we are trying to be honest and straight, this may not necessarily be the case. After all, we not only deceive other people from time to time; we also practise *self*-deception! We deceive ourselves about our real intentions; we cover up our feelings from ourselves; we rationalise – in private as well as in front of others; we run away from ourselves just as much, perhaps, as we run away from other people! We easily imagine that our 'act' is the truth, the whole truth and nothing but the truth about who we are. Furthermore, we easily forget that we can only get through consciously to others to the extent that we have managed to get through conscientiously to ourselves! We are often quite unaware of our own thoughts, feelings and behaviour; never mind other people's; and as a consequence, we may deliberately communicate far less than we pretend, while inadvertently revealing (to the skilled observer) far more than we may intend.

All these patterns are commonplace enough, and we shall spend some time in examining when, and how far, such deceptions and defences are necessary and/or counter-productive.

Commonly enough, we may feel too distanced from people we would love to get close to. But, let's not forget, there are also occasions when we feel too close to people whom we would like (and may need), to get away from! In some situations it's not so much that we feel isolated from others; rather, we may feel enmeshed with and/or overwhelmed by them. In other words, we would like to get away from others to some extent; to defend ourselves against what seems like their intrusiveness.

It is obvious to everyone that people cannot 'meet' if they are 'too far apart' from each other. Less obvious, but equally important, we cannot really meet if we are too enmeshed with each other. Thus, for example, I cannot meet you unless I have a sense of myself and of my own integrity that exists separately from you and your interests. Or, to put it another way, I cannot meet you unless I have a reasonable awareness of the boundaries that exist between us. You and I have to have a sense of 'me' and 'mine' and of 'you' and 'yours' before we can make contact with each other and formulate any notions of 'us' and 'ours'.

Finally let us remember that just because people have got together with each other and are talking, it does not necessarily follow that they actually want to communicate with each other! They may wish to observe each other but reveal nothing about themselves. They may wish to get hold of information without actually giving anything away. They may wish to steal some sort of advantage over each other rather than offer anything.

Communication may not always be the underlying motive, or intention, when groups of people gather together. It may be that, more fundamentally, they are in competition or in covert or overt conflict with each other. Truth is the first casualty in all warfare, and this is just as valid in relation to psychological struggles as it is in overtly military situations! In such circumstances, propaganda may be much more at the heart of the matter than honest communication. Each player in the competitive game may well want to get across to others; but he will not be struggling to present himself; rather it will be an 'image' or 'ploy' or 'style' that he will be wanting to get over.

We are often told that we have entered a new era of information technology (or 'I.T.' as the mania for abbreviated jargon would have it!). More and more messages are being sent ever more rapidly via telephone, telex, fax, television, satellite, cable, electronic mail, high speed rail, word processing, computerised databases and mailing lists; ever-cheaper desk-top publishing systems and ever-larger international media conglomerates!

'Our' specialists in advertising and public relations* are becoming ever more skilled and sophisticated in presenting a slick and enticing message. Indeed more cash, energy and talent is employed in TV advertising than on the programmes themselves. This has been the case in the U.S.A. for many years; but it is now true for TV throughout Europe and the rest of the 'developed' world.

In other words, there is a huge and ever growing communications industry. Everyone wants to communicate better; and almost everyone watches the various lifestyle advertisements that indicate how they can best present themselves according to their chosen image. In the process, of course, everyone discovers the products and services they need to buy this year in order to display, service and support their own particular style; whether this be country biscuits for the lovable old pensioner or sexy drinks for the fun-loving bachelor or new woman.

There is nothing intrinsically wrong in wanting to present an image or style to others. Indeed, the image we communicate will to some extent be a reflection of our personality and a means of putting ourselves across to the world. Everything we wear, use and choose says something about the sort of person we are, as well as having more utilitarian uses. And there is nothing new about any of this except that, possibly there is nowadays a greater variety of lifestyles from which to choose. (This, though, is highly debatable!)

The surface can reveal something about what lies underneath; but the danger is that, in a world that deals so much in surfaces and first impressions, we may end up in a situation where we are all surface and no depth. We may become, perhaps we have already become, hollow men (and women); stylish in our presentation, but barren underneath. It is silly to pretend that appearances are not important; but the public relations and advertising industries tend to deal with nothing more than appearances and fail to see anything else. The danger, then, is that our images become the only reality of any importance, and credibility becomes more significant than underlying truth. We then make the mistake of believing that to find ourselves we need do no more than check our overall appearance in the mirror. We lose our heart and soul and instead give ourselves over, at home, at work and with friends, to high-gloss hype or some other kind of superficial veneer.

* Don't forget, though, that advertising and P.R. specialists are 'yours' – if and only if you can afford to hire such people! In other words, 'yours' if you happen to run a government department or large commercial organisation!

Of course, advertisers may protest strenuously that this is not the case. They will argue that you cannot, and should not, deal in lies and deception; and that images cannot be manufactured for people, products or services unless the presentation reflects an underlying reality. In other words, says the ad-man, you have to find the underlying truth of what you are presenting to people if your message is to be effective. You cannot simply present any message you like.

This may well be so, but it is, nonetheless, a gross deception (or self-deception). Every civilised country has legislation that is supposed to prevent advertisers and image makers from telling out-and-out lies. Every advertisement in the U.K., for example, is supposed to be 'legal, decent and honest'. But the real underlying truth of the matter is that image makers do not *need* to lie overtly since they can do all they want by innuendo, and by bending or burnishing the truth, or telling only part of it. No advertiser actually says, "Buy this product and you will become a part of the lifestyle we are so seductively presenting to you". All he has to do is present the product with the desirable lifestyle where everyone seems to be living happily ever after. The product and our dream then become associated in our minds and we buy it, hoping against all hope that this will take us one step closer to our own particular nirvana (or arcadia).

What, you may by now be asking, has all this got to do with communication in our own day-to-day lives? Don't we all know that advertising, public relations and most of the media are concerned with profits, deception and stylish appearances rather than authentic communication? Don't we all realise that advertisements provide us with entertainment, amusement, a harmless bit of fun and a chance to appreciate the sheer virtuosity and creativity that is so often involved? Don't we all know that they shouldn't be taken seriously and that they don't actually influence what we do and how we present ourselves?

If they are so harmless then why do sober businessmen and politicians spend ever more time and money on employing such communication specialists? Why is it that most discoveries made by psychologists are harnessed for profit rather than for honest communication? How can we pretend that advertising is harmless fun when, for example, most children spend more time watching television than they do at school, and far more time sitting passively in front of this 'means of communication' than they do with family or friends?

Advertisers and other professional communicators undoubtedly want to 'get through' to their audiences; and they will stay in business only for as long as they can show that they are succeeding. But the 'getting through' that is involved is most likely to be the communication of an image, a facade, an illusion, rather than a reality. There *is* a difference, although we are in danger of forgetting this – drenched as we are in 'presentation' and 'hype'! Thus it is that the sophisticated communicator can become so adept at presenting an appearance that (s)he forgets who (s)he really is!

In a society of enchantments, distractions and seduction, we may lose our soul!

Dreaming (I)

We have a Dream . . .
And the next instalment will appear shortly.

There's a Heaven on Earth . . .
And it's slickly packaged.

Hope Springs Eternal . . .
And Hype rides on its back.

See the Universe in a Grain of Sand . . .
And Cornflakes in the Sunshine,

And Black Magic in a Lover's Face,
And Levi 501s on a Desert Trail.

Dreaming (II)

We have a Dream . . .

And that's all we have
And it's under investigation
And it's advertised everywhere.

We are, all of us, Unique
And there's something waiting, especially for You . . .
At your local Hype r *market.*

We all want to be loved
And if you buy the branded product
You will be as One.

There is a crock of Gold
At the end of the Rainbow
. . . And it's available on Credit.

They all lived happily ever after
Because they had Style
. . . On Sale Everywhere.

There is a Heaven on Earth
And it's in Marbella, at a private pool,
In the sun, with Martinis, and the owner drives an Audi.

It seems to me to be a tragic waste that so much genuine talent and creativity is presently employed cleverly and wittily to inform us, for example, which brand of coffee is chic or 'honest-to-good-ness-wholesome'. Just consider what could be done if such skills were employed to galvanise us into doing something genuinely worthwhile and fulfilling!

If the Public Relations industry addressed itself to real human and social needs rather than serving the interests of those who already have too much power, then just imagine what sort of world could be created. Moreover, what is the effect on children who learn, from a very early age, that adults spend so much of their time building slick, elaborate and expensive fantasy stories about boxes of chocolates, soap-powder and other consumer goods?* How, too, should we feel when we explain to our children that all these grown-ups who are trying to persuade us to buy products, are not doing so because they genuinely believe in them, but merely because they were paid to do so? What is a child to make of the fact that so many people can be paid to say and do one thing, even though they might really believe something else altogether? With such a discovery, what becomes of the real value of an adult's word, if it can be bought for a price?

Finally, what is the effect on our ability to communicate genuinely with others if we spend so much of our time trying to be a carbon-copy of the hero in the *Levi 501* advertisement?

Needless to say, I hope that I will be able to 'get through to you' in these pages. I will attempt to avoid all jargon and technical terms since I do not think it is helpful for writers to bamboozle their readers with displays of all the books they've read, the pseudo-professional language they have mastered and the training they have undergone. I will not be assuming that you have ever read anything about the psychology of communication, or that you have any specialist knowledge. But neither do I wish to

---

* In the U.K. twice as much is spent on advertising as on the entire education system – schools, colleges and universities!

assume that you will be content with a superficial approach to the subject.

I hope, and think, that it is possible to explore this topic in simple language without being simplistic in approach. Indeed, I want to move very deeply into some of the dilemmas and mysteries of human communication as well as looking at helpful hints and practical skills in day-to-day life. Sometimes, sophistication is used to cover up an underlying banality; while a simplicity of approach can help us get to grips with the profundities of communication. My intention is to stay with simple language, yet attempt a complex and deeply probing journey. You will have to judge for yourself whether, and how far, I successfully 'get through to you'.

Questions:

The following questions and exercises are designed to help you actively to explore aspects of 'getting through' in your own life. There is a great deal of material in these pages and at the end of every chapter. If you made a serious attempt to explore each question and try out every exercise then you would be kept busy for a very long time. You would also learn far more than if you simply read the book. Clearly, you must use your own judgement as to which questions and exercises are of particular use to you.

1. Who would you like to get through to more effectively?

2. What do you imagine it would be like if you could get through to this (these) person(s)?

3. Imagine a conversation with this person where you are both really getting through to each other. What would you be saying and doing? What would (s)he be saying and doing? You can make this imaginary dialogue come alive by imagining that this person is in a real empty chair before you. 'Be' this person by sitting in his chair and see what he has to say! Switch between chairs as appropriate.

4. How far are these fantasies realistic? How far are they just fanciful dreams or perfectionistic ideals? What would happen if you shared your fantasies with the person(s) in question? Do they have similar fantasies?

5. What problems do you tend to have in getting through to other people?

6. What difficulties do you think other people have in getting through to you? Is that because of them? or you? or both of you?

7. What are your strengths and weaknesses as a communicator? What skills do you possess, or lack?

8. How do other people assess your skills as a communicator?

9. What sort of impression do you imagine you make on others when they first meet you?

10. What kinds of people respond favourably to you?

11. Who responds unfavourably?

12. Why?

13. Is there anything you want to do about this?

14. What can you do about it?

Exercises:

'First impressions':

If you ever have (or make) the opportunity, the following exercises can teach you a great deal. As you will see, they cannot be done on your own. In each case, be aware of what you are, and are not, willing to share with others and why. Clearly there must be no pressure on people to reveal to others what they don't wish to reveal or what seems inappropriate to reveal. However, it is always worth asking: Are you protecting yourself? The other person? Both?

1. With a partner, or in a small group, take it in turns to complete the following sentences:
   "My first impressions of you are . . ."
   "I notice . . ."
   "I imagine . . ."

2. Share your views of the following: (to the extent that this seems appropriate and useful).
   "How I put myself over; what I reveal, what I hide".

   Be aware, in this and other exercises, of what you are not willing to share with others and why. Trust yourself that you can make adequate judgements about what you will and won't reveal. Don't be too harsh on yourself about this – or too complacent!

3. Be with, or imagine, a particular individual. Try saying to yourself, or out loud: *"If you really knew me . . ."* and see how you complete this sentence.

4. Take it in turns to ask ten questions of the other person. They can pass if they choose.
   What will you ask? How will you decide?

Find out how far your own impressions are in line with the other person's self-image.

And how far is *your* self-image the same as the impression you have just made on your partner? In other words, do other people see you in the way you see yourself?

To communicate at all we have to take *some* risk (of getting hurt; or hurting others; or being misunderstood). But if, on balance, you don't think it will be helpful to share an observation – don't share it!

Be aware of how you feel about these exercises.

Did the observations seem accurate? Inaccurate? Who spoke the most? How did it feel to talk about all this with other people? How did the group form?

These exercises can be completed between people who know each other well or between strangers. (In the latter case you might well prefer to attempt them only where there is an experienced group leader present who you trust!)

If you try these exercises with people you know well, remember that it is almost impossible to look at familiar faces as though they belonged to unknown strangers. We carry with us all our previous expectations, prejudices, pleasures, hurts and judgements concerning the people we know, and these, needless to say, colour what we see before us and how we interpret it!

Likewise, the person we know will present himself to us in a way that is influenced by all his previous experiences of us. (S)he will, for example, be actively trying to figure out our intentions; and the conclusions (s)he draws (in a fraction of a second) will affect how (s)he puts herself across.

2. Getting the better of You!

Coupled Together

We are
a military disaster under one roof
preying mantis versus the scorpion
blooded and bloody-minded
thin-skinned, torn and wretched
Spoilt brats crying for attention

We are
Like a pair of jousting sheep
Soggy with tears and tissues of issues
Entrenched behind our artillery
we fire away:
Blame! blame! blame! blame!
"Gotcha!" "Missed" ("It didn't hurt anyway"!)

We are
Drizzling all over each other
A deadly ambush at the next tricky pass
powder kegs in search of a spark
An 'in depth exposé' of each other
Thera-pistols at each other's heads.

We are
tired of all this
Searching for a peace formula
Researching a Starwars defence system
In our endless Psy-War.
Trying to save the slag heap of our mountainous face.
Slogging on, slugging it out,
Slagging each other off;

Looking for a better way.

In the Middle Ages, people who could afford to, lived in castles with thick walls, turrets and entrances from the top of which they could pour boiling oil on the heads of unwanted visitors. They owned lances, swords and battle-axes; and in troubled times they wore heavy armour.

Nowadays, governments that can afford to, own tanks with powerful artillery and armour; submarines that can lurk in murky chasms; aircraft that can duck and weave; and tens of thousands of nuclear warheads. Some of the less well-off make do, instead, with stock-piles of poisonous gas and other chemical weapons.

Most of us, we believe, are more civilised. It's the politicians, admirals, generals and the leadership generally, who let the rest of us down – innocents as we are! We do not go around with arms and armour, although many in the U.S.A. continue in the belief that they have an inalienable right and duty to carry their own personal hand-gun.

I want to suggest, however, that most of us, for much of the time, are more or less 'on our guard'. We, each and every one of us, have:
- our own 'Departments of Defence';
- our own propaganda machines;
- our own armaments and armour;
- our own abilities to manoeuvre and hide;
- our own specialist 'guerrilla units';
- our own 'dirty tricks' departments;
- our own censors, 'inquisitors' and public-relations specialists;
- our own secret weapons: delayed-action time-bombs, poisons, booby-traps, bull-dozers, battering rams and various instruments of torture.

Such specialisms, skills and abilities may be invisible in that they exist as psychological capacities rather than tangible military hardware; but they are none the less real for that! Of course, we do not need to use our psychological weapons of war all the time; but they are on permanent stand-by; and we can activate them to a state of full readiness in a split second. Also, just as nations tend to hide away their more sleazy and less savoury underside, so we, too, deny to ourselves and others that we can and do, strike out at the people around us.

A study of history shows that every nation that ever went to war always did so in the belief that God was on its side. There is no Department of Attack in any country; everybody is defending himself against attacks, threats and injustices from elsewhere. Every soldier has always been told that he is fighting for honour,

glory and virtue of one sort or another; for duty to God, Justice or
the correction of previous injustices.

No one has ever gone to war:

- for the sheer gory hell of it;
- or out of foolish pride, paranoia or prejudice;
- or out of boredom or arrogance;
- or in order to avoid internal dissent;
- or in order to rape and pillage and generally exploit other
  people.

Even when the aggression and oppression is particularly severe,
the aggressor/oppressor always has an alibi or, more grandly, a
view of his 'historical destiny' or 'duty' that justifies his behaviour:

- Empires were founded in order to educate and civilise the na-
  tives;
- Genocide was committed, because "these people are vermin"; or;
- . . . because "it is the only way their souls can be saved"; or;
- . . . because "they are a threat to civilisation/God/Socialism/the
  Fatherland/democracy as we know it".

I say all this because I think there are important parallels between
nations in conflict and individuals who are trying to steal an advantage over each other. The basic rule, generally, is that 'We' (whoever
we may be) are 'Good' and 'Right'; whereas our opponent (sometimes, even, our competitor) is 'Bad' and 'Wrong'. Therefore, whatever takes place that is nasty, unsavoury and malicious – IT IS NOT
OUR FAULT!

Even if I may suspect somewhere deep down that I am less than
honourable, my own propaganda department will work overtime
to come up with a rationalisation and 'world view' that puts me
in the most favourable light possible – at the expense, of course,
of my opponent. Consequently, so much of what passes for the
'history' that a nation or individual writes for itself is just a heap
of rationalisation and self-deception!

It is most important to remember this when we consider the
matter of 'getting through' to others. We all want to 'get through',
but the propagandist wants to get through by convincing others
with his propaganda; the competitor wants to get through by beat-
ing the competition; and the protagonist wants to get through by
defeating his opponents. So often, therefore, 'getting through'
amounts to little more than winning over the people around us
into seeing that we are basically good and right, and that they can
be so too, provided that they agree with us. Otherwise they are

bad and wrong, and their stubbornness is revealed to us by their ignorant refusal to see things the right way (i.e. our way).

We can all very easily observe such competitiveness and intrusiveness in others; and we have all felt the need to resist what we consider to be the invasive attempts of friends, colleagues and family to 'get through' to us. It's much harder, of course, for each of us to admit that, quite often, what we pretend is an honest attempt to communicate is in fact a dishonest manoeuvre to get others to give in to our own prejudices, preferences and preoccupations!

Each side can so easily take a position that they are anxious to communicate to the other. You must hear me out when I tell you my position, and you must then take the same position as me. Each of us clings to our position as though it was some treasured fortress that we must hang on to at all costs. Each of us, as it were, stands astride our 'fortress' and hoists our flag proudly for all to see. Little do we realise that we are not in fact 'on the battlements' of our position; we are in effect 'in the deepest dungeon' of our fortress. For our position, so often, captures and enslaves us; leaving us with no chance of vision or action. We each go on and on trying to tell everyone about our 'position' on this that and everything else; little do we realise that our 'position' frequently prevents us from communicating about anything.

This book is about communication, but there are many occasions when you would do well to ask yourself:

Do I want to communicate with this person or do I, first and foremost, want to control him/her?

If you are honest, you may well conclude that you are often more interested in control than in communication. On such occasions, honest communication may very well be abandoned or restricted; particularly if you fear that such honesty might put you at a tactical disadvantage. A dishonest approach may seem to be the most likely way of achieving the control you seek. You will be in the business of propaganda rather than authenticity, and your messages are likely to become ever more devious and manipulative when your opponent seems to be getting near to revealing the truth!

We are often closed and defensive with each other to a greater or lesser degree and it is very easy to slide, on a vicious spiral, ever deeper into defensiveness and conflict. In crude terms, the pattern is as follows:

- We feel insecure and threatened.
- We fail to notice that the 'other side' feels the same.

- We each deny our own home-grown insecurity, and instead blame our feelings on the action of others.

- Consequently, we label others as a threat; since it is much more congenial to accuse them of being threatening and aggressive than to face the fact that we may be neurotic and paranoid.

- We each put up a tough, competent, confident exterior in order to avoid our underlying fear. The other side does the same. Both sides find this threatening.

- If the other side differs from us in appearance, life-style, values and beliefs, then we find the differences that we don't understand even more threatening.

- If our opponents have different positions from ourselves about important issues we may very well find these differences threatening to our own positions.

- We look for subtle ways of undermining the confidence and self-esteem of the other side because we (mistakenly) believe that this will secure our own position. They do the same to us. This really is threatening to each side.

- We each slip into more overtly aggressive, undermining and defensive styles of behaviour.

- Each side is now feeling increasingly threatened, fearful and undermined by the manoeuverings of the other. We each slip ever more rapidly into the Pit of Misunderstanding.

At each stage we fail to look more deeply into our own motives and behaviour, and we fail to empathise with the perceptions of others. Moreover, we look only at our short term costs and benefits and, as a result, we fail to see what may be the long term costs of conflict.

As a result of all this, unrealistic feelings of insecurity within ourselves are converted, via our self-defeating behaviour, into a genuinely dangerous and insecure situation. We blame others for aggressive behaviour, yet our consequently defensive actions create the very aggression we feared. We rarely learn from this experience, however, since we conclude that we were obviously 'right all along' to accuse the other side of being a threat. Over and over again, we attempt to increase our security at the expense of the other side, since we continue to make the mistake of believing that we will be more secure if the other side is less secure. Over and over again, the other side draws the same conclusion, and so we all end up armed to the teeth and feeling less secure than ever!

When the winning of a conflict is seen as more important than successful communication, there are a number of possible outcomes:

1.   'Control versus Control':

The most obvious outcome is where each side refuses to back down and the power struggle just goes on and on. In this scenario each side tends to consider that the other is 'bad and wrong' and thus they do whatever they can think of to get the opposition to 'accept their guilt' and feel appropriately apologetic and compliant.

There is a variety of ways of undermining the security and self-esteem of your 'opponent':

- You can be directly (or covertly) threatening. Your partner can then be made to feel anxious and insecure unless and until (s)he fits in with what you want.

- You can directly (or more subtly) ridicule him so that he feels stupid and uneasy for as long as he holds out against your position.

- You can take a moral (or pseudo-moral) approach and thus assert or imply that unless others agree with you they are morally reprehensible in some way. It is amazing how, when it suits our own interests, we can increase the number of moral commandments that must be applied to other people until they run into thousands. *"You should . . . You must . . . You ought to . . .* gets extended to include not just the old virtues and vices, but many more exact and specific details. For example; *"You should . . .*
  . . . mend my shirt
  . . . come out with me this evening
  . . . do my aunt a favour this afternoon
  . . . listen to me whenever I want someone to talk to
  . . . keep your upsetting feelings to yourself
  . . . let me get my feelings out
  . . . re-arrange your priorities when I want you to." etc. etc.

All of these are personal preferences rather than absolute moral imperatives, but many of us are quite good at pretending that our own particular desires are ordained by cosmic laws that must be obeyed at all costs; and we will have a wide array of devices to get others to feel anxious, stupid and guilty for as long as they dare to hold out against us. Furthermore, such is our guile, we may be very skilled at operating these tricks in a subtle way that can be extremely difficult for others to track down. If and when our manoeuvres are ever uncovered we will, of course, be amazed and appalled that anyone could ever suggest that we are capable of such dastardly action and we will quickly invent new cover and rationalisations. Like foxes, we will dig ever deeper below the surface of other people's awareness of what we are doing, for as long as they continue to try to flush us out!

We can all tolerate, and even enjoy, a certain amount of conflict, of course; and we all employ a variety of dirty tricks from time to time when we feel threatened and embattled. However, small-scale conflicts can escalate steadily upwards into large-scale wars; until we find ourselves arguing with the other person about more and more (trivial and not so trivial) issues. Of course, if we are sufficiently armoured, then the direct (and snide) attacks of our opponent will bounce off us relatively easily. Alternatively we will learn to dodge, weave and parry some of the more offensive remarks and non-verbal stratagems insinuated upon us.

Nonetheless it is painful in itself to have to be on our guard the whole time and, in the nature of things, many of the offensive comments and manoeuvres that others try out on us, which are designed to hurt, will do just that. Like good soldiers, we will try to make light of our wounds, since we will not want our opponent to see that (s)he has scored a hit. (Alternatively, we may decide manipulatively to display the injuries in order to get the wicked perpetrator to feel suitably guilty.) None of this will take the pain away however; and, with too many wounds, we are likely to become highly sensitised to, and intolerant of, even small slights and insults. Consequently, with a thin and raw skin, and accumulated resentments on both sides, we will discover that finding a peace formula is far more difficult than beginning the conflict in the first place!

Worst of all, perhaps, is a situation where two evenly matched, strong-willed, manipulative, aggressive, stubborn, punishing, defensive and proud individuals grind away at each other in an effort to get the other party to give way, fit in, shape up, see sense etc. If they are also malicious, revengeful and unforgiving, then the scene is set for a psychological version of the First World War stalemate; with 'trenches', 'mud', confusion, lies, agony and despair that can be piled up for as long as each side has the resources, will and energy to continue in the struggle! (Each side, of course, will continue to insist that they are fighting for Honour, Dignity, Freedom, Principle etc. right up to the moment, if it ever comes, when they finally admit that the whole sorry business has been destructive and futile in the extreme.)

Thoughts of War

The arrow, they thought
Would stop all wars.

The War to end all Wars
Was followed
By the Second World War.

Starwars, they told us,
Would end all war.

There is a new weapon:
With this Device
The mere thought *of the death of your enemy*
Will kill him.

Penny for your thoughts?

2.   'Control versus Compliance':

Some people go on and on and on with whatever war they are fighting; and neither side ever really gives in. Not everyone, though, is as persistent, (stubborn, pig-headed) as this. And so very commonly one or other party in the conflict will, sooner or later, give in to the other side and let them have their way.

In the short run, this may seem like a solution to the problem and, let's face it, some arguments are not worth pursuing. Sometimes, the wisest thing I can do is hold my piece, restore the peace, fit in with someone else's preference, go along with their opinion and keep my own views and preferred options to myself; if only because it is not worth the bother to make an issue out of the matter. Life, after all, is short. It is simply not worth pursuing every minor altercation, hurt or injustice, where the effort involved is out of all proportion to the issue itself.

However, if I am too much the compliant sort of character, I may be purchasing peace and quiet in the short term at the expense of my long term well-being and self-esteem. It is all very well to give way to others on some occasions; and, if I never do, that in itself tells me something about my stubbornness and underlying insecurity. But to make a habit of giving in to others, and particularly when I do so on important matters where my own integrity is on the line, leaves me feeling resentful towards myself for failing to stand up for myself; and angry with the person I have allowed to 'walk all over me'.

Such anger can grow and fester, and it will not help me if I deny that it is there or repress it or 'make the best of it'. Sooner or later I will find that I will have grown cold to the person whom I have habitually allowed to dominate me. There may still be, inside me, a hot fire of fury that I might usefully direct both towards myself and the other person for letting all this happen. Such anger, if only I knew how to deal with it, could drive me into a more constructive and fulfilling relationship. Alternatively, the anger, growing colder, may be turned in on myself and, if there seems to be no way out of my predicament, my mood may sink into depression and despair.

As for the person who has managed to get me to fit in with him/her: I shall tend to see him as a steam-roller, bully, arch-manipulator whom I shall dislike. And, if I make a habit of giving in, he will tend to look upon me as weak, unreliable, with no mind of my own, without self-respect and therefore unworthy of respect from others. I shall be looked down upon and so my efforts to fit in will, in the longer run, have got me nowhere.

The other extreme (of always getting my own way instead of endlessly giving in to others), can look much more attractive. But the attractions are only superficial. To begin with, undeniably, it can seem sweet and fulfilling to 'win' and to get what I want. But I soon take my victories for granted and, when surrounded by a compliant opposition that I have successfully managed to intimidate, I realise, somewhere inside, that others are merely going along with me and no longer revealing their true preferences and feelings. Consequently, I begin to feel isolated from others; sensing that I am not really in relationship with them. Furthermore, I feel uneasy when I suspect the degree of resentment on their part that may be smouldering beneath the surface.

Quite frequently, conflict is avoided (but unresolved) because one person habitually complies with the other. This may seem to produce a quiet and happy situation on the surface; and peaceful marriages of this sort can seem luminously happy right up to the moment that the marriage dissolves. This it may do when, for example, one or other party finds a person with whom they can negotiate more constructively. Alternatively, the partners may go away and find new people who are in fact just the same as the old model. With these they can repeat their futile patterns of dominance and submission – for as long as they can pretend to themselves that they are doing something fresh and new.

In a workplace setting, the enforced compliance of subordinates can be equally destructive. Some 'macho' managements see all workplace disagreements as trials of strength that must be won at all costs in order to prove their own virility and determination of purpose. If the management has the power, then it may indeed enforce its decisions and get its own way. But resentments will accumulate in a workforce that is always forced to comply rather than persuaded, respected and genuinely consulted. Sabotage, low productivity and a sullen atmosphere will predominate. And outright rebellion will occur as soon as market conditions change and it looks as though the workforce can gain the upper hand.

As a footnote: it is worth mentioning a particular pattern of conflict that can *seem* to involve compliance, but which doesn't. This is where one party goes through the motions of complying with the other person's wishes, but then exacts such a price and/or launches such a major (direct or devious) counter-attack that it eventually becomes clear that they have not given in at all. In other words, this is a variant of 'category 1' conflict, 'Control versus control'! One combatant lies down and 'Plays dead' as it were; his sword and shield roll away and he lies limp. But when you lean over to inspect your vanquished foe, he goes for your throat with a hidden switch-blade! And so the battle continues.

3.　'Control versus Withdrawal':

You may think that I have drawn too graphic a caricature of the nature of the conflict. That may be. Certainly we all tire of this kind of battle from time to time and yearn for peace. With luck, we will actually make peace with our combatant and find ways in which we can be rewarding, helpful and constructive with our partner(s); at home or at work. In later chapters we will be looking at ways in which we might be able to move towards such greener pastures!

However, to continue first with our grim litany of the destructive options; the third category of conflict worth avoiding is where one person, quite possibly sickened, pained and exhausted with chronic argument or slavery, withdraws, emotionally if not physically, from contact with his/her partner/friend/colleague. To begin with, quite possibly, such withdrawal will be a feint, a tactical device designed to punish the other person and get him or her to come into line.

In other words, I may very well pretend to withdraw in order to get the other person (spouse or department) to take me more seriously, accept my views and do what I want. My withdrawal-strategy, thus, will be yet another device that I employ in order to win the struggle. I will not have withdrawn at all, but will simply be trying out a new way of getting the upper hand and scoring a point.

You can often tell if withdrawal is real or merely tactical. In the latter case the person who has 'withdrawn' will be keeping an intense, though quiet, eye on the reactions of the partner in order to see if this strategy is working!

Sometimes this kind of tactical withdrawal (*"I will no longer love you, co-operate, attend, or want to be with you anymore if you behave the way you do"*), can work very successfully. The other person, faced with such punishment, may very well fall into line. However, withdrawal tactics may begin another vicious spiral. As I sulkily withdraw, you may try all the more to establish control with punishments of your own. For example, you may come after me with ever larger displays of temper, tears, moral blackmail, 'rational proof' that I am an unspeakable scoundrel; or whatever other weaponry comes to hand. This may drive me still further away. Consequently, we may each go on and on with our own particular brand of punishment; striking back with our own weapons each time we are hit by the tactics of the opposition. This takes us to the final category of conflict to be explored here:

4. 'Withdrawal versus Withdrawal':

As above, the parties may begin by only pretending to withdraw from each other. Each may punish the other person by withdrawing, and in the process looking sulkily hurt, injured, morally outraged, furious, despairing, tearful – whatever might seem likely to get the partner to comply and apologise for being so bad and *wrong*! Such conflict can become a form of siege warfare. It is a waiting game where each side holds on to see if the other party will crack first. Such an argument takes the form of long deafening silences, and subtle (or blatant) displays of misery and injuries. You may be able to cut the atmosphere with the proverbial knife. Each party vies with the other to look the more injured or abused or indifferent to the whole thing. Some 'tactical withdrawers' lie around for hours, days, weeks, months, *years* looking hurt, sullen and sulky. Others go out of their way to look busy, preoccupied, content, quite unneedful of the other person; and they may fleetingly smile in triumph if this provokes a raging outburst from the other side!

But, like all manoeuvres, we may eventually tire of such a burdensome and self-defeating method of getting attention, love or respect. And thus we may eventually move beyond the stage of merely pretending to withdraw and become genuinely indifferent to each other.

You might think that, in the case of marriages, such mutual withdrawal and mutual indifference might signal the end of the partnership. Far from it. We simply do not know how many relationships fit under the general heading of 'devitalised but stable'. There is reason to believe that the number is large. Such a situation does not have to be desperately painful or dramatic. On the contrary. People simply reduce their expectations, or discover that these never really were very large, and thus they may find that they can live quite peaceably with their 'partner'.

Nothing very bad goes on between the people concerned, simply because nothing very much goes on at all. Such partners can be like distant neighbours to each other who just happen to live under the same roof with the same front door. They may, indeed, have smooth and well-oiled working relationships concerning daily chores, routines and responsibilities – which operate to the genuine satisfaction and convenience of both (or all) the people concerned. It may very well be that, in the past, many (even most) marriages took this form; and they lasted because people had much lower expectations about their marriage, and were simply too tired and otherwise preoccupied to give the matter much thought. Nowadays, with higher expectations, people are less prepared to tolerate mutual indifference and may prefer, if they can, to get out and find someone else. A peaceful marriage like this, which imperceptive outsiders may consider to be a model for others to emulate, may crash very suddenly if one person finds genuine passion elsewhere. Alternatively it may continue for a lifetime; where neither party aspires to more, or both are consoled by a quiet satisfaction at having 'done their duty'. Worst of all, perhaps, one or both partners may be steadily deadened into quiet depression and despair.

Mutual withdrawal and indifference seem a rather tragic state of affairs in a marriage where, these days at least, we tend to expect rather more from our relationships than mere domestic convenience. In a workplace, obviously, we do not anticipate such high degrees of co-operation, intimacy and mutual respect. Nonetheless, the quality of human relationships at work not only affects how people feel about their employment, it also has an influence on how productively and efficiently an organisation is working.

I am not, of course, suggesting that an employer ought to be as concerned about the overall well-being of staff as a spouse is to his or her partner. But there is no doubt that if managers are indifferent to the quality of communication at work then output, sickness and absentee rates will all be influenced; and everyone will pay a price.

The problem of *overt* conflict ('control versus control') in commercial and industrial settings has been the subject of intense study. Less publicised, though probably far more commonplace, is the situation where staff have withdrawn from each other to a very considerable degree and are thus essentially 'ploughing their own furrow'. They may have decided, long ago, that it is useless to try to co-operate with particular colleagues, and in order to avoid what they see as inevitable conflict, they simply get on with things on their own as much as this is humanly possible. In this way the efficiency, productivity and creativity of an organisation can decline until it is locked into a conservative stance of merely continuing to do what it has always done before; in the way that it has always done it. Anything else requires too much staff contact, discussion, co-operation and mutual respect to be seen as achievable.

Some organisations die because they tear themselves to pieces with internal conflict. This, though, is comparatively rare. Much more commonly, an organisation will become ossified and die because of a failure of internal contact. People will have stopped talking to each other about anything more than well-established 'pleasantries' and procedures. And so, when changes need to be managed, the organisation will simply be incapable of adapting rapidly enough and unable to respond creatively and to adopt new methods.

There is a less extreme, and sometimes less damaging, variant of mutual withdrawal that deserves mentioning. This is where both parties withdraw from arguing about an issue, not in order to try to gain a tactical advantage, nor because they each feel so battered by the damaging effects of the conflict. Rather, they withdraw because they are both/all compliant individuals who are so afraid of disagreement that they back off whenever it looks as though they might see things differently from their partner. In some cases, people can be so compliant that it is very difficult to get them to take a decision or offer an opinion about anything – in case this is out of line with the views and preferences of others.

Such compliant people will try to get others to make all the

decisions and offer all the opinions, which will work for as long
as there are others around who are willing to take control. But
when equally compliant people get together and try to decide
anything, then you can wait and wait forever as they each of them
ask "What do you think? What would you prefer? I don't mind.
It's up to you really. I'll be happy to go along with you. I'll leave
it up to you to decide. I'm sure you know best. You're the expert
on this one." etc. The only thing that the compliant individual is
certain and decisive about is that (s)he does not wish to take the
risk of making a decision. This may be because (s)he is reluctant
to take responsibility or to risk disapproval. Such reluctance may
have arisen because (s)he has been previously traumatised by the
destructive effects of watching (or participating in) aggressive conflict where no quarter was given and no compromise made. Alternatively (s)he may just be timorous by disposition.

When two compliant people get together, the decision-making
process can be slow and tortuous in the extreme, with neither side
being willing to make a decision or even give an opinion. This can
be frustrating for both parties, and one may well blame the other
for his indecisiveness. Thus the paradox: while some compliant
individuals resent their partner for being domineering, others will
complain because the partner will not take a lead and give an
opinion. In both situations, the compliant individual will tend to
be unwilling to face up to his/her own role; and will instead be
content to blame the other person! In each case, the would-be
powerless individual will stay that way until she takes responsibility for her own behaviour. After all, it is we who allow others to
walk all over us. And it is we who decide to put off making a
decision. Such indecisiveness is itself a decision, for which we are
responsible.

5.　'Controllers' and 'Compliers':

. . . (Getting on top versus *Giving in)*

How do you fit in to the above categories?

- Do your conflicts tend to take the form 'Controller versus controller'? 'Controller versus complier?' or 'Complier versus complier'?

- Do you tend to withdraw? Do you have a growing number of
'no-go' areas which you seem unable or unwilling to discuss?

- Have you sometimes found yourself in a situation where both/all of you have withdrawn from contact because of difficulties in resolving a disagreement?

- Have you ever been in a situation where you are both/all mutually indifferent?

- In particular, are you the sort of person who insists on getting his way; such that you go on and on trying to control the outcome and 'win the battle'?

- Or do you prefer to keep the peace and therefore comply with other people in order to try to preserve 'good working relationships'?

- Quite possibly you may find that you are a 'hard' controlling sort of individual with some people while taking a 'soft' compliant approach with others. If so, why do you think this occurs?

Compliant individuals tend to approach disagreements from a different perspective than people who are more insistently controlling. It is worth summarising some of the major differences:

The compliant approach seeks *agreement* first and foremost, since the compliant personality likes to avoid a contest of wills and does not like to apply pressure to other people. This is likely to be because (s)he wishes to preserve the friendship/relationship first and foremost. Consequently the compliant approach tends to be 'soft' on people, even if this means having to be soft in the approach to the problem. Compliance involves making offers and concessions; accepting one-sided agreements that are disadvantageous to oneself; and generally searching for an answer that the other person will accept. Consequently, the compliant individual has to be willing to change his or her position and opinion, even to avoid having one. (S)he seeks to trust the judgement of the other person or, at least, to accept it without complaint – in order to keep the peace and preserve the relationship intact.

The danger in all this, of course, is that if you are too compliant you may well lose the respect of people in the longer run, even though they may be happy that you fit in with them in the short term. Furthermore, an organisation is unlikely to make the wisest decisions if the talent of compliant individuals is under-utilised; and this will happen when a domineering minority is insistent on proving itself to be 'right' all the time.

The controlling individual, naturally, approaches disagreements from a very different perspective. The controlling approach seeks *victory* first and foremost and the controller is quite willing to engage in – even relishes – a contest of wills and the use of pressure on other people. Getting his/her own way is much more important to the controlling individual than preserving the relationship; indeed (s)he is quite likely to demand that concessions be made as a condition of the relationship. The controlling individual, in other words, is the one who takes the attitude: *"You must fit in with me or else you are spoiling things between us."*

Consequently the controlling approach tends to involve more of a hard-nosed attitude to tackling an issue, even if this means being hard on the people concerned. Control involves making threats rather than offers; and demanding concessions from the other participants in the discussion – who tend to be seen as adversaries rather than friends or partners. One-sided gains are demanded by the controlling individual as the price of agreement. Not surprisingly, therefore, the controlling person tends to be the one who 'digs in' to his position and who sees any kind of flexibility or concession on his part as a sign of weakness and defeat. Controlling individuals, who are obsessed about getting the better of people, tend not to trust the motives, feelings, intentions and opinions of others; and regard them with suspicion, as a potential threat to their own precious position.

Games People Play:

It is very hard to get through to someone who is determined to see every disagreement as a contest which (s)he must, at all costs, 'win'. Not surprisingly, therefore, there are times when compliant individuals, in particular, prefer to 'Get through *with* You' rather than 'Get through *to* You! If disagreements are likely to degenerate into major, possibly malicious, contests of will then compliant people are likely to try to avoid such conflict if they can and restrict themselves to superficial and uncontroversial matters.

Of course, there is always the possibility that we will inadvertently slip into a discussion or activity that could lead to a quarrel, and the less we are able to predict the sort of things that we might say or do the more likely it is that this will happen.

Unpredictability, in any case, tends to be seen as a source of insecurity for most of us; if we were to be really open and open-minded with the people around us, who knows what might be said and done? Therefore, in order to avoid such anarchy, there is a tendency in all of us to discover and develop rules and roles which govern the sorts of things that can, and can't, be said and done in different situations. Over a period of time, these rules tend to harden and the roles that people adopt, both formally and informally, become more and more tightly played. Once these guidelines (or constraints) are firmly established, our various public performances become more safely predictable for us. We become more certain about the sort of things we will say and do among different groups of people; and confident, too, about the way in which we will perform. Equally, we will be able to predict, with a high degree of confidence, what others will do and what styles of personality and presentation they will adopt.

A brand new social situation can seem like travelling across open country without a map. We are uncertain about where we are going and how we ought to be travelling. As the social scene around us becomes ever more familiar, it feels more as though we are travelling along a railway line to a known destination. Others, too, move safely along their own particular tracks; the risk of anarchy, uncertainty and destructive conflict is minimised. We all get to know where we are, where we are going and what is expected from us along the way. Our social world becomes safe and secure.

The trouble is, of course, that it might also become dull and boring. We can feel stifled by the roles thrust upon us. We can feel inhibited by the (generally unwritten and undiscussed) rules that seem to govern everything we do. A social framework that initially helped to give us our bearings and a means of expressing ourselves can, by degrees, turn into a prison from which there seems to be no escape and through which any kind of genuinely authentic behaviour and communication seems impossible.

Sometimes we find ourselves in situations where the fundamental spirit, or principle, that governs what everyone says and does can be summarised as follows:

> *Given that we don't really want to meet each other, how can we pass the time? What games can we play?*

The notion of a game as a useful concept to describe many social situations was first introduced by Eric Berne way back in the nineteen sixties in his classic bestseller; *Games People Play* (Grove Press, U.S.A., 1964; reprinted many times).

A game, let us remember, has certain, well-known, attributes:

1. There is an agreed set of rules that all the players learn and understand in advance and which they have to know and follow if the game is to be played at all.

2. There is generally a fixed number of players and the rules govern their role and the way they must play it.

3. There is a limited number of possible outcomes, and although there may be winners and losers there has to be a payoff for all the players. In other words, each player must know that (s)he will get some sort of benefit/enjoyment from playing the game. (Some people, being masochists, get the benefit of punishment/abuse/ridicule from others which, if nothing else, at least proves to them that they are not being ignored!)

4. Generally, there are few major surprises. Variations all take place within a fixed framework of certainty and predictability.

Eric Berne described over one hundred 'communication' games; and devised for each a somewhat zany title designed to attract the reader to move beyond the front cover and buy the book (eg. Rapo, Harried, Sweetheart, Schlemiel, Uproar, Corner and Wooden Leg). If you want to know what these names describe, you too can buy the book and add to Eric Berne's already enormous royalties. The trouble is that naming and describing games has in itself, I suspect, degenerated for many people into yet another sterile pastime! There are literally thousands of games that we can play, and really there is no limit to the number that might exist; it simply depends on our own creativity. People are inventing new games all the time and there are, of course, particular preferences and fashions that come and go.

We can, and often do, turn any recurring social situation into a game by tightening the roles and rules, limiting the outcomes and establishing the payoffs.

For example, arguments (even bitter ones) can be turned into games where, say, the reward for one person is that they have a noisy tantrum, while the other gets the pay-off of being allowed to feel holier-than-thou. Some people deal with many of their regular quarrels by turning them into games. The game might get a bit rough at times, but some games, after all, *are* rough. They provide safety and security, nonetheless, since the range of possible outcomes and pay-offs is known in advance. You may yourself have come across couples who argue quite noisily and intensely with each other but whose disputes, you come to suspect, are not really serious or even malicious. Such games give the players the chance to go through the same old motions without there being any real risk.

Committee meetings are often turned into games where there is merely a pretence that something new is going to be achieved. The pay-off is that everyone's self-interest is protected, no one betrays anyone else and everyone pretends that serious business is being transacted and that a major breakthrough is imminent. (I wasted three hours of my time at one such meeting only this morning when I could have been writing instead!)

Report writing within organisations often becomes a kind of game. It may suit everyone to pretend that a significant project has been completed; or a new resource material developed; or that a major piece of research is under way. Such pretence, that something important has happened, is generally less costly and time consuming than the real thing; indeed, if you are engaged in genuinely significant work, you may not have very much time to write a glossy report about it. Consequently, I suspect that an inverse law frequently operates: the inflated presentation of a report is in inverse relation to the amount of real work that was done. I am sure I am not alone in thinking that a plethora of report writing is often a sign that people are under-employed! However, such is the injustice of this world, those who have the time to promote themselves and their own department may very well secure the limelight, at the expense of their busier colleagues, and ensure that they are promoted to still more agreeable, game playing, heights within their organisation.

Discussions of all sorts can be turned into games. No one need listen to anyone else; different players are allowed to sound off in whatever (predictable) way suits them; and various partners can run out whatever favourite, and familiar, theme or melodrama is reserved for them to play. We all will know who will say what, when and how; and we all get the pay-off of pretending that this is a new, real, risky, creative and genuine situation/problem/dilemma.

Our habitual emotional response to certain people or situations can be turned into a game. We may pretend that our feeling is fresh, original and useful; yet it may well be that we are simply running along the same old tracks with the same old outcomes governed by the same old rules.

In the end, *our whole life can become little more than a series of games!* Everything and everyone can get to become entirely pre-determined and over-controlled. Everything can be turned into an *act* where there may not even be a glimmer of genuineness or authenticity. Some people can so lose track of themselves, heart and soul, that just everything they say and do becomes phoney and 'gamey'. In some cases you can ask someone, "What do you *actually* think/feel/want right now?" and their (unspoken) reaction will be to try to figure out, "What is *your* game?" In the light of your reaction, they will come up with whatever seems an appropriate gamey response in reply. There are a few people who are quite convinced that genuineness does not exist and that everything people do is a game. And so they are endlessly looking out for the games that others are trying to promote. And, it has to be admitted, even genuineness and intimacy can be turned into phoney games; where the rule, or spirit, of the thing is that I 'win' by being more genuine and intimate than you!

Now, I am not suggesting that we must never play games and never run along predictable tracks in relation to each other. Some games can be harmless fun, or exciting, or a means of filling in the time. But if we only ever play around in our lives, following whatever rules the game allows, we turn ourselves into little more than robots. This reminds me of the story of an Indian religious teacher (Krishnamurti I think it was) who was asked, "What is your opinion of people who commit suicide?" He paused for a while and then replied:

"As far as I can see, most people have already committed suicide!"

You may by now be feeling somewhat disheartened as we journey through the shadows and the seamier aspects of human communication (and non-communication). Bear with me. I think it is quite essential that we face up to the reality of all this and get beneath some of our habitual rationalisations and righteousness. However, there are ways out of the gloom; we are capable of better things; and we even manage to achieve them from time to time!

Questions and Exercises:

These can be answered individually or in a group:

(For Small Groups): share your answers in pairs (3's or 4's) (to the extent that you wish to do so).

(For Large Groups): share what came out of small group discussion in the larger group (to the extent that this seems appropriate and useful).

1. Who would you like to get round, get the better of, get away from?

2. Who do you want to get out of the way or under control?

3. Who wants to get *you* out of the way?

4. What changes are you trying to make in other people?

5. What changes are others trying to make in you?

6. How do you reward others and how do they reward you? Can you think of recent examples?

7. How do you punish others and how do they punish you? Can you think of recent examples? Who have you sentenced recently to punishment? What form does this punishment take? How long is the sentence you have inflicted on them? (Hours? Weeks? Months? Years? A *Life* sentence!) Do you offer remission for good conduct? What do they have to do to earn it? Who is presently putting you under a punishment regime? Can you forgive each other, or, at least, shorten the sentence?

8. (For young couples): what are the 'little things' in your partner that, you are quite sure, you will easily be able to change? And what agenda for change is (s)he planning for you?

9. What rules and roles govern the way you behave in different situations?

10. Do others operate by the same rules? What rules and roles do others adopt? How did these rules come about? Are they your rules? Are they shared by the group? Or were they imposed on you by someone else? (If so), What led you to accept this imposition?

11. How far do these rules help/hinder effective communication? Do they help us to fulfil ourselves in the group or are they more a source of frustration?

12. What changes in the rules would you like to see? Are these changes realistic?

13. What other roles do you wish you could adopt?

14. What games do you play in your life? Are you happy with them? Would you like to play some new ones? Would you like to play games rather less often? What might this involve?

15. What have you done recently to build up self-esteem in other people?

16. What have you done to undermine it?

17. How do you cope with disagreement?

18. What do you do when someone does not fit in with your plan for how they ought to be?

19. How do you respond to perceived hurts and injustices that others have inflicted on you?

20. Look again at the various patterns of conflict described in this chapter. What approach to conflict do you take? Do you try to control? Do you tend to comply? Do you withdraw? Does your approach vary with different people? Why is this?

21. Can you think of occasions where you only wanted to *seem* to be 'getting through'? What were you really after?

22. Now that the Cold War looks like it has come to an end, do we need to find a new Enemy? Who will it be?

3.   Is Anybody Listening?

A man who listens because he has nothing to say can hardly be a source of inspiration. The only listening that counts is that of the talker who alternately absorbs and expresses ideas.

Agnes Repplier, 'The Luxury of Conversation', *Compromises* (1904)

There is a tendency, still, to believe that listening is a passive process that takes care of itself. Our ears, we imagine, are like microphones. They simply pick up whatever sounds are around and send the signals on to the brain. Similarly, we may believe, our eyes are like cameras; the light pours in as though through a window and the image on the retina is faithfully transmitted to, and through, the brain. A similar view is generally assumed of all our senses; they cannot help but pick up the stimuli around us and so we cannot avoid becoming aware of our world.

We still have a great deal to learn about the physiology of perception; yet a detailed account, even of what little we do know, would still go far beyond the confines of this book. Suffice it to say, though, that it has for a long time been absolutely clear that our perception of anything whatever is far from being a passive process akin to the action of microphones or cameras.

Let us take the simplest possible example of a clock ticking: with each tick, an electro-chemical signal is, initially, transmitted from the ear to the brain. Each tick is faithfully reported as an electro-chemical pulse; but only for a short while. The brain soon becomes habituated to the sound, or, to put it in psychological terms, we get tired or bored with hearing the clock. We lose interest. As a result, the ear soon stops transmitting the signal to even the lowest centres in the brain. Somehow, the ear is instructed to refrain from reporting any more clock signals. We no longer hear the clock. There are many other such barriers within the brain itself that shut out unwanted information. This is just as well, because there are far more stimuli around us than we could possibly have time, or reason, to process and understand.

However, whenever something new and interesting takes place that might require a decision on our part, we will be quick to take note of it. And so we may notice when the clock *stops* ticking, despite being unaware that it was! More dramatically, the roar of an airliner's engines may soon, for the seasoned traveller, fade into unconsciousness. But we will hear it immediately if the engine starts to cough and splutter or cuts out into silence!

In other words, there is physical evidence that clearly supports what we ought long ago to have realised from experience; we hear (and see) what we *want* to hear (and see) and we 'tune out' sources which do not interest us.

Hearing, moreover, is not just a question of picking up, or tuning out signals. It is also a matter of understanding. When someone speaks in a foreign language, all you hear is a high speed jumble of sounds. You will notice that some are harsh or soft; high or low pitched; slowly or rapidly pronounced. The occasional sound might remind you of words found in your own language. But you will find it difficult to attend for long. Soon, you will ignore this meaningless stream of sound, unless you are keen to learn the language; in which case you will attend carefully to the context, tone, volume and gestures in an effort to figure out what is going on.

People often use the expression "*I see*" or (more recently) "*I hear you*"; and these phrases provide a significant clue to the nature of perception. When I say "*I hear* you", I am not just saying that I heard the sounds you were making. Rather, and crucially, I am saying that I understand the meaning and intention behind your words. That is why we don't say "*I hear you*" to someone talking in Chinese. We hear the sounds, but we don't understand the meaning, and so we are not really hearing anything of significance at all. Moreover, we will see no sense in uttering any sounds ourselves if we know that the person does not understand, and does not wish to understand, the language we speak.

In other words, to speak at all, we have to make the (sometimes very considerable) assumption that our listener might eventually understand us. Similarly, to listen at all, we have to assume that we can get behind the speaker's words and reach the underlying meaning. Communication, then, is not just about sending signals; it involves believing that their meanings can be usefully interpreted.

Despite this, we still tend to assume that we perceive the world around us and *then* try to make meanings out of it. This is quite inaccurate. What actually happens is that we perceive the world around us in the very process of making sense of it! Sensing and making sense are inseparable. I 'see' often means I 'understand', which is why only car mechanics can see carburettors, filters and clutches. The untrained observer can only see a tangled confusion of metal and wire.

This poses quite a problem, because it indicates that perception of any sort can be full of pitfalls and dilemmas which are very difficult to pin-down. As far as listening to other people is concerned, such difficulties may be summarised in the following – contrary – statements:

1a. *"Knowing you, I really know what to listen for."*
1b. *"Knowing you, why bother to listen?"*

2a. *"Not knowing you, I can listen with an open mind."*
2b. *"Not knowing you, how do I listen and what do I listen for?"*

3a. *"Hearing you brings up my feelings."*
3b. *"Feeling as I do shapes what I hear."*

4a. *"Hearing you sets me thinking."*
4b. *"Thinking of you, I stop attending to what you're saying."*
4c. *"Thinking of you, what I hear makes sense."*

5a. *"I know what to expect, so why listen?"*
5b. *"To listen at all I have to have some expectation."*

6a. *"I really hear you by interpreting you right."*
6b. *"I am so busy interpreting that I have failed to listen."*

7a. *"I find it difficult to listen when you don't make sense."*
7b. *"I see no point in listening when I have the exact sense of what you're saying."*

8a. *"My mind constructs my experience."*
8b. *"My experience broadens my mind."*
8c. *"My mind narrows my experience."*

'Sensing' and 'making sense' are inseparable, and the language we use provides some clues to this. For example, I recognise, or re-cognise, the objects around me. Re cognition, in other words, involves cognition, (thinking), and this is part of the very process of perception.

We have to think, then, in order to make sense of what we hear; but the danger is that this very thinking may prevent us from paying attention. Furthermore, the interpretation that we have of any message, and which we have to make if we are to understand what is being said, is our own personal construction, (influenced by our own attitudes, history and expectations), which will put an individual bias on any message we hear.

To repeat, we have to interpret the messages we receive in order to be able to understand them at all. But, in consequence, my sense of your message may only vaguely resemble the sense *you* make of it; what you *intended* to say; and what other listeners *thought* you said.

It wouldn't be so bad if we could make a clear distinction between our experience of what someone says and our reaction to this experience. To some extent we can, but some (in the professional counselling fraternity for example) over-estimate the degree to which this is possible. The professional counsellor is trained to hear what the client is saying while putting her own reactions and responses to one side. Personal reactions, it is thought, get in the way of pure attention, and so trained counsellors are expected to keep their reactions quite separate so that they can have a reasonably objective perspective on what the client is saying. This is all worthy enough up to a point, but the trouble is that our reactions, expectations, interpretations and intentions are themselves part of the construction of what we 'hear'. And so there are severe (and probably unknowable) limits on how far 'what I hear' and 'my response to what I hear' can be separated, even in principle, never mind in practice! 'Experience' and 'reaction-to-experience' are welded intimately together. There is no such thing as 'pure experience' since all our experience is corrupted/constructed by expectations, attitudes, beliefs and interpretations. I experience what I *construe* to be the case; my ideas, feelings and reactions to what you say are my experience of what you say, to a very considerable degree at least.

We each carry a tool-kit of concepts, interpretations, and maps of the world; and these are necessary in order, for example, for us to be able to put the sounds detected by the ears into a jig-saw that makes sense to us. Yet this tool-kit is also a baggage and set of blinkers that imprison us.

Thoughts, feelings (and actions), then, focus, construct and make sense of what we sense. They also act as a filter on our view of the world; and we can only ever swap one filter with another. Even in principle, there is no such thing a 'pure' perception, untrammelled by subjective response. We are, at one and the same time, supported and stifled by our knowledge.

Let's see how all this works when, say, you are trying to get through to me: I, like you, am no passive listener and so, if I am not careful, (and even if I am careful!) I might indicate that *"I hear you"* when in fact I am 'hearing' . . .

- What I *expected* you to say.
- What I *wanted* you to say.
- What I thought you *should* say.
- What *I* would have said in what I think is your position.
- What seems to me to make sense for you to say given what you have previously said.
- What seems to me to make sense for you to say given my understanding of where you are, what you are experiencing and what you are trying to do.

Whatever I do, I am faced with dilemmas:

- I try to *figure out* what you are saying; and in the process I often run ahead of your words.
- I *rehearse* the reply I want to make to you.
- I *review* what I have previously said.
- I make *judgements* about what you have said.
- I am *reminded* by what you said of a dozen other experiences.

By doing all this, I just might get a broader and deeper understanding of what you are saying. Equally, though, I might produce a very quirky interpretation quite different from the impression you are trying to make. I might even stop paying much attention to you at all, and drift off, instead, into my own reactions and preoccupations. In my efforts to understand you, I might fail to hear what you have said beyond your first couple of sentences!

In the light of all this, how can we ever get through? Can we ever piece together the meaning of other people's messages so that they can really know that they were heard? How can we be sure that we heard aright? How can we show the speaker that we heard? How can they confirm that we got it right?

Undoubtedly there are times (for some, maybe, precious few!) when we feel that we have really got through to another person. And not just about simple things like getting them to pass us the salt; but about deeper matters. We really feel that we have got through to someone when we have communicated what seems like 'the bottom line' about our present state of heart and mind. On those, (rare?), occasions when we have reached, and shared, the *root* of our presently experienced feelings, yearnings and beliefs, we feel that we have made a real connection with another person. On (most) other occasions we may wish to share, or succeed in sharing, only more superficial aspects of our experience. In any case, with day to day run-of-the-mill situations, there may only be superficialities to communicate about. We would not wish to, and do not, 'move over deep waters' of experience all the time. And so, for example, over an average breakfast I might have got to the (shallow) heart of the matter when I have successfully got it across to you that I want you to pass the butter.

Generally, I manage to get such simple messages across. But we do not consider that the listener has successfully empathised with us when our activities are as simple and straightforward as this. And it is empathy, I want to suggest, that lies at the heart of 'getting through'. I have got through to you when I feel that you have really heard something that is of importance to me, and is of more than passing concern. Moreover, it is not enough that you have heard it purely from your own perspective.

For me to believe that I have really got through, I need to know that you are able to see the matter in the way that I see it. You don't have to agree with me, and you can have your own reactions too. But, we have fully connected only when it seems that you are able to get a glimpse of what the world looks like from my experience; with my spectacles; 'from my shoes'. Indeed, if we really communicate, we will be able to go deeper into, and understand, our own and each other's experiences more profoundly than is possible alone. The ultimate in communication is where we each can explore the mysteries of our experience, our yearnings, feelings, beliefs and the meaning of all this – more deeply than if we were alone.

Consequently, and commonly, the ultimate frustration can be when one person in a relationship wants to go deeper in this sharing process, while the other is happy to coast along at a more superficial level. In such (tragic) circumstances, one person will be clearly or dimly thinking *"if only we could get through to each other to what really matters; to the heart of all this"*; while the other will, if asked, say, *"Oh yes, we seem to get along fine, don't we dear?"*

Communication, at its rare ultimate, almost becomes a form of communion. We may not be able to talk about it. But probably all of us, whether we realise it or not, yearn for it; (though we may also fear it!)

How can such a level of communication ever be achieved? – (and particularly in the light of all that has been said above). How can we get through? How can we empathise? Are there particular skills we can learn and/or habits that we need to unlearn? Needless to say, I believe that we *can* learn to get through more effectively and, specifically within the confines of this chapter, there are, undoubtedly, ways in which we can improve our listening.

There are times, though, when our listening is a sham, and only rarely do we listen with full intention and intensity. In any case, we only rarely want our lives to be lived with great intensity; and so low levels of attention are more the norm than the exception. We can pretend to ourselves and others that we are listening and empathising. We can go through the motions of listening; we may even convince others that we are listening. Yet still we may not be listening.

Nodding and grunting and making eye contact do not prove that you are listening. These may reassure the other person and encourage them to speak; but you can do all of this and still not be listening. And so, in order to be sure that you have heard, it is often necessary to repeat back to the person:

- at the appropriate moment,
- in your own words, yet from *their* perspective,
- as succinctly as possible,

. . . the heart of what they seemed to be saying. Then, and only then, can they tell you if you've got it right.

However, not even this is enough on its own. Computers can nowadays be programmed to function like counsellors; although at present they do so only in a very primitive way. Yet (who knows?), some day they might be programmed to be quite subtle and varied in the way they respond! Some people, already, are happy to spend hours with such a confidante; and, in a world where machines are taking over what were previously considered to be human functions, (and where many humans seem to behave more like machines), it becomes ever more important to see just what it is about being human that is, and will remain, unique to humans.

Let's see how a computer might be programmed to listen to and deal with a person's problems. Consider, for example, the following confession, that might be made by the customer of a 'computer-counsellor':

"I want to build more of a life for myself rather than stay around the house all day. I need to get up and go and do something new."

The computer (through analysis of the grammar) will first reflect back some of this in order to show that it has 'heard'. It will have a library of grammatical principles and constructions stored away and so it will not need to repeat sentences parrot-fashion. It might say something as follows:

"I hear you saying you want to build more of a life for yourself. Staying in the house is not enough for you. You feel the need to begin some new venture."

Of course this, on its own, sounds a bit wooden and mechanical. The machine has proved it heard or, rather, *received* the message. But more is needed if the machine is to create the illusion that it is not a machine. For example:

- Some empathy
- Some reassurance
- Some placing of this problem into a wider context
- Some expression of sympathy
- Some questioning that shows interest
- Some questioning that encourages the client to tackle the problem.
- Use of the client's Christian name to show that this is a personal(ised) contact.

Thus a more sophisticated program might respond, using its database of phrases and pearls of wisdom, as follows:

"This must be hard for you Jean; I think that I too would feel frustrated if I was in the house all day. But many others have faced this problem and have found ways of tackling it. It is a difficulty that lots of people have to go through. Jean, I really do sympathise, and you do know, don't you, that you can really let your feelings out when you are here? Eventually, though, you are going to need to sit down and see what you yourself can do to tackle the problem. Do you know others who are faced with similar difficulties? Would it be possible to share your problem with your neighbour Sally or your husband John? What first steps do you think you could take, Jean, to tackle the problem?"

Actually, this would be rather too voluble (and syrupy?) a response to such a short statement; and so it would probably not be wise to give out all of this in one statement. But it illustrates some of the principles that might be successfully programmed.

Such responses might still be detectable, sooner or later, by most customers at least, as that of a machine. Nonetheless, the client might also decide that it seemed more caring, constructive and considered than the actual grunts and shrugs that they received from other human beings who were themselves more pre-occupied with their own problems and concerns! Moreover, such a personalised program might indeed be quite helpful in getting a person to release and clarify his feelings, thoughts and wishes. It might also be quite a good guide in getting him to adopt a serious approach to practical problem solving.

A machine, then, with a well thought-out 'counselling' program, might be an aid to help us to get through to ourselves. But, insofar as we thought that the machine was getting through to us, or we to it, we would be living in the fantasy that it was itself a sentient being to which you could 'get through'! (I suspect that some people's obsession with computers is, indeed, a means of avoiding genuinely human company!)

Humans can, of course, do far more, and respond with far more subtlety, than in the 'caring response' outlined above. Let's face it, though, we may often do far less! Nonetheless, with practice, and when we feel so inclined:

- We can respond in a tone of voice that gently mirrors the tone of the speaker; and thus show that we have 'caught the mood'. With skill and practice, we can do this without either over-stating the tone, so that we seem melodramatic; or understating it, so that we come across as indifferent.

- With further skill, we can gently switch our tone; thus empathising without becoming trapped or enmeshed in the experience of the other person.

- We can learn the appropriate use of silences; ensuring that they are not so long as to seem embarrassing; nor so short that no one has a chance to feel their feelings and reflect quietly on what has just been said.

- We can learn to use other non-verbal behaviour that shows interest. For example:
  - Leaning forward a little, but not intrusively so.
  - Sitting up, without being too stiff nor slouching.
  - Avoiding fidgety behaviour and other irritating mannerisms.
  - Making appropriate eye contact, without being intrusive and without turning the contact into a staring match.
  - Mirroring the posture and facial expression of the speaker in order to discover what this feels like. In this way we can 'feel with' and 'feel for' the person and thus inhabit their experience. Such mirroring also can show the speaker that you know how they are feeling and that you are able and willing to feel as they do. With practice, the right balance can be found: if you mimic too often and too closely the style of the speaker, it can seem wooden or offensive, or else it may appear that you are allowing yourself to be engulfed by the speaker's experience. Such mirroring ('mimicry' sounds manipulative and cynical) needs to be very subtle and light; yet if it is too slight the speaker's experience may feel too distant.

- We can learn to become aware of the category of imagery that a person tends to use most and adopt the same category in our replies. Images can be:

  – Visual: ("I see; I get the picture; *I have an* over-view *of the problem; It's in perspective, fuzzy..*" etc.)

  – Auditory: ("*I hear you; the* tone *of the meeting was all wrong; he* dropped a real clanger; *we* whistled *through it...*" etc.)

  – Tactile: ("*Revenge was* sweet; *he leaves a* sickly *taste; he was so* abrasive; *a real* smooth *operator; we really got* squelched *that day.*")

  – Olfactory: ("*It was a* fishy *business; I didn't like the* smell *of it; it was a* heady *experience.*")

  – Kinaesthetic: ("*It turned me* inside out, upside down; *I was* flat *on my back;* knocked *for six;* torn *apart;* ripped *open; badly* hurt.*")

The skilled listener learns to 'get a focus' on the first, 'tune in' to the second, 'reach out' to the third, 'get the smell of 'the fourth' and 'feel the guts' (or heart) of the fifth! The unskilled listener replies using mental images that are in a different sensory category. The original speaker thus feels that he has been talking fruitlessly to someone who 'takes a different view', is 'on another wavelength', 'out of touch', has 'lost the scent' or is 'lost in his head'.

All these skills can seem artificial and contrived when they are first consciously and conscientiously practised. That is because *any* new behaviour or belief tends to feel unnatural; whereas old habits and prejudices, however self-defeating, generally seem comfortable and proper! With constant practice and persistence, and a genuine wish to change, such skills are gradually internalised so that we are able to use them spontaneously, without conscious reflection. After all, when we really know what we are doing, we don't need to be excessively self-conscious about it, but can merely trust ourselves to get on with the job. (Take, for example, driving a car.) When we are first learning a new skill, though, we are bound to be halting, clumsy and highly self-conscious. Indeed, if we are trying to change our bad old ways in relation to deep-seated old habits, then we may very well find that our performance actually gets worse before it gets better; (e.g. learning to touch-type after years of two-finger typing).

In recent years, such listening and communication skills have been studied very carefully by Public Relations specialists, advertisers, 'organisation development' consultants, politicians and other professional communicators. As a result it can be observed that the quality of public relations, advertising, and human resource management expertise has improved enormously over the last thirty years. All these practitioners are very eager to convince you personally that 'We are really listening'; 'We really care'; and that 'You are really important to us'.

In a democracy, Public Opinion is seen to be of enormous concern to every state and private sector organisation. This is all very well; and potentially great things can come from new skills and insight. Professional expertise costs money, of course, and so, for example, the best PR consultants tend to be hired by those with the most money. The question then arises, will the Voice of the People really be listened to and acted upon by caring, sophisticated (state and private sector) corporations? Or will the ordinary person be managed and manipulated? The risks of being bamboozled – even hypnotised – by sophisticated communicators are, I believe, very great indeed.

It might be said that we are making genuine progress when our masters are forced into hypocrisy! Governments and ruling establishments have only in relatively recent years celebrated the virtues of universal freedom, justice, respect for every individual and equal opportunity for all. That they do so now, in virtually every country on Earth, is not to be lightly dismissed.

However, let's be realistic, the temptation to *seem* to be living by such ideals, while not actually doing so, is going to be very great for those who would otherwise have to make a real sacrifice of power or material wealth! The 'master' now has to listen; or, at least, pretend that he is listening. Pretence may be a cheaper option than the real thing. On the other hand, in the process of going through the motions he may in fact become convinced by his own propaganda and take a genuine interest in human well-being. Alternatively, the whole exercise might remain cynical – yet effective!

Sadly, it sometimes seems that more skill and attention is given over to the manufacture of images and appearances nowadays than to the realisation of the real and the genuine. Effort is given over to making it look like we care rather than to actually caring; to make it seem as though we are listening rather than actually listening.

Even at the level of individual communication we need to be aware of these dangers. Do you really want to listen? ...Even to the extent that you genuinely empathise, feel with and feel for, the other person? To do so will require that you authentically respect and support the integrity and right to self-determination of other human beings. Alternatively, do you want to listen carefully only in order to know how best to manage and deal with this person?

Do you want to know what others want because you genuinely want to meet their needs? Or do you want to know what they want in order to *appear* to be helping them while in fact helping yourself first, foremost and, if necessary, at the expense of everyone else? Do you really want to reward others? Or do you want to find out what minimal rewards are necessary to keep control of the situation?

These are tough questions because, if we are honest, we will have to face up to the extent to which all of us are attempting to manage and control others rather than meet and co-operate with them.

In other words, it is the underlying intention and spirit of what we do that really counts. Listening, for example, involves a whole variety of skills that can be learned and practised. But listening-in-order-to-'get-through' is quite different from listening-in-order-to-'deal-with'. Listening and other communication skills, like all skills, can be used for good or for ill, and we won't face up to this dilemma, and get to the real heart of the matter, if we merely think of the whole business of communication in terms of the acquisition of skills.

"Have a nice day!"

Those who are hungry for power might think that the ability to listen is the last thing they need to learn to do. After all, if *my* wants are all that matter to me, why bother to find out what you want? We commonly fail to listen because we are so pre-occupied with our own insecurities, concerns, fantasies and plans; and many conversations consist in the 'listener' going through the motions of seeming to listen while all the while impatiently waiting for his turn to speak.

Yet, it has to be admitted, and it is more and more being disco-vered, the ability to listen is an extraordinarily powerful skill. It can be used to bring you closer to fellow humanity. Just as easily, though, it can be used to give you power and control over other people!

The key to success in business is to get people to keep paying over their money to you while feeling happy in the process. Similarly, success in democratic politics requires that voters feel pleased as they put their cross, once again, by *your* name. Getting people to feel happy involves knowing what they want. Knowing what they want requires careful and attentive listening.

An honest communicator will say how far (s)he can, and will, try to meet the needs of others. A sophisticated communicator might instead decide to give the impression of meeting needs, and to deal in illusions rather than realities.

If you are selfish, and an unskilled communicator, then you are likely to get into a great deal of conflict with others. You and they will polarise; you will take defensive positions; you will try to punish each other; you will both get hurt – in all the ways that have been outlined in previous chapters. If, on the other hand, you are selfish, but skilled in communication and an excellent listener, then you will find that there are many ways of oiling your interactions with others. You will avoid head-on conflict. You will look for, and find, ways of providing rewards to the other person at little cost to yourself. You will appear to give a great deal while in fact giving as little as possible. You will empathise with the other person, and this in itself will seem highly rewarding to them. But your empathy will be a means of achieving control rather than genuine contact. With a hidden rudder, you will steer the conversation while seeming to be following in a direction set by your victim. You will set the agenda while appearing to be following theirs. You will get what you want while seeming to have given away nearly everything to the other side. You will maintain control, while appearing to be 'non-directive'.

In later chapters we will examine some of these skills in managing conflict; and we will see how they can be used for good or ill depending on the nature of our deepest attitudes, intentions and underlying spirit. As regards listening, I will mention just one more method of achieving contact – or control:

This is the matter of paraphrasing; i.e. reflecting back, and seeking to clarify, what a speaker has just said: when we operate with integrity, we will reflect back what seems to us to be the heart of what the speaker was saying; he will tell us if we are right; and this will help him to move deeper to an understanding of what he thinks, feels and wants to do next. If, however, we wish to achieve control, we will reflect back what the speaker will recognise as true; but it will be a partial truth designed to shift the agenda in our direction. A skilled listener has enormous power to steer a conversation even if he does no more than attend to what the other person has said. Sometimes, we do not even need to introduce our own preoccupations and preferences; we may attend only to the other person's agenda – insofar as it fits in with ours!

For example, every message has a feeling component, an ideas component and possible consequences in terms of action. A seemingly non-directive counsellor can have her client drowning in feelings, lost in thought, or planning her actions simply depending

on which component of the client's message she decides to clarify
and to ask the most questions about. Thus it is that some non-directive therapists find that their clients muse a great deal about
their childhood; others have enormous cathartic releases of emotion; others analyse goals and behaviour; others confront their
'basic aloneness', ..or travel down whatever pathway the therapist
sought, passively, to 'clarify'.

Similarly, a good salesman will listen carefully to what the customer wants and ask for clarification about this. But the questions
will steer her in a direction that suits the salesman. Little by little
the customer will discover for herself ways in which some of the
products on offer will help her to meet some of her needs. Likewise,
the politician will listen carefully to the preoccupations and concerns of members of the electorate. The canvasser will ask the voter
to elaborate on some of these concerns, and little by little we will
discover how this party's policies are designed to get to grips with
the things that bother us.

Of course, there are limits to this. You can't fool all the people
all the time. Sometimes you can do no more than work at the
margins in your efforts to steer people's preoccupations. But, if
you are skilled enough, and more skilled than your opponents,
you can fool enough of the people enough of the time to get your
way while seeming to be following the public. And that, after all,
is all you need to do.

Big Brother (Big Sister?) is not out to get you. Indeed, she wants
you to know that she loves you and that's why she's here. That
is why she is watching and listening. She will be at your side
listening when times seem hard. She will be nice to you. She will
show that she has heard what are your very, very real concerns.
She will show just what she is going to do that will meet these
concerns. She will be so fulsome in showing how she has 'inhabited
your experience' and followed you down your own road that you
may well fail to see how your other potential concerns and preoccupations have quietly disappeared from the scene. She will be
genuinely rewarding (when the price is low enough – and often
it is very low). She will make good eye contact; her posture will
be appropriate for the occasion, it will look, sound and feel as
though she really knows, really cares and really feels for you. She
will manage, or handle, you so well that you will feel respected,
free, supported, understood and well on the way to wherever you
are trying to go. You will give her your vote; keep on making the
payments; do precisely what you want; and she will, merely, follow.

All this illustrates the general point that there is nothing under the Sun that can't be misused. If your intentions are fundamentally dishonourable then your acquisition of skills will be destructive. People may imagine that they will not be caught out and that they can always tell the genuine from the illusory. If only this were true. The facts seem to indicate that if the other person's skills in presentation and listening are much greater than your powers of perception, then you will be fooled. Conjurers make their living from powers to create illusions; there are growing numbers of Conjurers in Communication creating equally impressive illusions. The only way we can fight back is to learn their methods and thus see through the tricks. We have to hope that our abilities to flush them out will be greater than their own capacities to create ever more new, and intoxicating, decoys.

When you are doing no more than practising a skill, while having lost touch with your underlying intentions (some would say your 'soul'!), then the very activity is in itself phoney. What's real is when we want to be with people because we want to be with them. This is not the same as managing them, handling them and doing something to them. But we can go to great lengths to pretend to ourselves that we want to be with people without actually being with them. Counsellors, for example, if they are merely practising a skill, are not being with people. Rather they are indulging in a phoney kind of intimacy that gives them an illusion of contact with few of the risks.

Similarly, other types of sophisticated communicator may find that ultimately, their efforts to get through to others, even their own spouse, are sterile for as long as they are merely exercising a variety of skills. Two 'smooth operators' may live together in a marriage that seems to have everything going for it. The quality of their relationship, the subtlety of their communication, their sophisticated powers of negotiation might seem, to an envious outsider, a model to emulate. But if their heart and soul is not in it, if they are 'dealing with' each other rather than making genuine contact, then there will be no ultimate fulfilment. With intelligence and sophistication we may be able to look more deeply into the heart of ourselves and our relationships; *or* we may become ever more skilled at dissimulation, at 'seeming', at rationalising, at evading. With dishonourable intentions, we may become too clever for our own good.

In public life such artful sophistication can be observed in its most developed form. For example, in a radio or television interview, notice how the interviewer does all he can to set and steer the agenda using questions that are anything but innocent. Notice too, though, that this skilled professional interviewer these days must 'do combat' with the skilled professional public speaker. And so, for example, we will find, over and over again, that the politician is given a loaded question, but he simply refuses to accept the agenda that the question presupposes. Instead, as like as not, he will answer some other question that was not even asked! This will be the question that the politician wanted to have asked and which he was going to answer regardless of whether or not it was put! And, if he's a really smooth operator, he will steer his response in a way that gives the impression that he is actually answering the interviewer's question.

A final word: let us remember that there is a time and place for everything and that different intensities of listening, too, are appropriate or inappropriate, depending on the circumstances. There are degrees to which we may wish to become intimate with another; there may be times when we need to speak and make judgements rather than listen; times when we are, in any case, incapable of listening; times when we need to protect and defend ourselves rather than listen; times when we simply have more pressing priorities and concerns. We cannot be 'real' if we pretend to listen when we don't want to. And we will not be authentic if we try to become more intimate with people than we really wish.

Nonetheless, there is a famine of well-intentioned listening; a glut of advice; and an ominous growth of 'listening-to-control'. What we do in relation to all of this is in the hands of each of us.

Questions:

Think of a time . . .

1. When you were *not* heard:

    What did the other person think you said?
    Why do you think they interpreted you in this way?
    What could you have done to improve your chances of being heard?
    What might happen if you tried to discuss the above with them?

2. When someone accused you of not hearing them:

    What did you hear them say?
    In what way, in their view, did you get it wrong? Do you know?
    Why do you think you misinterpreted them?
    Do you still maintain that you interpreted their real underlying intentions accurately?
    What went wrong with the way they sent the message?
    What went wrong with the way you heard it?
    What might happen if you tried to discuss the above with them?

3. When you really *were* heard:

    What was the secret of your and their success?

4. When you really did manage to hear someone else:

    Is this just your opinion, or is it shared by the other person?
    What was the secret of your and their success?

5. When you *pretended* to listen:

    Were you being polite? devious? controlling? compliant? bored? lazy?
    Do you think you successfully fooled the other person?
    If not, how do think they felt about it?

6. When you think someone was only *pretending* to listen to you:

    Were they being polite? devious? controlling? compliant?
    How did you feel about it?
    What, if anything, did you do about it?
    What else could you have done about it, and what, do you think, might have been the result?

7. When you gave advice/blamed/made a judgement:

> Did this help the other person? How do you know?
> Were they grateful for your advice/blame/judgement? How do you know?
> Did they act upon your advice/blame/judgement? How do you know?
> As a result of your advice/ blame/judgement were they more/less willing to open up to you? How do you know?
> What would happen if you shared your answers with the person concerned?

8. When you were judged/blamed/given advice:

> Did this help you? Does the other person know?
> Were you grateful for their judgement/blame/advice? Do they know? (And how do you know they know?!)
> Did you act upon their judgement/blame/advice? Do they know?
> As a result of their judgement/blame/advice were you more/less willing to open up to them? Do they know? Are you sure?
> What would happen if you shared your answers with the person concerned?

9. When you labelled and interpreted what the other person was saying:

> Did this help the other person? How do you know?
> Were they grateful for your labelling/interpretation? How do you know?
> Did they accept your labelling/interpretation? How do you know?
> As a result of your labelling/interpretation were they more/less willing to open up to you? How do you know?
> What would happen if you shared your answers with the person concerned?

10. When what you were saying was labelled/interpreted:

> Did this help you? Does the other person know?
> Were you grateful for their labelling/interpretation? Do they know? (And how do you know they know?!)
> Did you accept their labelling/interpretation? Do they know?
> As a result of their labelling/interpretation were you more/less willing to open up to them? Do they know? Are you sure?
> What would happen if you shared your answers with the person concerned?

11. When you found it quite impossible to listen to a person:

> What was it about the way this person spoke and their overall manner that you found so difficult?
> What was it about the topic of conversation that you found so difficult?
> What was your internal reaction to this person?
> What was your external response to this person?
> What might happen if you tried to talk about this to the person concerned?

12. When you listened in order to meet a person.

13. When you listened in order to co-operate with a person.

14. When you listened in order to control a person.

15. When you listened in order to get the better of a person.

16. When someone listened in order to meet you.

17. When someone listened in order to co-operate with you.

18. When someone listened in order to control you.

19. When someone listened in order to get the better of you.

> How did you differentiate between one kind of listening and the other?
> How did you feel on each occasion?
> How do you think the other person was feeling on each occasion?

Exercises:

1. A talks to B; and B simply 'reflects back'/paraphrases...
   at the appropriate moment,
   in B's words,
   from A's point of view,
   as succinctly as possible,
   the 'heart' of what A was saying.
   B does <u>not</u> offer advice, or make judgements, or ask questions (except if essential to clarify what A has just said), or make conversation, or drift off somewhere else. B listens to what A is saying.
   A corrects B if B has got it wrong and then continues.
   A and B discuss the overall 'tone' and 'atmosphere' of the session.

A and B then swap roles. (10 minutes each way is about right to start with).

2. A talks to B and B tries to clarify what A has said by asking appropriate questions. B tries to avoid:

Too many questions
Poorly timed questions
Invasive questions (where the person is not ready to answer given the level of trust between you)
Leading questions (where the expected answer is contained in the question)
Pseudo-questions (which are statements disguised as questions)
Closed questions (where the possible answers are limited and directed by the question) Hint: ...*how, who, what, where, why* questions tend to be 'open'; i.e. they leave open lots of possible answers. Questions that begin with a verb tend to lead to closed answers; e.g. *Can, should, must, will, have, did, is, are.* Try it and see. There are exceptions of course; e.g. *"Can you tell me what are the options now?"* is actually open because *"Can you tell me"* is just a polite entry to the real question *"what are the options now?"*

A then tells B why the questions seemed helpful/unhelpful. In particular, A and B consider how B's questions may have steered A in particular directions.

A and B then swap roles. (15 minutes each way is about right to start with).

3. Repeat exercise '1', and see if you can spot any of the following:

Direction and control by the listener
Judgements, blaming, moralising, advising
The emotional state of the listener (was it helpful? hindering?)
The listener talking about herself
The listener protecting herself with humour and unnecessary reassurance
Excessive labelling and interpreting
Distractions and irrelevancies
Effects of the pressure of time (was this helpful? hindering?)

4. Repeat exercise '1', but in addition pay attention to non-verbal behaviour:

Posture, gestures, eye contact, length of silences, nodding head, encouraging noises and other encouragements to talk, position

of furniture, (too far apart? too near? too directly facing? too
oblique to each other? big versus small chair? desk in the way?
desk needed to come between us?)

5. Repeat exercise '1' but in addition see if you can consciously
mirror the tone, postures and gestures of the speaker. See how
far this helps you to get into their shoes, inhabit their experience, feel with and feel for them.
Speaker then says if this was helpful, wooden, melodramatic,
controlling, understated.

6. Repeat exercise '1' but in addition see if you can use the same
category of imagery as the speaker. Also, take a particular image
and find six possible responses using all six categories of mental
representation. Which image do you prefer? Which image does
your partner prefer?

4. Getting through to Myself.

Man can be defined as the animal that can say 'I', that can be aware of himself as a separate entity.

Eric Fromm, *The Sane Society* (1955)

We are all serving a life-sentence in the dungeon of self.

Cyril Connolly, *The Unquiet Grave* (1945)

Philosophers have puzzled for centuries over the mysteries of experience and personal identity. On the one hand, our day-to-day lives can seem perfectly familiar, obvious and straightforward; and yet, when (if) we start to ask a few probing questions about who we think we are and what we think we're doing, our ordinary everyday existence can become awesome, deeply baffling, and enigmatic in the extreme.

For example, I burn my hand under the hot tap and automatically pull it away. I tell you I have burnt it and you immediately consider that you understand what I'm talking about. You, after all, have probably had similar experiences with taps, burning etc. And so you assume that the pain you felt was probably similar to the pain I'm experiencing now. This strikes all of us as a perfectly reasonable assumption of the sort that we are making all the time. Yet an enigma remains. My pain experience is mine and mine alone, (along with all my other experiences). Others cannot experience it directly; they can only infer that it is there given my behaviour and the surrounding circumstances. But can we ever know for sure how far my pain is similar or different from yours, and can such a question even be sensibly asked if there is no possibility of an answer?

Perhaps you suffer from chronic pain of one sort or another. Perhaps you find it deeply depressing and exhausting. If I could feel your pain would I conclude that this pain is really very mild and that therefore you are making too much of a fuss? Or would I be overwhelmed by the experience and amazed that you have managed to cope at all? And what am I talking about when I imagine feeling your pain? Suppose that nerve fibres could be run from your burnt hand to my brain. Would I then be feeling your pain or mine? Could I then be sure that I was having the same experience as you? And what if it became possible for me to have a brain transplant? Would I be feeling your pain then? Would 'I' even exist then?

We take our pains along to the doctor and, although he can't feel them, we expect him to be able to make a diagnosis and tell us why we are having this pain and what can be done about it. He listens carefully to our description of our experience; observes our behaviour and body and, quite possibly, arranges for a number of other specific physiological tests. And so, although he can't experience our pain, we can get through to him about it to some considerable extent even if he himself has so far had little direct personal experience of illness. We don't, after all, assume that the best doctors should have actually suffered from the illnesses they treat.

We are quite happy to allow that a doctor of the body knows more about its workings than the patient, and that he should be better than we are in explaining some of the causes of our experience; (of our aches and pains, at least, though perhaps not our pleasures, joys and woes). Similarly, most people are willing to accept that a doctor of the mind should be able to know more than we do about the underlying meanings of our experience. Moreover, he may very well suggest causes as well; not just of aches and physical sensations but also of our moods of elation, anxiety and despair.

Sigmund Freud, (still the most well-known psycho-analyst), was himself trained as a doctor. He took the view that there was little point in the patient making a conscious effort to get through to the analyst about the causes and meaning of her (generally her) experience. The patient, Freud considered, could describe her dreams, sensations and fantasies and, indeed, ought to do so, since the analyst could not read her mind if she was unwilling to talk. But there was no point in the patient attempting to sort out, interpret and understand her experience. She was not in a position to do so since she had insufficient perspective, no training, and, in any case, she was probably running away from a great deal of what was going on inside.

Freud considered that we needed to face the truth about ourselves if we were to grow up, move on from neurosis or, at least, transform hysterical misery into common unhappiness. We could not do this alone since, without outside help, we would remain unwilling and unable to face ourselves as we really are. (Freud seemed to place himself in a special, and unique, category since he never personally underwent the analysis that he considered to be so essential for everyone else! But that's another story.)

'Know thyself' was the principle that provided the underlying rationale for Freud. And this required us to face up to the ways in which we ran away from ourselves and our reasons for doing so. He suggested that we all of us made use of a variety of 'defence mechanisms' that kept away from awareness insights that would otherwise make us feel anxious and uncomfortable. For example:

1. We *rationalise*: i.e. we invent seemingly reasonable excuses for our behaviour when we are unwilling to face our real (possibly rather shabby) motives.

2. We *repress*: For example we avoid becoming aware of a fantasy of murdering our mother, or we avoid accepting that we are, right now, feeling extremely angry.

3. We *deny*: i.e. Even if we have failed to entirely repress our anger, we try to deny to ourselves (and certainly to others) the full nature of it.

4. We *displace* our anxious or angry feelings away from their real source and onto safer targets or causes. For example, we may take it out on the kids when we are really angry with our spouse.

5. We *project* our own unacceptable problems onto others. For example, we may spend a lot of time getting our spouse to deal with her anger when much of the anger that needs to be dealt with is our own.

6. We *react* from one unacceptable feeling by acting out the opposite of our real emotions. For example, we go out of our way to smile and be nice to our spouse when we are actually feeling murderous towards him.

7. We *introject*: i.e. we attribute to ourselves desirable qualities that we may find (or imagine) in others. For example, we may pretend that we are like some calm and serene person we much admire, when in fact we are very different.

8. We *regress*: i.e. We retreat to a more childish way of behaving in order to escape from the responsibilities and pains of adult

life. Or, a more childish response seemingly bursts out when an unresolved early trauma is triggered by something happening here and now.

9. We *fantasise*: i.e. rather than face what is happening here and now, within and around me, I might prefer to drift off in my thoughts into some happy land of my own making where everything is going just as I would like it to be!

In all these ways, we fail to get through to ourselves, and we erect barriers to self-awareness and acceptance. How, then, can we expect to be able to get through to others when we are not even being honest with ourselves? For example, how can we deal with our conflicts with others when a great number of these are triggered and fuelled by conflicts within ourselves that we refuse to face? Many of the battles that really are within ourselves get displaced and projected into battles with the people around us. So often, we make war on each other because we are not at peace with ourselves.

Even when we are alone, our rationalisation and defensiveness can get complicated enough. But when we are with others we get into a whole new league of complexity. This is because the way I see myself, my experiences, motives and intentions, interconnects with the way I see you and the way I want you to see yourself! Likewise, the way you see yourself has consequences in terms of the way you see me and the way you want me to see myself. No wonder then, that personal relationships can become convoluted.

Our lives are intertwined, and so once I have set up a story about the who, what and why of 'myself' this immediately has consequences for you. If I am going to be able to keep my story intact it is going to be essential that you accept the various walk on parts that I have allotted for you in my act. For example, if I'm going to play the role of 'Strong male hero' I might consider it imperative that you accept that part of 'Helpless little woman'. Or, to bring this rather more up to date, if I am to play the part of 'Exploited progressive feminist', I might require that you accept the role of 'Defensive, domineering, male patriarch'. And, if you refuse to accept it, that only goes to show what a defensive, domineering, male patriarch you really are!

Whatever our roles or rationalisations, they have consequences for others who, we will insist, must 'see sense' and 'face reality' . . .

- How can I be a doctor if you won't be a patient?
- How can I be a peace-loving activist if you won't be a stiff, repressed and violent member of the military establishment?

- How can I father you if you refuse to act like a child?
- How can I feel self-righteous about you if you fail to behave like a pig?
- How can I be a powerful caring saint if you won't play along with the role of helpless wounded sinner?

In other words, as we approach each other, we are not merely trying to pick up from each other information about who we each are. We are also trying to plant on each other our own views about what we want each other to be! This is of vital importance to us. I cannot run my role, act, style, ploy, game or pretence if you refuse to fit in with it. Consequently, there are many occasions when we say "I just want to *get through to you*", when what we really mean is, "I just want you to *go along with me*"! (And act the part accordingly!)

As we meet, therefore, we each place considerable pressure on the other to play along with our own defences, pretences, rationalisations, games, ploys, image and roles. We will generally be quite unconscious of the subtle negotiation that may be going on about this. Each of us will be trying to find a way in which our own rationalisations can successfully mesh together with the pretences of the other person. Thus, for example, friendship, when both parties are highly defended, can be defined as the state of affairs whereby "*I go along with* your defences and rationalisations if you will *go along with* mine". Needless to say, we each deny that there is anything of the sort going on between us. Instead we say that our friend is "a sensible sort of person who sees most things realistically." (i.e. They agree with us!)

The more weighed-down I am with defences and pretences of one sort or another, the more I will find it crucial to get others to collude with my story. Because, if they don't, I may very well see it as a threat to my very survival and integrity. And so I am going to take it very personally if you refuse to play your part. My very identity will be built around my rationalisations and pretences; so if you won't go along with these you will (seem to) be threatening aspects of my very existence!

Given such delusion and collusion, how can we ever get through to ourselves? Is it essential that we are assisted by a Freudian, or other, analyst? If Freud managed to get through to himself without outside help then why can't we? And how, with or without help, can we ever be sure that we have successfully 'broken through'? Certainly we may get very excited from time when we discover some powerful new insight about ourselves. But how do we know that this isn't yet another illusion and pretence? Maybe we have just swapped one rationalisation for another. And how can we be sure that the outside analyst is any nearer the truth than we are? He, after all, may have his own games to play. Can we be sure that he has freed himself from all self-deception just because he's been through five years of psycho-analysis, or meditation or whatever? His training may merely have strengthened his fantasy of being a perceptive observer rather than improved his powers of observation.

In any case, what is this 'Self' that we are trying (or trying not) to get through to? In one sense I may know perfectly well who I am in that I could answer any of the questions that might be asked of me at an interview or in court. Yet, on the other hand, isn't there always more to say and see about me that I remain unaware of? How do I know when I've said it all? Is there an 'all' that could, even in principle, be finally said?

There are, if you like, (at least) two ways in which we can look at ourselves. On the one hand, we are the sum total of a complex idea about who we are; an idea that we have built up over many years. We are the totality of all our roles, moods, intentions, fears, fantasies, history, strivings, behaviour, opinions and so on. We may even identify ourselves with all our achievements, possessions and relationships. And were these to be taken away from us, we would very likely have a crisis of identity! Such crises are not at all uncommon, because whenever we face major losses, or changes, our sense of who we are may wobble. For example:

- "My job was a part of me, and now I have no job! . . . Who am I?"
- "My husband was a part of me, and now I have no husband. . . Who am I?"
- "My beautiful young face was a part of me, and now I see this old wrinkly mask that never used to be there."
- "My children were a part of me, and now they have left and gone."
- "My (singing/writing/dancing/walking/seeing/hearing) were a part of me, and now I can no longer . . . "

This (idea of) self that I contemplate and make inferences about can never in fact be observed in its totality. I can look at my whole body (with a mirror). But I am not just a physical object. I can observe the movement of my thoughts and feelings. But I am not just the thoughts and feelings that I am presently experiencing. I can watch the way I am behaving with the people around me. But I am not just a pattern of behaviour. Whatever I may observe, hear, smell, touch, witness, say and do, I am more than this. Or at least, I have the thought that I am more than this. But what more am I? Indeed, am I any of these things if I would, and will, continue to exist when most of them have changed and gone?

In addition to the Self-as-object; that can be thought about and observed (though never in its totality), there is the Self-as-subject, that actually does the observing and the thinking. Yet who is this 'I' that, right now, is thinking and observing?

Whoever or whatever I am, I (mercifully) don't spend too much of my time asking who or what I am! Indeed, I may feel least at home with myself when I am endlessly gazing into my own image. I am most comfortable when I get on with something else; when I lose myself in unself-conscious activity. On such occasions, my life feels richest, most full, most real. I don't have to keep on reflecting about myself in order to live right now. Indeed, the more I try to grip on to any idea of myself, the more this 'self' gets in the way of whatever I am actually seeing and doing here and now.

This is no abstract difficulty. Enormous amounts of very real energy are probably wasted because people are so desperately interested in being right about, and defending, whoever and what-ever they (think they) are. Instead we might live a fuller life if we allowed ourselves to discover rather than construct and defend ourselves. In other words, I might live more fully and with more integrity if I found myself by *living* instead of trying to *live in order* to find myself. The self that we found would then be an experi-enced, though indefinable, reality rather than a well-defined and (necessarily) well-defended concept.

In other words, trying to pin down our idea of 'Self' is like trying to nail a butterfly or catch a fish. If you ever succeed, you end up with a corpse, since the very nature of butterflies and fish lies in their change and movement. We try to get a grip of some notion of self that is constant, separable and unchanging; but change and interconnection is the real nature of self. It is not a constant at all. 'I', like 'x' in algebra, is a variable. By its very nature it takes on a different value, shape, meaning and identity in different contexts.

The ever elusive 'I' can be compared with the equally elusive 'fundamental particle' that physicists have been searching for throughout much of this century. Surely, we ask, there must be some basic and indivisible 'brick' of existence from which every-thing else is built? And, if so, it must have a clear shape and identity of its own that is not dependent on what is going on around it?

Physicists have tried for years to find this basic grit of existence that can't be broken up and which is solid and hard enough to be able to withstand the forces around it without distortion. Yet they have failed. Or, rather, they have succeeded in showing that no such ultimate substance exists. When physics gets to the fundamentals, we find that the world does not consist in forces and things: the *forcefulness* of things and the *thinginess* of forces are aspects of one inter-related process, so that, for example we can look at basic 'things' as particles or waves, and they are both, and we will choose one or the other depending on our frame of reference. This suggests that no 'thing' (and no person) is ultimately coherent, or definable, independently of what is happening around it. And so, for example, the perennial debate about free-will ("I can force things") versus determinism ("I am forced by things") loses much of its own force ("We are thinginess and forcefulness"). Consequently it no longer makes the sense we might have thought to ask, "Can I triumph over the world around me? or will I, ultimately, be overwhelmed by these greater forces?" If you are like a wave in the sea – part of a greater process – then how can you triumph or be defeated? Victory, Defeat... both presuppose an ultimate separation between Self and World that may, it seems, be more of an illusion than a reality.

Similarly, there is no absolute boundary between the stuff of the universe; the space within which it sits; and the time it spends in sitting there. On the contrary, objects bend the space they are in rather in the way that a cannon ball on a rubber sheet would bend the sheet. And curved space provides the line of easiest movement for the things that are 'in' it. Time, too, itself sits as an interacting variable in the equations that describe the Dance of Life.

The implications of this holistic perception of existence may take generations to percolate through to everyday consciousness, since we have for centuries assumed that there must be a firm handle of 'thinginess' somewhere that we can take on ourselves and our lives. Yet it seems that, with ourselves as with elementary particles, we have a choice: the more we try to pin down where and what we are, the less do we have much notion of where this is leading to and where we're heading. And the more we are willing to go with where we going, the less can we cling on to what and where we presently are. (The analogy with fundamental particles is interesting: quantum physics suggests that – in principle – the more accurate your knowledge of the position of a particle, the less can be known of its momentum, and vice versa).

To move and live we need, eventually, to let go of our strangling grip on our position and identity. People are understandably reluctant to do so since we fear that if we have nothing solid to cling on to we will fall back into anarchy and chaos. Yet nothing could be further from the truth. Physics, for example, may have shown that there is no basic, independent and unchanging entity anywhere in the universe; yet the existence it attempts to describe is far from chaotic and random. Indeed, the 'chaos' that it does find is itself part of a greater coherence within which chaos and order interconnect according to deeper principles that, in our developing mathematics of chaos, we are beginning to unravel. (And which were described poetically by Taoists more than two thousand years ago).

The fantastic, and awe-inspiring beauty of this interconnected world, as revealed by twentieth century science, requires a poetic rather than a prosaic description, and we are very far from understanding its implications. Breakthroughs in physics cannot be translated in any simplistic, or mechanical, way into a corresponding insight within Psychology. Therefore, the parallels I have drawn between, for example, fundamental particles and a fundamental self, are suggestive rather than descriptive. What is clear, though, is that we do not live in the empty and arid clockwork universe described by nineteenth century science (and which is still the picture offered to children at school). This is a world drenched in its own symphony; whose melodies echo and re-echo out of every part of it, each reflecting the all. The world is one great Song of Itself, and the smallest part of it is part of the chorus – whether we realise it or not. If we saw more than a small glimpse of its beauty, it might well blow the lid right off the self we think we are. Not that this dance of life (or 'dance of Shiva', as the Hindus call it,) is always pleasant and congenial; we have to listen to and move with the whole interconnected lot of it; including all its horror and pain and dread; its darker moods and its more tragic melodies.

More prosaically, though, and more often, we tend to spend much of our time shut away from the Music of the Spheres all around us; living instead within our 'dungeon of self'. I don't, however, think Cyril Connolly is right to say this is always a life-sentence (see quotation at the beginning of this chapter). We all 'come out of ourselves' sometimes for air, sunshine and exercise; though how far we are willing, and able, to step beyond the perimeter fence of 'me and mine' is unclear. Cyril Connolly's remark is itself one that, if only for a split second, can free us from ourselves. We probably manage to forget to be locked up, just as we forget to be depressed, more often than we may realise. The trouble is that, as soon as we do realise we are experiencing something beyond our own petty attempts at significance, we try to hang on to the experi-

ence and thus lock ourselves away once again within our own
self-centredness.

When locked into any idea about the sort of individual we are
and the sort of person we're supposed to be, we will often feel the
need to defend these ideas from the depredations of others. When,
on the other hand, we no longer cling on to such ideas we can,
instead, simply trust that 'we are'; even though we can't define
ourselves. Then we no longer have to work towards 'integrity' or
defend it; we simply discover it as a given reality, that was there
all along!

We cannot help but be ourselves; but we lose touch with this
because we try so hard to 'find ourselves' (i.e. build up the perfect
idea, or conception, of who we really are). But we don't have to
conceive of ourselves (conceptually) since we have already been
conceived (literally!).

In other words, I get through to myself when I am no longer
attached to any idea about who I am. Such ideas about personal
identity have their place, but I am free only when I can witness
them and look in on them, rather than looking out at the world
through them. Such a 'witness' cannot be defined since it is not
an object but rather the subject. Even this formulation is more
wordy than it might best be. After all, 'subject', too, is a concept
that has particular meanings within English (subject-verb-object)
grammar but a more uncertain reference outside of that language-
world of conception.

In summary: I may dearly want to get through to you. But how
can I do so when I am so concerned to ensure that you behave in
a way that fits in with my idea of myself? And how can you ever
get through to me if I am more interested in the blue-print I've got
planned for you than the reality that you are? We may love to meet
each other as we really are; and yet, when we are attached to ideas
about who we are, we cannot meet because we are much more
keen to mould each other into the 'proper' shape than face each
other in the shape we are actually in. In other words, we may say
that we want to get through to ourselves and each other, but
perhaps we are more interested in making contact with our ideas
of our respective identities rather than the ever changing and often
mysterious reality? In the process, as we have seen, we find it
imperative to inflict these precious ideas onto everyone else around
us.

We seem to want to be right about who we are rather than alive
to ourselves and others! And, in consequence, we prefer to be right
about each other rather than allow another to get right through to us.

The prospect of facing myself in a genuinely honest and open way can be difficult, because the reality is so often so very different from the ideal. For example, we like to believe that our personality is reasonably free from darker, disreputable, malicious and seamy features; and yet each of us is capable, and guilty, of extreme forms of cruelty, ruthlessness and hatred. Beneath all our arrogance and bravado we are generally terrified of facing our more evil manifestations.

So many of us may strut around in one way or another, and it is painful to realise that this need to prove how wonderful we are generally masks an underlying lack of faith in ourselves. After all, if we really felt ok, about ourselves, what need would there be for us to continue to have to prove that we are ok?

Similarly, facing up to ourselves is difficult for as long as we cling on to the notion that there is a tidy, observable, coherent and consistent self to face up to. My real self, some imagine, is like a steady shining beacon that beams out through all the apparent confusion, interpersonal conflict and inner turmoil of everyday living. In other words, we hope that our doubts, fears, chaos, destructiveness, contrary and contradictory natures are not really present, but are merely a surface layer below which we can find our real, eternal, stable selves.

Our turmoil, however, is real enough. Not infrequently we will have 'platoons' of contrary and contradictory yearnings and responses passing through; each bouncing off, and reacting to, its opposite. We are in conflict with ourselves at least as much as (generally more than) we battle with anyone else. We have three or four contrary views about many topics, which is why, when one person has taken any position on any matter we find it very easy to adopt its opposite. We may very well do this even if, the previous day, we had been taking the same line as the person we now oppose.

In relation to this, it is worth remembering the defence mechanisms referred to earlier. We may be unhappy about the conflict that goes on between people but so much of this arises because we fail to look at, and learn from, our own *internal* conflict . . .

- We *project* our own issues onto others and pretend that the trouble is coming from them rather than from inside ourselves;
- We *displace* our own internal frustrations with ourselves onto frustration with the other person.
- We *compensate* with one person because of feelings within ourselves that we are running away from.

- We *introject* qualities in other people, and pretend that they describe who we are because we don't want to look at the reality of who we are.
- We create *fantasies* about the nature of another person and then, maybe, have a conflict with this fantasy, because we don't want to look at the truth.

The examples can be replicated endlessly.

We may like to think that one day we will finally arrive at some celestial inner destination known as 'myself' where, at last, there will be eternal peace, tranquillity, certainty and the chance of an error-free, hassle-free life. But this, too, is fantasy! There is no such option. All we can do is come to terms with this as well as we can and then there is indeed peace of a sort, but despite and within the turmoil, rather than in the absence of it.

In later chapters, we will be looking at more of the interpersonal skills that can help us to get through to others. But, as I have said before, what really matters most are our underlying attitudes and intentions. Any skill can be co-opted to serve our basic goals; regardless of whether or not the goals themselves are worthy. And so, for example, if the underlying spirit of what we do is malevolent or manipulative, then the skills we learn will simply become new weapons, and means, to serve our disreputable ends.

Thus, more specifically, if your main aim is to get other people to fit in with your fantasy, then your new-found interpersonal skills will simply be used to help you in this somewhat shabby task. Many skilled and sophisticated communicators do no more with their skills than co-opt, bedazzle, stroke and hypnotise their victims into sharing their own illusions. To put it another way, the very same skills and abilities that can be used to get us closer to ourselves can also be used to take us still hopelessly further away from ourselves (and from each other). Instead we may inhabit a smooth and glossy world of our dreams and take ourselves ever further away from authenticity. My very great fear is that this is precisely what is happening on a gigantic scale in 'civilised' Western consumer society.

Such sophisticated, yet dishonest, patterns of behaviour amount to a sorry waste, and they are brilliantly documented in a hilarious, and very unsettling, novel by Cyra McFadden, entitled *The Serial*, (Pan 1978). The book describes Liberated Life in Marin County, California where everyone is busy committing themselves in 'LTRs' ('Living together Relationships'), 'renewing', 'revising', 'restructuring', and 'evolving' in their progressive lives. Everyone wants to 'get through' and 'get clear'; everyone learns all the necessary life-skills and psycho-babble jargon. But, because everyone is essentially unwilling to face himself with *genuine* honesty, the whole business is corrupted and futile. Which reminds me; I was told that in Los Angeles, in some networks, the phrase *"I really hear you"* has decayed into a statement of sarcasm and abuse! This expression has been so much over-used and abused that it has now really come to mean *"Why don't you just piss off!"* – which, sadly, might be nearer to some people's 'bottom line' than the trendy 'humanistic' original. (Nearer still to the heart of the matter, though, will be a good deal of hurt and loneliness!)

It is tempting in such circumstances, to react against sophistication of any sort, and hanker instead for the wholesome, honest, child-like world of innocence. We might think that we have all got far too clever than is good for us. Why can't we see the world once again with the simple honesty of the child who (if young enough) is uncluttered with self-consciousness and schemes to emancipate or defend itself? The child, generally, has a raw zest for living, free of schemes and wheeler-dealing. It just celebrates the joys of being alive with a bounce and spontaneity which we can envy. It has no idea of itself and, we might imagine, it is all the more fortunate for that!

This, though, is just so much romantic fantasy. The very young child certainly does not have any conception whatever of 'Myself'. But we soon find that it is busy working away to build up just such a conception, regardless of anything we may do, or not do, to encourage it. Indeed, the whole of childhood (and early adulthood) is given over to patiently constructing an ever-more sophisticated idea of who I am. The child is fascinated by its own name and will soon want to be able to write it. It is keen to learn what it possesses and what does not belong to it. It wants to know what it is entitled to, what is expected of it, what it can do, what are the boundaries of its existence and the main characters within these boundaries. It wants to know what are the rules that govern our behaviour. It is soon keen to tell you what it likes and doesn't like. What it wants and doesn't want.

Furthermore, it is not long before even quite young children begin to try to mould parents and siblings to fit in with the personality they are constructing for themselves. And not long, too, before youngsters learn how to boast, undermine and torture each other as well as co-operate and show concern. The child's affection may be simple and open, but so too is its cruelty, denial and posturing. Only later does it learn to 'behave like an adult' and thus manoeuvre for position in a way that covers its tracks!

(I remember as a young child how we would manoeuvre and compete with each other with questions like: "Have you got a fridge?" "We've got commercial television" "Haven't you got a washing machine yet?". And I can remember feeling the need to keep it a secret from some rivals that we hadn't yet had our TV set adapted to take ITV! As adults we can look with smug condescension laced with liberal unease at such childish antics. Yet I would maintain that the only difference between adults and children in respect of, for example, their material competitiveness is that the children are upfront about it whereas we like to pretend that we are above such mundane concerns!)

In short, the last thing the child wants to do is remain in child-like innocence, quite unaware of the boundaries between self and 'not-self'. It is keen to grow up; to discover, construct, learn about and exercise its ever growing and ever-enlarging personality. To seek to prevent it from doing all of this would be folly and a sign of our ultimate despair.

Similarly, in early adulthood, it is important that, having moved away from the protection of our parents, we learn to find a place for ourselves in the wider society. We have to carve a space that is for us and ours, and take on our roles and responsibilities – both the ones we have chosen and those others that are expected of us. We have to discover just how far we have freedom to move within the constraints of the world around us. We have to find our powers, opportunities and limitations. We have to continue, in other words, in the long (and never-ending) process of working out who we are and, by implication, what we are not, and cannot, be and do.

Throughout our lives, we face different chapters and turning points; marriage, job, promotion, unemployment, separation, growth and departure of children, death of parents, ageing and loss of one's own powers and responsibilities. At each stage we are forced to revise our conception of who we are, since so much of what we may have thought was central to our personality in fact changes and moves away. This can, for some, feel like a tragedy that they never come to terms with. They refuse to face up to change and loss, and refuse to go through the mourning process that such reconciliation requires. In other words, they imagine that their finest self is the self of their supposed hey-day when they were at their most fit and strong and successful. They cling on, fruitlessly to this lost self and thus can never find themselves as they are here and now.

Some people, on the other hand, learn to accommodate and attach themselves to a revised conception of themselves. They look

into the mirror and – eventually – after much unavoidable hear-
tache, they are willing to accept the grey hairs, the wrinkled face
and all the rest. But best of all is where we can learn, not only to
be ever revising our precious conception of who we are, but to sit
more loosely in relation to any conception of self whatsoever.

Our ideas of 'Myself' (like any idea) can serve a useful purpose.
The labels and descriptions help us to clarify goals, options, styles,
roles and all the rest. But they are, in the final analysis, just a bunch
of ideas; the nature of which will need to be changed as the years
go by. The sun shines regardless of whether or not it is called 'sun'
or 'soleil' or whatever. And we can shine too, regardless of our
latest fancy notion about 'who we really are'.

At some, difficult to define stage, every idea, including our ideas
of 'Myself', ceases to be an aid to insight and action and becomes
instead a blindfold and a prison. Our view of who we are gets set
in plaster and then we wonder why we don't feel free! No description of ourselves can ever be final and complete and, far from
letting this be a source of frustration and insecurity, it can be a
cause for awe, excitement, wonder, exhilaration and release. When
asked "Who are you?" we may give a long list of predictable, or
clever, answers. Alternatively, we may decide that there is no need
to rush for an answer. Instead we might sometimes choose just to
watch and witness and see what's next, without pretending to
know at all. In the last moment of our lives, when all that we ever
became attached to may have passed away, we might face the next
moment with the same eternal awe, and wonder "What's next?"

Questions:

(Reminder: there are many more questions and exercises available in this, and other, chapters than you could possibly manage to tackle at any one time. You are invited to explore only those that seem most useful, as and when the time seems right).

1. Which parts of your personality do you most like to display to others?

2. Which parts do you try to hide from others?

3. Which parts do you even try to hide from yourself?

4. Which parts do close friends consider that you hide?

5. What is the worst thing that could happen if you revealed . . . (hidden part) to . . . (particular individual)?

6. What is the best thing that could happen?

7. Think of particular individuals who are close to you: what do they like to display to you? And hide from you? What are the worst and best things that could happen if they were more open?

8. What might happen if you talked about your answers to the above questions to particular individuals?

9. Can you think of occasions where others used one or other of the various defence mechanisms listed in this chapter?

10. Can you think of occasions where you have used such defences? Could others suggest to you the sort of defences you tend to utilise?

11. What weaknesses, failings (and strengths!) in yourself do you tend to attribute to others? In other words, in what ways do you blacken others with your own shadow? Equally important, in what ways do you illuminate others with your own light? Could you talk to the people concerned about this?

12. What sort of behaviour in others tends to cause you to over-react or 'boil over'? Could you talk about this to the persons concerned?

13. Is there anyone you know who, you consider, knows you better in many respects than you know yourself?
What do they know that you don't know?

What makes you think they know?
How do you feel about this?

14. Can you think of a time when you were not being true to yourself? In what way were you being phoney and why? Is there anything you could have done about this? What can you learn from all this? Who could help you answer this question?

15. Can you think of an occasion when you were so unsure of yourself that it was a hindrance? What did you need to know in order to be more confident? Who could help you answer this question?

16. Can you think of an occasion when you were so sure of yourself that it was a hindrance? What prejudices and perceptions did you need to let go of in order to be more open and effective? Who could help you answer this question?

17. What kind of internal battles have you been having with yourself recently?
What effect have these had in your relationships with others?
Can you look in to your internal turmoil (from a peaceful place inside) as well as simply looking out from it? If you can, then you will gain perspective. You might even have a sense that there is harmony and meaning in the conflict.
For as long as you are lost within your own inner turmoil, and identifying with one or other part of it, you will look out on the world from this struggling part of yourself and blame the world for all your inner tension. Your own wounds will be etched across your view of the world and you will find it difficult to differentiate problems that are out there from the ones that are inside, within yourself).

18. In what respects do you refuse to accept yourself as you are?
What is the best/worst thing that could happen if you accepted these parts of your personality?
Who told you that you mustn't accept these parts of yourself?
Who might be able to help you to accept yourself a little more?

19. Is your voice of conscience generally a firm and supportive friend or a harsh and domineering tyrant? What are the consequences? As well as being kind and considerate to others, what about trying to behave like this to yourself? If you could forgive yourself, perhaps you would find it easier to forgive others?

20. What major crises and turning points have you faced in your life?
    What effect have these had on your self-image?
    What have you gained and lost from these turning points?
    What could you gain from them?

21. What major crises and turning points are you likely to have to face in the future?
    How will you deal with them?
    What effect will these have on your self-image?

22. Can you think of occasions where you would find yourself and get through more effectively:
    - If only you would talk more?
    - If only you would talk less?
    - If only you did more?
    - If only you did less?

    We can find ourselves:
    - In silence and reflection; and
    - In action and interaction.

    Do you think you have got the right balance between these various ways of being in your own life?

In relation to all these questions and exercises ask:
    What have I learned?
    What positive action can I take as a result of what I've learned?

Exercises:

1. Write a letter to yourself, where you tell yourself all about the more important thoughts, feelings, fears, fantasies and intentions that you have been running away from. See if you can adopt a tone with yourself that is firm and uncompromising, yet also caring, compassionate and forgiving.

2. Write the letter that, you imagine, a very close friend or Wise Old Person would write to you if they really wanted to help you get to know yourself better. Choose a person who respects you and who is genuinely seeking to be of help to you. What would it be like to show this letter to the person concerned?

3. If particular parts of your body could speak what would they say (about the way you treat them and the way they respond

to you)?! Have a dialogue with parts of the body that are of particular interest and concern to you, and with the body as a whole.

4. If a particular dream recurs or seems important to you, have a dialogue with the dream or parts of the dream. If people and objects in the dream could speak, what would they say? Which particular parts would be really worth listening to? If you continued the dream as a day-dream what would happen next? What would you like to happen next? What can you learn from all this?

(Getting a dreamed image, or body part, to speak seems somewhat fantastic and strange when you first do it. It is a simple device for unlocking the symbolic meanings we have attached to the people and things around us).

5. Imagine that you have available to you a very Wise Old Person who you can go and consult about any matter whatsoever. Create a vivid fantasy of the place in which this Wise Person is to be found. Go and have a dialogue with this person and ask any questions you care to ask. See what answers you get. (And the notice that this 'Wise Person' is in fact a projection of your own wisdom!)

6. Imagine a dialogue with a person you are close to. Begin the first sentence as follows: "You tell me that I am (like this . . .) But really/also I am (like this . . .)".
Imagine their response.
Imagine them using the same two sentences directed at you. What can you learn?
Can you each escape from your respective power plays; at least in this fantasy?
Would it be safe to share what you've learned with the person concerned? Or would you each use it as further ammunition to get the better of each other?

7. Think of a person who is very important in your life and fill in the gaps in the following sentence:
"*I am . . . and so I expect you to be . . .* "
You can do this for as long as useful insights keep on coming to you.
Then: reverse the 'I'; i.e. imagine that this person is now doing this exercise.
What would they write down about their view of themselves and their consequent expectations of you?

You can, if you wish, repeat the entire exercise in relation to other people who come to mind as worth considering.

8. In pairs. A asks B "Who are you?"
B replies with whatever first comes to mind and (if she can trust the other person sufficiently) without censorship.
A says *"Thank you. Who are you?"* (A makes no other comment whatsoever and seeks to build up a steady, firm, inquiring yet unaggressive rhythm to the questioning).
Later; A and B swap over roles.

You can take five minutes each way for this exercise (or five days!) The aim is to assist a person to gain an overall perspective of who they think they are but also, more crucially, to loosen any attachment to whoever they think they are.

9. Sit yourself down in a quiet and comfortable position where you will not be disturbed for fifteen to twenty minutes:
Watch the stream of visual images go rushing by.
Listen to all the imagined conversations.
Notice all the idle thoughts and fantasies.
Do not either resist or hang on to any of this.
Notice that it all arises and passes away.
Notice that none of these thoughts and feelings are necessary to support your personal identity.
Notice what you can, without even trying, learn from all of this.

10. Draw your life as though it was a journey. Draw the 'map' with all the major milestones, pitfalls, havens, confusions, peaks and troughs. Use whatever images come to mind.
Extend your road map into the future using three possible routes:

The worst outcome
The best outcome
The most likely outcome.

What do you learn from all this? What positive action can you take as a result of what you've learned?

11. It is sometimes difficult to be honest with others. How far can you be honest with yourself? . . . Keep a Journal where you write down whatever thoughts, feelings and observations you have that seem worth recording and which might help you to gain some perspective on yourself as you look back over the years.

12. How far are you able to describe the sort of person you are? How far do others agree with your description? If you were a car what make of car would you be? (What 'personality' of car best describes your own personality?) Similarly, if you were an animal, what sort of animal would you be? What sort of dog? tree? landscape? weather? country? music? object? How far do your friends and family agree with your answers?

13. Plan your autobiography and see how this can help you gain perspective on your life as a whole.

14. Go, regularly, (in your mind or in reality) to a Temple of Silence, Lake, Hill, Mountain, Woodland, Garden, Sea Coast or wherever else you might find peace and perspective. See if you can 'sit loose' to the Self that you know and can define and which will continue to 'chat' on about this and that for most of the time. In an enormous Silence there lives the Self that cannot be defined. If you chase after it then all you will find is a frenetic chasing. Is there a 'witness' to your life or are you allowing yourself to get lost in the details and daily manoeuvring?

Don't forget: we can find ourselves; though never finally - and so our lives remain alive. How dull life would be if we ever got the final measure of ourselves and our lives! There is no final self to find! There is always more. Thus the awe, mystery and fascination of being alive at all!

The truth about ourselves and others is multi-faceted. This is why it is possible to discover and express different facets of our personality in different situations with different people. Any of these facets and potentialities may become real depending on the circumstances. They cannot all do so, though, since in one lifetime there are only a limited number of people I can be with, places I can go to, and projects that I can take on. "Who I am" is a matter that is not entirely separable from "Where I am" and "Who I'm with".

However, the 'I' that I am is not to be entirely determined by other people and surrounding circumstances. For, if I pretend to be whoever you want me to be, then I will be no more than your fantasy; and will reveal nothing of my own possibilities at all.

5. Getting through: some Rules and Verbal Skills.

A fool uttereth all his mind.

The Bible, *Proverbs* 29.11

Talk does not cook rice.

Chinese Proverb

Talking is like playing on the harp; there is as much in laying the hand on the strings to stop their vibration as in twanging them to bring out their music.

Oliver Wendell Holmes, (1858)

It is very rare, and would generally seem rather strange, for anyone to bother to write down, or even explicitly discuss, the rules and principles that govern, and help to promote, effective communication in groups. Few individuals ever consciously think about the standards that they see operating among their particular circles of friends or colleagues. Large, formal organisations might well be more explicit about some of the codes of conduct that are expected; but these will not probe very far into the dynamics of human relationship *per se*. Certainly it would be unusual (though it might sometimes be useful?) for people within families and informal groups to ask *"What rules do we adopt and need to change?"* or *"What skills do we need to improve if we are to communicate better?"*

And yet in every network of people there will be such rules even though no one might ever have systematically thought about or promoted them. Somehow or another the rules take form and, without consciously knowing what or how, we learn what they are and try to put them into practice.

Human beings are, in fact, pretty good at learning rules; and this is just as well. We would be very restricted in our ability to learn anything if we did not, first and foremost, try to grasp the principles that bind together what we learn. Otherwise, we would be faced with what would appear to us to be totally disparate bits of information. Thus, for example, young children learn the language they are born into by learning the rules of grammar. No one teaches these to them and yet, somehow or another, they have a built-in propensity to 'sniff them out'. We can discover this by observing the nature of the grammatical errors children make. Over and over again, you will find that the error is not random or chaotic. Rather, it has arisen because they have applied one rule and have not yet learned that there are exceptions and complications. Thus, say, a child might talk about "two sheeps". And if you offer him a fantasy animal and call it a 'wuk'; he will happily say that "here are two wuks"; and thus apply a rule about plurals without ever being told.

However, we don't always do quite as well as we might when it comes to being aware of, and applying, the rules. And so it is worth examining the principles that govern effective social interaction, so that we can see where we might be going wrong. Of course, individual groups and communities will differ in the rules they operate. But there is a substantial number of fundamental principles that apply to just about any group of people. It is these basic principles that deserve particular attention.

Let's begin with some of the more straightforward (and superficial?) conclusions drawn from research evidence. They will, I think, produce few surprises:

1. Popular people, throughout the world, tend to be cheerful and friendly. They take a genuine interest in others; they are helpful and kind; interesting and amusing. Unpopular people, on the other hand, (and are you surprised?) are gloomy and hostile; boastful and mainly interested in themselves. They try to get others to do things for them rather than offer very much to others.

2. Some individuals, on the other hand, may be popular because of their *position* as well as their personality. The roles they occupy in society may mean that they are able to offer tangible help of one kind or another. Thus, for example, Power can in itself be an Aphrodisiac!

3. Physically attractive individuals, of either sex, tend to be more popular. (It's an unjust world!) To some extent, obviously, physical attractiveness is something we are born with, or without, as the case may be. But an attractive personality will in

fact radiate out in a decidedly physical sense – smiles, posture, eye contact, physical health, a sprightly, outgoing style. Conversely, an unattractive personality will be able to destroy the finest good looks that Nature has endowed.

4. We are more likely to be popular if we know how to provide people with appropriate rewards. Many of these are non-verbal: for example; smiling, looking, touching, using a friendly tone of voice. (We will look at non- verbal aspects of communication in more detail in the following chapter.)

5. Intimacy can be rewarding (and not just physical intimacy): for example, we tend to find it rewarding when people share good news with us and disclose intimate thoughts and feelings, (providing they don't disclose to us substantially more than we are willing to reveal to them.)

6. Emotional and material support is rewarding. And, not surprisingly, we tend to be more favourably disposed towards people who support and reward us than we are with those who try to undermine, threaten or punish us!

You may well say that all of this is just plain obvious and that we scarcely require scientific research to prove (or confirm) what we have known all along. Yet, there are times when the obvious needs to be re-stated because, if we look carefully at our own behaviour, we will often find that we are simply failing to put these obvious principles into practice and that we, as well as others, are suffering as a consequence!

Take, for example, the question of rewards versus punishments. We all know that we like to be rewarded rather than punished (unless we are real masochists!). We feel more favourably disposed towards people who are rewarding; and we are more willing to be positive and accommodating to them. Conversely, when people punish us, we are more likely to want to strike out at them, to resist them and, if they force us to fit in with them, we will be prone to seek revenge whenever an opportunity presents itself. When we have been heavily punished and have been unable to punish in return, we will very likely want to 'even the score' in one way or another if ever the opportunity arises.

We all know this. We know that a punishing approach to people is contagious, destructive and tends to lead to resistance and retribution. It also leads us to feel bad about ourselves inside because, even when our powers of attack are greater than the retaliatory powers in others, we know in our hearts that we have simply created a wasteland of hurt, resentment and hostility around us. This hostility may be hidden if we can successfully intimidate others, but it will be there beneath the surface all the same, even if no one is conscious of it. We will feel its latent presence however much we try to repress and deny it. We will find no peace.

Punishments, of course, can take many forms; some are loud and obvious, others are covert and subtle. Language, for example, can be used to punish in a wide variety of ways:

1. We can be *insulting*; either directly or by innuendo.
2. We can be *abusive* and condescending.
3. We can label, name, and *interpret* in a manner that punishes and undermines rather than informs and supports.
4. We can be *sarcastic*.
5. We can *ridicule*.
6. We can make sweeping *allegations*.
7. We can *accuse* people of wicked motives and generally offer *mean-spirited* interpretations of their behaviour – in a way that is designed to punish rather than enlighten.
8. We can attempt to *slaughter* people with 'the truth' as we see it.
9. We can *blame* and *threaten*.
10. We can *complain* and *nag* – in a way that wears people down rather than inspires them to change.
11. We can *exaggerate* and distort; for example with the over-use of expressions like; *"You must"*, *"This is awful"*, *"The way you behave is terrible and I can't stand it!"*
12. We can go on and on and on so that the sheer *length of time* we speak is itself a punishing experience.
13. We can give *orders* and provide *'answers'* when this is inappropriate and undermining to others.
14. We can be deliberately, but sneakily, *provocative*.
15. We can *manipulatively* parade our 'hurts', 'oppression', 'martyrdom', 'powerlessness' and 'despair' in powerful ways that are designed to punish and wound.
16. We can be *passively aggressive;* by withholding positive behaviours unless others fit in with us.
17. We can place a *'sting in the tail'* of our words.
18. We can go in for a *'hit and run'* approach; i.e. drop an insulting or otherwise offensive remark on someone just as we, or they, are leaving the room.
19. We can *criticise* in a way that seeks to undermine rather than support.

20. We can hide our malevolence and our punishing tactics by ensuring that we communicate in a vague, indirect and *dishonest* way.
21. We can try to 'corner' a person and show them no mercy if ever we succeed.
22. We can *brood* and complain about past grievances, and use these to exact *revenge* and to threaten and undermine other people.
23. We can *reject* or belittle any efforts at reconciliation on the part of the other person by saying, or implying, that it is too little, too late, and less than we are entitled to.

A long list like this may seem too depressing and debilitating. It is, however, important that we are aware of our negative behaviours so that we can face up to their destructiveness and thus, hopefully, resolve to change. We can't make positive changes, though, unless and until we can get a clear picture of what these might be and how they might really be rewarding, not only to others, but to ourselves as well, at least in the long run. And so let's get to the more important part of this discussion, and see what we could do if we wished to turn the above destructive options into something more positive and constructive:

1. We could show *praise* and appreciation of the good that we see in a person. And we could do this openly, directly and unconditionally rather than in a vague and half-hearted and manipulative fashion.
2. We could be *supportive* and show due respect.
3. We could offer our own interpretations in a tentative and *tactful* way rather than intruding on others with them.
4. We could be *sincere* with others yet gentle in relation to their feelings of vulnerability.
5. We could *reassure*.
6. We could be specific, *practical* and limited about what we might wish from a person.
7. We could be *compassionate* about the motives of others, pay more attention to our own and try to see, and work with, what's positive in all of us.
8. We could have some *humility* about what seems to us to be the truth, and tell it, with tact and humane intentions; when people are ready, willing and able to listen to us.
9. We could *set an example* and offer incentives.
10. We could share, and *take responsibility* for, our feelings, opinions and preferences, and be willing to negotiate.

11. We could be *realistic*, responsible and sincere. We could use statements that take the form "*I . . . (preference)*" rather than "*You . . . (blame)*". In this way we could avoid 'musterbating', 'awfulising', 'terribilising' and indulging in 'can't-stand-it-itis.

12. We could avoid long monologues and give others *a chance to speak*.

13. We could *state preferences*, make requests, and mind our own business.

14. We could assertively and sincerely *defuse* hostility in others; without being evasive.

15. We could acknowledge our power yet *reveal our hurt* in order to communicate rather than control.

16. We could *reward* others without demanding that they owe us anything in return.

17. We could find '*a positive note*' to end on when we suspect that what we say will be hard for someone to hear.

18. We could ensure that others have *plenty of time* to speak when we have something to say that they might find hard to hear.

19. We could turn any criticism and complaint into a specific, practical, yet negotiable, *request*.

20. We could try to be *clear, direct* and *honest* (yet tactful).

21. We could try to ensure that there is always a '*face-saving*' way forward for others that is in both their interests and ours.

22. We could look for, and discuss, the *positive* steps that we could take in the future that would be practical, healing and rewarding to us both.

23. We could *acknowledge* any favours offered by the other person in a way that rewards them for their efforts.

The first list can look daunting and depressing. The second (above) looks too good to be true since, we know, we cannot really expect to live up to such high standards all the time and thus become a kind of 'Saint'. These are all, clearly, ideals which, being human, we can only expect to meet some of the time. But, provided we're not insistently perfectionistic, it is worthwhile to state and re-state our ideals from time to time. Moreover, the above are, I hope, specific, practical and detailed, rather than vague and woolly. That doesn't mean that we will always put them into practice; but they will, I hope, provide some sort of map or guide for those occasions when we really do seem to have got lost, or stuck in the mire, in our relationships.

Thanks to our ability to use language, therefore, we have a variety of ways in which we can be punishing or rewarding in our dealings with other people. It has been shown, over and over again, that rewards are more effective (let alone more desirable) than punishments. Moreover, such rewardingness is desirable, not only when we are listening to and fitting in with other people, but also when we ourselves have requests, preferences, opinions and emotions to share. We are more likely to get what we want if we use 'the carrot' rather than 'the stick'; so that, in addition to meeting our own needs, we also help others to get something *they* want.

Of course people will never find out what we think, feel and want if we do no more than offer rewards. We also need to know how to make requests and, generally, to assert ourselves with messages of our own.

To assert yourself at all, of course, you have got to believe that you have a right to your own thoughts, feelings and wishes and, moreover, a right to communicate these to others. (I certainly want to suggest that you do have such a right; provided, as always, that your underlying intention is essentially honourable). This may seem obvious, but many people find it difficult even to begin to be assertive because they are imprisoned in the belief that others have got to give them a 'permit' before they can have, or express, any view of their own.

The second basic assumption that we have to make before we can assert ourselves is that, however difficult, it is possible to communicate our thoughts, feelings and wishes with good-will; and without violating the integrity of others. Again, this is not an assumption shared by everybody. Some compliant individuals take the view that, if they were really to say what they thought, it would have a destructive effect on the people around them. This is a particular problem in relation to the expression of anger. We are so used to using anger as a weapon with which to threaten and wound other people that we may be quite at a loss to know how it could ever be expressed with any sort of honour, dignity or humanity. And so a key part of any training programme in assertiveness needs to be to help people get a glimpse of how a constructive expression of anger might be possible.

Thirdly, people need to be reminded that being assertive does not have to, and should not, involve finding new ways of winning, punishing, outmanoeuvring or generally trampling on people. I have found that, with every course on Assertiveness that I have ever taught, more than half of the customers have (sheepishly) agreed that they have come to the course primarily in order to *get*

the better of spouses, friends, relations or colleagues at work. Assetiveness courses, in the U.K. and U.S.A. are presently doing very
good business; but I do fear for the outcome of all this if people
simply use what they have learned as new, 'smart', weaponry in
the unending struggle to get ahead.

No wonder so many of the spouses and colleagues of Assertiveness students report that they feel suspicious and uneasy! They
may well be right to ask *"What's the catch? What's the game? What
are you going to lay on me now?"* Assertiveness is going to get a very
bad reputation if the skills involved are merely added to our 'armoury'; and, I must say, I do get the impression from some authors
of books on Assertiveness that they are positively, though covertly,
encouraging the emergence of a new style of sophisticated *smartass*
who learns how to win while looking virtuous and (ever so slightly)
smug!. Assertiveness will, however, be welcomed by all if it is seen
as a way of promoting a 'Win-Win' scenario (to use the jargon!),
where both parties get as near as possible to getting what they
want, and both learn to treat the other with respect and dignity.
(The latter, of course, is a somewhat old-fashioned term; but I
should like to see it revived!)

In other words, assertiveness is based on the idea that we can
avoid both the roles of 'doormat' and 'steam-roller' and that we
should try to find compromises that are acceptable to all. At the
very least, we ought to be able to agree to outcomes that do not
do damage to either party.

The practical skills involved in asserting ourselves are relatively
easy to describe and understand. It is putting them into day to day
use that is more difficult! This is because most of us have deeply
ingrained habits – of aggression, or compliance, or manipulative
punishment of one sort or another. And these habits may go very
deep indeed. It is only by practising and practising and practising
over and over again that we can shift these old habits and substitute
them with something more constructive. It is much easier to learn
and practice such skills in the company of others; thus I do recommend that you consider the list of recommended addresses at the
end of the book.

The best courses on assertiveness will spend only a limited
amount of time on the theory; most attention will be given to seeing
how the theory works out in practice. This is done by role playing
examples of situations where students have found it difficult to
assert themselves. Such role play also gives people the chance to
try out different ways of saying the same thing, and to get clear
feed-back from the group as a whole as to what seems to be working

or not working. Essential, too, are homework assignments where the individuals concerned go away and attempt to put what they have learned into practice between sessions. They then report back and there is further discussion with practical suggestions offered in a supportive, informal and encouraging atmosphere.

It is surprising what rapid progress many people can make when provided with appropriate advice and support. Of course, miracles should not be expected; set-backs, doubt and confusion are inevitable; but we can learn to set ourselves small and realistic goals, work towards these and feel good about ourselves because of the efforts we are making.

People differ enormously in their abilities to assert themselves. For example, within one evening I have worked with three students who were at very different levels of skill and who felt blocked for very different reasons. The first had difficulty simply in speaking at all to a group of a dozen or so others. For him the immediate target that was of interest was to simply put together a few coherent sentences that other people could hear. He prevented himself from doing this with the following beliefs:

- *"I have nothing of interest to say."*
- *"I have to rehearse everything I say in advance; by which time the moment for saying it has passed."*
- *"I have to watch myself very carefully as I'm speaking so that I don't make a mistake. This, though, makes me too self-conscious and so I make lots of mistakes."*
- *"It's terrible to make mistakes; it's unbearable to make a fool of yourself; I am bound to spend a lot of my time thinking how terrible it is."*

This little package of beliefs (which are quite commonplace) was a lethal mixture that effectively prevented any speech. To fight them gives them more power, but we can substitute them with other beliefs that are more realistic and more attractive. For example:

- *"People take more interest in me when I stop trying so hard to be something or get somewhere."*
- *"I can find out what I want to say, by saying it."*
- *"I can pay attention to what I'm saying rather than to myself saying it. Then I won't keep tripping over myself."*
- *"I don't have to make a 'perfect speech'. In fact I come over as more human if I just let the words come out and trust myself. Some of what I say may seem a bit confused or unclear but so what? In any case, how else can I sort out my ideas?"*

With encouragement, when the moment is right, such a tongue-tied individual can let himself just see what words come out without rehearsing anything at all. He then finds that the less he tries the more he succeeds. The coherence of what he is saying simply emerges rather than having to be forced into clarity in advance of speech!

The second candidate for role play on this particular evening had a problem about aggression. She was quite able to speak, but the trouble was that she felt that certain individuals around her were so provocative and so irritating that she found it very difficult to avoid 'blowing her top'. This didn't seem to get her anywhere since others then labelled her as moody and aggressive, and dismissed anything she had to say. She was well aware that her present response was not working; and wanted some suggestions about what other, more effective, responses she could make. To change her behaviour she needed to accept the following:

- *"I can be heard more effectively if I don't raise my voice in a threatening way."*
- *"I may need to say what I want many times before I am really heard. I can be quietly and firmly repetitive and insistent about being heard without turning this into a contest."*
- *"Others are more likely to listen to me if I am genuinely willing to listen to them and if I take the trouble to prove that I have heard."*
- *"I don't have to be overcome by my rage when others try to provoke me. I can pause for breath, step outside my feelings and see if I can find a more constructive response. I can make light of provocations and pay attention to what I really want to say. I will not allow myself to be distracted by people's efforts to 'trip me up'."*

The third candidate for role play had no problem about communicating her own thoughts, feelings and wishes and never allowed herself to be provoked. She was confident, competent, intelligent, sensitive, sophisticated. Indeed she seemed to be a role-model that everyone else could emulate. She never seemed to put a foot wrong. And yet she reported that certain people around her were mystifyingly furious with her, and chaotic and unpredictable in their hostility and aggression towards her. They seemed to want to 'get even'; and yet what, if anything, had she done that provoked such reactions? The answer, which was revealed during a particular role play session, was that she was rather poor at allowing others to *save face*. She would out-argue her less intelligent and less-perceptive colleagues, even her own boss. She was more principled, more coherent, more consistent, better informed and more compe-

tent and confident about presenting her own views than most of
the people around her. All this was absolutely fine except that it
created enormous difficulties for her given that she was not particularly skilled in being tactful and in respecting the self-esteem of
colleagues. (Confession: I have great sympathy for those with this
particular human weakness since allowing others to save face is
far from being one of my strong points!)

We all meet people who are more intelligent and perceptive than
ourselves or who are much better organised and informed than
we are when discussing a particular topic. This is all very well,
and we can cope with the experience, although it can knock our
self-esteem a bit to discover that we are not as bright as we thought.
But we will become hostile in the extreme if people 'show us up'
too much. It's bad enough when ill-informed people maliciously
try to put us down. But even worse is when *well*-informed individuals mercilessly show up our own inadequacies, and without even
meaning to! It may seem that there is no way to 'get back at them'
and that, in any case, we are being unreasonable to want to hit
back. Nonetheless, we are very likely to try to 'get even' with them
in some way or another!

In short, there is nothing worse than a 'smartarse' – who really
is smart; or the 'clever-clever' person – who really is clever!

We all want to protect and preserve our own feelings of security
and self-esteem. In the West though, undoubtedly, too little attention has been given to this topic and I have seen far too many
books about Assertiveness which pay no attention whatever to the
importance of protecting the self-esteem of others as well as,
merely, one's own. Indeed, far from protecting it and even attending to it, we actively go out of our way to undermine it!

Western observers of the Japanese, on the other hand, often
suggest that they pay too much attention to the importance of
saving 'face' – to the extent that people rarely communicate their
own views for fear of offending others. That may be (though I am
in no position to judge). Certainly, though, we in the West, operate
too far down the other end of the spectrum; thus, for example, the
brash New Yorker's demand that you "Get out of my face" is not
itself an entirely face-saving request. On the contrary, we mistakenly believe that we will be safer if we can throw our rivals off
balance and unsettle them in some way. Quite a few people put
a great deal of energy into securing their own position by undermining that of others. In the short run this can work, but it creates a
lot of enemies. Your continued security and well-being then becomes dependent on your ability to ceaselessly outwit and further

undermine what is likely to become an ever more determined opposition.

The lower our self-esteem becomes, the more desperate will be
our efforts to preserve what little self-regard we have left. And so
we will be ever more defensive when others continue for too long
to make accusations or criticisms of us; particularly if they are less
than tactful (or positively offensive) in the way they tackle us.
Beginners to assertiveness training imagine that with their new-
found skills they will have an ever more powerful capacity to hit
out, or hit back, at others, when they are criticised and accused.
They also hope for ever stronger defensive armour or ever more
skilful means of deflecting and avoiding the onslaughts from others.
A strong defence, with strong retaliatory powers to act as a deter-
rent are, we imagine, the means to preserve our much cherished
self-esteem. The reality, however, is very different.

It is one thing to put across your message. It is quite another to
hit out with it; and the whole point of assertiveness is that it ought
to help us to move away from militaristic images and attitudes
concerning communication. Thus, not only do we avoid being aggressive in the way we send out messages to others, we also try
to avoid being defensive in the way we receive them. This may
seem too good to be true and impractical as a means of surviving
in the day to day world. However, an ability to avoid defensiveness
is not only desirable as an abstract moral ideal, it is also sound
practical advice as a means of communicating effectively.

Attack creates defence; and defensiveness produces an ever more
determined aggression. Therein lies the key! The more you attack
someone, the more they are likely to be defensive and to hit back.
Similarly, the more defensive you are, the more you will encourage
the other side to find further deadly ways of punching through
your armour. Likewise, the more skilled you are at being able to
duck and weave and deflect and evade, the more strenuously will
the other side try to find ways of coming after you; cornering you
and capturing you.

If, however, we see communication as an opportunity to learn,
rather than a competition or conflict, we can completely transform
our attitude to accusation and criticism. Those who communicate
to win see their critics as their enemies. But those who, genuinely,
communicate to learn see their critics as their greatest teachers.
Our friends, after all, may well be far too polite or tactful to point
out things about us that, in the longer run, we would do better to
hear. Our enemies, on the other hand, have no such inhibitions!
We, all of us, have a shadow side; which consists in all those

seamier aspects of our personality that we don't like to face up to. Our closest friends, sensing that we feel sensitive, defensive and vulnerable about this side of ourselves, will tend to refrain from drawing it to our attention. (As long as we tacitly agree not to bring up the subject of their own shadow!)

Our enemies on the other hand, sensing our vulnerability, and wanting to win, will tend to home in on those areas where it seems that they would be most able to wound, undermine, unsettle and discomfort us. These, generally, will be precisely those areas where, we feel, we must defend ourselves, at all costs.

But just suppose that we didn't defend ourselves; just suppose that:

- When criticised, we agreed with anything that seemed to have some truth in it.

- We saw our critics as providers of useful information rather than threats to our self-esteem.

- We felt better about ourselves as a result of being open to criticism and willing to face ourselves.

- We discovered our critics making remarks with, at the very least, some truth in them. (And particularly when they know us well.)

- We actually asked our critics to specifically elaborate on their criticisms so that we could more clearly assess, and learn from, what they had to tell us.

You might think that if you adopted such a saintly approach you would simply be annihilated by your competitors. But consider further. The critic elaborates; you focus on what seems useful and (tactfully) reject what seems false. What now can the critic do? He is much less able to go on and on once you have made it clear that you agree that he has a right to his views, that you have listened to them carefully and actively considered them. The force of his attack will now be spent. The principle is the same as in Judo; where you go with the force of the blows of others and make use of their energy without making yourself an actual target. If, on the other hand, you shut someone out or counter-attack you actively fuel their determination to 'have another go at you'!

In other words, we fear that to drop our defences would be to lose all, whereas when we let go of our defence we may find that we have lost nothing at all. Indeed we may have gained. We have not fuelled our critics and instead we have learned from them. Furthermore, we have not lost any self-esteem nor any tactical advantage.

Of course, you are not likely to agree with all the criticisms of your 'teachers'. In particular, manipulative critics make use of a number of standard ploys designed to undermine you which you would do well to reject. For example, we often feel defensive because we are only human rather than superhuman and manipulative critics often play on this. Superhuman people:

- Have endless reasons, explanations, excuses and justifications for everything they do, and they can go on giving them indefinitely.
- Can solve everyone else's problems as well as their own.
- Never make mistakes.
- Never change their mind because they were never wrong in the first place.
- Know and understand everything.
- Care about everything and everyone.
- Are liked and loved by everyone.

Superhuman people do not, of course, exist, and once we really appreciate this and feel at peace with being merely human, then, all of a sudden, it doesn't matter at all if manipulative critics say:

"Your reasons aren't good enough." "You must help me." "You've made a mistake." "You've changed your mind." "You don't understand." "You don't care." "I don't like you".

Human beings . . . don't have to have reasons for everything; don't have to, and can't, help everyone; can change their minds and make mistakes and be indifferent and uncaring at times. Human beings will not be liked by everyone in any circumstances nor anyone in all situations!. Assertive human beings, furthermore, will not expect to be so liked and will not therefore feel threatened and undermined when critics point out that in fact they are just – human beings!

The trouble with being defensive when shrewd critics move in to the attack is that we end up trying to defend the indefensible. And even if what we defend *is* defensible, do we really have any need to defend it? If your self-esteem is dependent on your pretending to yourself that you are better than you really are then you will, of course, be vulnerable to the manipulations of others. But what if you decided to feel ok about yourself, warts and all? What if you continued to feel ok about yourself regardless of the skeletons your critics could haul from various cupboards? You would then be immune to all manipulative attacks and able to learn from valid criticism.

In other words, we will become much stronger if we can face up to, and live with, our weaknesses rather than find new ways of defending them. Thus a major key to assertiveness, paradoxically, lies in learning how to listen to criticism from others without feeling the need to defend ourselves. The energy that we waste in defending ourselves can then be put to more constructive purposes and all valid criticism becomes a source of gain rather than a terrible set-back. Moreover, we will gain from valid criticism even when the underlying intention of the critic is manipulative or malicious; and even when we feel hurt by the ill-will of our critic!

To be open to criticism from others is not to be immune to hurt. On the contrary, it is to be open to the fact that people can and do hurt us! However heavily defended we are, we can be, and will be, hurt by others at times. We may hide our hurt and even deny to ourselves that we are hurt. But this will not make the hurt go away. Alternatively, we may parade our hurt as a means of trying to hurt or undermine our opponent. We will, as it were, be saying: *"Look what you've done to me! How can you be such an insensitive, malicious bastard?"* (etc.) And the covert message will be *"I hope you feel terrible, remorseful, guilty, ashamed, apologetic."* (etc.) . . . *"and then fit in with what I want!"*

Assertiveness, though, is about avoiding such shabby manipulations and insecure defensiveness. It is about seeing that we are at our strongest when, paradoxically, we face ourselves in all our weakness and limitation. This, further, requires us to face the fact that, being human, we can be hurt!

The general tendency is to believe that we will be stronger if only we can avoid getting hurt and that, when hurt, the 'tough' person avoids feeling it. This, quite simply, is a fallacy. Being human, we will not want to get hurt; and there is no virtue in masochism. But when we are hurt, we will be all the stronger if we are able to face up to this experience and communicate it to others without either repressing or indulging our feelings.

You might think, since it is generally thought, that to show our hurt will put others at an advantage. After all, when they've been trying to hurt us, won't we be allowing them a victory over us were we to give away the fact that they have scored a hit? Consider this more carefully, though. What, in fact, does the malicious individual gain when (s)he discovers that (s)he has been successful in her attempts to wound? If faced with a compliant individual, she may gain in the short run because she may succeed in intimidating her opponent. The compliant, and cowardly, individual, as we have seen, will fit in with the preferences of others rather than allow themselves to be hurt any more.

But what if you decide that you are not going to comply even though you have been wounded by the other person's remarks? What if you show that you have been hurt without trying to counterattack? What if you continued to stand up for yourself while at the same time showing respect for the rights of others? What if you managed all this with tact so that the other person did not suffer loss of face? What indeed? You might well avoid self-defeating forms of (non)-communication and you might well help the other person to be less aggressive and defensive. But there are no guarantees. Furthermore, it is a long list of 'What ifs...?' and so we can begin to see just how much easier all this is to describe than it is to put into practice! It is much easier to destroy than to build. . . . Much easier to throw abuse than to deal with disagreements constructively. . . . Much easier to slip into old habits than change fundamental attitudes and learn new skills.

Clearly, we are never going to become the sort of paragon of virtue and skilled communication described above. To hope for this is to cry for the moon. But that doesn't mean that all our efforts are bound to be fruitless. The wisest policy, surely, is to see just what would be a more effective means of communicating and then take whatever small steps we can to move in the right direction; remembering all the time that, being human, our progress is likely to be slow, fitful and limited! In this respect I am reminded of David Smail's excellent analogy, (described in *Taking Care: an Alternative to Therapy*, Dent, 1987): human beings he suggests, cannot be re-programmed like computers, with all previous experiences and errors wiped clean at the touch of a button. They are more like plants that need care and cultivation. With the right sort of care, positive changes are possible. But if, through a lack of care, the person has been damaged early in life, then that damage will never be entirely erasable and will be etched into the heart of the person in the way that the history of a tree is etched as rings in its trunk. In good seasons it may begin to grow straight and tall. But the deformities produced by earlier storms, droughts or barrenness can never be entirely overcome, and will be written into its gnarled features for all its days.

We all have aggressive and defensive tendencies, and, having regard for Smail's sober observations, it would be a nonsense to pretend that these could ever be abolished. But it is worthwhile to learn at least to limit their damaging effects and try to understand how they operate. As a child, I remember we sometimes used to chant "sticks and stones may break my bones but words can never hurt me". We found out soon enough that the words hurt too; and in civilised societies most people, most of the time, restrict their violence to verbal abuse rather than physical attack. The words hurt because it's painful, even, to realise that someone is intending to hurt us. But what really hurts, and let's not forget it, is when someone criticises us, maliciously or otherwise, about something in ourselves that we too are unhappy about!

All of us try to get our way, at times, by trying to get others to feel 'awful' about themselves in this, that or the other respect. Often we do this with malicious intent. But our efforts, be they spiteful or benevolent, are generally doomed to failure unless the other person is already predisposed to feel awful about what they have done! In other words, people can chide or punish me most effectively by handing me the stick I use to beat myself! They say, "You should feel bad about this", and I do feel bad about it, if and only if I myself believe that I should!

What all this means, in short, is that you can't really get at me except by getting me to get at myself. Insofar as I am terrified of my own guilt and shame I can be terrified of your efforts to get me to feel guilty. But, were I really able to face myself, I would have no need to defend myself from criticism from you or anybody else. Indeed, I would welcome any such criticism as a chance to learn, and I would then know that you could never cast a shadow over me. All you could, and can, ever do is draw attention to the shadows I cast over myself!

I hope that this throws some light on the matter of our defensiveness. I hope, too, that it is clear that, being human, many of our shadows, and therefore much of our defensiveness, will remain intact!

So far, we have been considering situations where we are faced with people who are being manipulative, threatening and generally undermining. But, let's not forget it, even when there is good-will on both sides, we may still disagree with each other – sometimes quite fundamentally.

Faced with disagreement, some people, as we have seen, tend to comply; even in the absence of threats or malice. This is because, for compliant individuals, disagreement itself feels threatening; and they would rather go along with the wishes of others sooner than, as they see it, risk their friendship. There are others, of course, who are more domineering; and they will tend to shift the outcome in their preferred direction if only because of the loud and forceful way in which they negotiate.

For the compliant individual the aim is to agree with the other person in order to keep the peace. For the 'hard' bargainer, on the other hand, the aim is victory. Both approaches are likely to lead to undesirable outcomes.

A 'third way', therefore, is needed; and, in an effort to find it, Roger Fisher and William Ury, of the Harvard Negotiating Project, wrote *Getting to Yes*, (Hutchinson, 1983). This is somewhat dry in style but the contents are of great interest in suggesting ways of dealing with disagreements that avoid both the 'soft' (compliant) and the 'hard' (domineering) approach.

Fisher and Ury's 'third way' is described as *Principled Bargaining*. Its aim is to reach a wise outcome efficiently and amicably; and this requires a reasoned approach where you neither apply, nor yield, to pressure. Instead, you yield, if that is the right word, to the force of the argument and the evidence rather than the forcefulness of the person who is presenting the evidence. You reason, and you are open to the reasons offered by others; but you avoid, if possible, any ego-centric attachment to the argument. As a result, it is not a question of my reasons versus your reasons, or my position versus your position. Instead, we both of us simply explore the arguments and evidence – with an open mind and without taking sides.

In other words, the principled bargainer tries to avoid an adversarial approach and attempts to reach a result that is independent of the will-power of the parties concerned. He sees himself as a problem-solver rather than an adversary or a friend; and he attempts to be 'hard' on the problem (in order to get the best outcome) yet 'soft' on the people (in order to avoid personal antagonism).

So often, when we disagree about anything, we start to talk and think in terms of *my* arguments rather than *the* arguments. Similarly, we tend to polarise around *my* position – as supported by *my* arguments. In no time at all we are likely to find that the opponent has become equally entrenched into *his* position and we are both stuck. We freeze our options into just two: either my way or your way; my position or yours; I win or you win. As soon as we move into this polarisation of options we become defensive and resistant to any of the arguments, insights or ideas of our opponent. We might secretly recognise that much of what they say is of value, but we will never admit this to them because this will seem to imply that we are giving way and in danger of losing.

With an adversarial approach to disagreement we face each other – eyeball to eyeball as it were. With a principled approach to disagreement we both face in the same direction and together confront the problem we *both* want to solve. Each of us wants to move forward and meet our various needs but here is this problem that is presently blocking our progress. Our task is to find a wise solution to the disagreement, with mutual respect and good-will and as efficiently as we can. This solution must help both of us to meet our needs and preserve our integrity.

In order to do this we need to scrap the idea that there are only two options; my way versus your way. We also need to scrap the idea that there are positions that have to be attacked or defended. Instead of thinking in terms of positions we need to think in terms of our various *interests* and *needs*. When we do that, we can begin to see that there are dozens, or scores, of ways of compromising in a manner that is attractive to both sides. Adversaries tend to assume that there is only one prize and so it had better be mine rather than yours. Co-operators work on the assumption that we can produce all kinds of different prizes and rewards for all participants if we let go of our tunnel vision and begin to think creatively about the various ways in which we might both benefit.

So much of our energy is wasted when we think only in terms of *"how can I win?"* The flip side to that question is *"how can I get you to lose?"* and it puts each of us into a frozen state of wariness and defensiveness. An enormous amount of creative energy can be released if, instead, we each ask, *"how can we win?"* With this sort of question we can relax a little, we can co-operate, we can start to listen to each other and pool our ideas.

Let's take a specific, and very simple, example of what all this might mean in practice. Suppose that a couple are disagreeing with each other about what they want to do one evening. One says *"I'd like us to eat out."* The other says, *"I'm tired and I need to prepare for some work I have tomorrow."*

1. Those who take an adversarial approach will each want to 'win'.

2. Adversaries will consider that there are only two options; either we eat out tonight or else we stay in. Both combatants will go to their battle stations.

3. Each side will consider, no doubt, that it would be right and proper for them to get their way. Thus, for example:

   We haven't been out this week; Who wants to cook anyway? I suppose you expect me to prepare something?
   Versus: *I really am tired; Let's just have a snack; We can't afford to eat out so much; I have a very important meeting tomorrow.*

4a. Domineering adversaries will take a position about it and consider that *"this is a matter of principle, my integrity is on the line, I will lose face if I don't get my way"*.

4b. Compliant adversaries may also take a position and feel very resentful if they give in – 'yet again' – to the other side.

5. Each side will tend to present slanted and exaggerated arguments that prove how right they are to hang on to their position. For example:

   "We never do anything anymore; All our friends go out more than we do; You don't give a damn about me!"
   Versus: *"I'm feeling really ill; tomorrow's meeting is 'make-or-break'; You never seem to want to cook me anything; You don't give a damn about me!"*

6. Each side will try to suggest ways in which their partner's position is illogical, incoherent, immoral, insensitive etc. For example:

   "How can you go to this meeting if you are so ill? Don't you think it's time you thought about me for a change?"
   Versus *"It's absurd to say we don't go out; why do you have to nag when you can see I'm feeling hassled?"*

7. Each side will begin with persuasion but, if this doesn't work, they will be likely to start punishing each other, verbally or non-verbally, overtly or covertly. The punishments quite possibly will involve reference to previous (perceived) hurts and injustices, and derogatory labelling. For example:

   "You're just so selfish, you don't care about what I want, you've taken me for granted for years."
   Versus *"I'm just so sick of your whining and nagging. You're always making accusations. You're just a punishing bitch!"*

8. Ultimately, and at worst, (although of course such arguments don't always deteriorate so badly) we end up throwing everything at each other with sweeping statements about all the terrible weaknesses, failings and evil that we have ever suffered in our partner!

Compare this, point by point, with the approach taken by 'principled bargainers':

1. Each of us will co-operate to find ways in which we can both gain. We will have won if we can both win. We will have both lost if either of us thinks we have lost. For example:

"I might be able to finish this work at a push, but could we eat late? . . . Go somewhere inexpensive? . . . Get a takeaway meal? What else would be fun this evening? What shall we do over the next few days if we can't sort something out for tonight?"

2. We will look for lots of options that are acceptable and desirable to both of us. For example:

"Cinema? Dinner out? Quiet evening together? Invite friends in? Time for each of us to do things as individuals? Ten minutes each to unload what our day has been like for each of us? Joint planning of future evenings?"

3. There will be no question of 'right' versus 'wrong'. We will both be right to find, and look after, our own and each other's interests. For example:

"If you feel stuck indoors we must do something about that. If you feel over-worked, how can I help? If you are feeling tired, bored, frustrated, what would you like from me that would help?"

4. We will not take a position about going out, or staying in, but instead explore our interests and then suggest ways in which these could be met. For example:

"You want more contact with people? A chance to unwind? More intellectual stimulation? More excitement? More attention from me? Shall we make a list? We can do all of these things over a period of time, one option doesn't have to prevent another from happening."

5. There will be no need to exaggerate or distort or prove or attack or defend. For example:

"I'll probably feel better in half an hour if I could just sit down now." "Let's eat out another time if you're really tired now." "Let's make some definite arrangements and let's make them soon."

6. There will be no need to undermine the other person's suggestions. Rather we will attempt to build upon whatever seems promising in what the other person has suggested. For example:

"Yes, tomorrow would be fine. Yes, let's eat later. Let's make arrangements earlier from now on when we've only got a limited number of spare evenings. Yes, you finish what you're doing, and we can be ready in an hour."

7. There will be no need to persuade or punish since we will be sharing and co-operating on the same task of finding options attractive to both of us. Each of us will be looking for ways of

rewarding the other person and suggesting ways in which we ourselves would feel rewarded.

8. Ultimately, we will agree to a solution that seems most attractive to us both. We will have chosen this from a large number of other solutions that might be almost equally attractive. For example:

> *"It's hard to choose between the cinema or dinner or a walk or swim or friends or conversation together or some quiet time pottering about. Let's eat in, then go for a swim on Friday. Or the other way round; it doesn't matter all that much."*

The above principles are exactly the same regardless of whether we are talking about a couple arranging their social life; two companies bargaining over a contract; two nations negotiating a peace treaty . . . or whatever. Nothing works perfectly, of course, and so we shall never become shining paradigms of principled bargaining. If we did, and thus avoided all malice and perversity, we would seem almost inhumanly 'nice'! But there is so little danger of this happening that we don't need to worry about it! Undoubtedly, though, we can all benefit enormously if we can manage to put such principles into practice:

- Just sometimes!
- Just for a little while!
- Just to some extent!

In other words, we can gain as soon as we start to try. We don't have to worry about becoming too successful; nor do we need to be despairing when our progress is so limited. So many people have, in effect, said to me; "Never mind perfection; it would be wonderful if just once (s)he let down his/her armour and stopped trying to score points. And, maybe it would be good if I did the same; if only for five minutes!"

It might be useful to summarise the differences between soft (compliant), hard (domineering) and principled forms of bargaining. Here is what I hope you will find to be a useful table (*from Fisher & Ury*):

'Soft' Bargainer	'Hard' Bargainer	Principled Bargainer
Participants are friends	Participants are adversaries	Participants are problem-solvers
The goal is agreement	The goal is victory	The goal is a wise outcome

'Soft' Bargainer	'Hard' Bargainer	Principled Bargainer
Make concessions (to cultivate the relationship)	Demand concessions (as a condition of the relationship)	Separate the people from the problem
Be soft on people and the problem	Be hard on people and the problem	Be soft on the people and hard on the problem
Trust others	Distrust others	Proceed independently of trust
Change your position easily	Dig in to your position	Focus on interests, not positions
Disclose your bottom line	Mislead as to your bottom line	Avoid having a bottom line
Accept one-sided losses to reach agreement	Demand one-sided gains as the price of agreement	Invent options for mutual gain
Search for the single answer – that they will accept	Search for the single answer – that you will accept	Develop multiple options choose later
Agree with the other party	Insist on your position	Insist on objective criteria
Yield to pressure	Apply pressure	Yield to reason and principle, not pressure

It comes as a tremendous relief when we realise that we can deal with disagreements, however strong they may be, without having to go to war with people. It really is an exhausting and demoralising experience to have to go around armed and armoured all the time. Even the successful warriors might, if they were willing to look deeply enough inside, come to the conclusion that they were paying as much of a price as their adversaries in the long run, even though they generally win. It is bad for your health and well-being if you are locked into the view that most of life is a struggle against others who are out to get you and who must be defeated at all costs. Such attitudes are contagious, as we have seen, and they can become a self-fulfilling prophecy. And yet it always possible, and never too late, to make changes.

People are often so starved of genuine good-will, supportiveness, empathy and co-operation that when they come across someone with a sunny rather than a stormy disposition they are enormously grateful. Indeed, if you can show that you genuinely do want to do something constructive about meeting other people's needs rather than 'pulling one over on them' they will often want to move heaven and earth for you, such will be their gratitude. In other words, if you shine on others rather than groan or glower at them, they will more likely take a shine to you! Rewarding behaviour is contagious, too, thank goodness!

Having said all that, though, let us not be too naive and innocent. Progressive managements, for example, can be characterised as the ones that adopt the 'carrot' rather than the 'stick' approach to employee relations. They look for rewards rather than punishments. They listen, they search for compromises, they adopt a principled approach to bargaining. They avoid threats, rigid positions and a domineering approach to their staff. But, as I have stated earlier, there is no good thing under the sun that cannot be misused; and so it is possible to be unprincipled in your approach to principled bargaining and use it as a tool with which to manipulate others.

Our surface agenda might be that of the genuinely principled bargainer; where we utilise empathy, compromise, mutual respect, mutual rewards . . . a genuine partnership. But our hidden agenda might be quite different, and consist in seeking the minimum reward for others and the maximum for ourselves ..as far as we can get away with this using our (possibly considerable) powers of agenda setting, image making and 'non-directive' control. (You may remember that we explored the latter in some detail in Chapter Three on *Listening*).

It would be quite mistaken, however, to suggest that every large corporation these days utilises sophisticated skills in bargaining. There are still plenty of examples of crude macho approaches to conflict in the commercial world just as much as between individuals. And on the international stage we are still living in an era that is often characterised by little more than crude brutalism and anarchy.

For example, peace between the Super-powers is still far too dependent on the ever-present terror of 'Mutually Assured Destruction' (MAD indeed!). West and East attempt to co-operate because they don't wish to annihilate all life on the planet. And yet this leaves us open to the possibility of Armageddon-by-accident where, for example, a flock of geese and a series of human and computer errors, could lead to massive retaliation. With tension presently lessening very substantially between the U.S.A. and U.S.S.R. we can hope that this prospect is less likely. But what of the longer term prospects, when most nations continue to develop ever more lethal capacities to wage war?

It seems that we are reaching a turning point in human evolution. Sooner or later any species, like ours, with the capacity for technological advance, will develop the means to destroy itself and all the life around it. It is simply a matter of our growing power. Any power, of any sort, can be used to create or to destroy; and we are now so powerful that we can inflict lethal, and final, destruction upon ourselves and our environment.

When we were weak, we could afford to fantasise about finally conquering Nature and our enemies. But now that we are strong, and we can actually do it, we have got to abandon such primitive notions.

In these new circumstances, the old 'Win-Lose' approach to conflict is going to have to be scrapped; and sooner rather than later. It is one thing for us to try to defeat each other, and to win at the expense of our opponent, when neither of us is powerful enough to do each other very much harm. But co-operation becomes a gritty matter of basic survival, rather than an 'airy-fairy' ideal, when the alternative is an apocalypse.

For centuries, the established religions have argued that one should do good, love thine enemy etc. because, if you don't, you will be punished in the afterlife. This hasn't always cut much ice because the short term rewards of aggression have sometimes been much greater than the risks (in this life at least). But with our new-found power to destroy ourselves and our planet it is soon going to become a basic necessity for us all to abandon the idea that we must conquer either Nature or our enemies. I see no long-term future for a species that adopts 'Win-Lose' mentalities towards people and the environment when its technological powers are as great as ours. We must learn to co-operate – or die! With the powers that we now wield we shall, from now on, be punished in *this* life if continue to try to destroy our enemies. And therefore, paradoxically, our own survival and security is dependent on our making quite sure that our bitterest enemy feels safe and secure!

One specific consequence of the abolition of 'Win-Lose' is that armed forces chiefs must abandon the idea of winning conflicts. If a military conflagration breaks out they must avoid sending in reinforcements and trying to win; since this will rapidly lead to the complete destruction of all combatants. Instead they must look upon themselves as 'fire-fighters'. When the flames of war appear the question will be *"how can we put this out before it overwhelms us all?"* The armed forces and politicians on all sides will need to get together in advance and share this problem so that humanity as a whole can find a way past it.

The stark reality of all this is clear when we consider the outcome of every war-game that has been played on the European battle-field since the last World War. Over and over again, military leaders simulate different scenarios of war in Europe; (and these days they use very complex computer simulations). Over and over again the outcome is the same – Europe ceases to exist; and catastrophe occurs regardless of whether or not nuclear weapons are used! War between the major powers can't be won; there can only be losers. And therefore it is no longer just morally repugnant, it is practically obsolescent as a way of meeting anyone's needs. Moreover, as our ability to kill on a mass scale improves still further, it won't just be war between the Super-powers that becomes 'out of bounds'. Even quite small nations (and terrorist groups!) will be able to kill millions through missiles, chemical, biological, and who knows what other, means?

There have always been a minority of mystics and other spiritually aware souls who have known that I am diminished by your suffering; that the bell at our neighbour's funeral tolls for all of us; that 'no man is an island'; that we are all ultimately united 'as One'. Such insights have generally been seen as desirable in theory but somewhat too lofty and inaccessible to be of practical use in the market place. All this must change. Either we will learn to co-operate within the living system that is 'Mother Earth', or we will grow at the expense of all around us and, like the malignant 'cancer' we will then have become, we will be shrugged off into extinction.

On the international stage, then, we have got to learn to co-operate since there is no attractive alternative. But we cannot pretend that this is the case at a personal level. Assertiveness, in a nutshell, is all about using what powers you have to the full, provided that this is done with integrity and good-will. But even if you do use your powers to the full there will be times when you do not have as much power as others. Furthermore, there will be times when you are negotiating with people who do not have as much incentive as you to reach an agreement.

It is worth bearing in mind that failing to agree is sometimes a perfectly viable, attractive and even desirable option for one or both of us. For example, in the market-place we might discover that I don't want to sell and you don't want to buy at the sort of prices we are each talking about. My not-selling and your not-buying might turn out to be the most attractive option for each of us. In which case there is no point in us trying to make a deal.

Some forms of power are fairly obvious; for example, wealth, intelligence, negotiating skill, political connections. But others are less obvious. When non-agreement is far more attractive to you than it is to the person you are bargaining with you are placed in an incredibly powerful position even if, in other respects, your power is weak. For example when one partner is not much bothered if the relationship continues or not, (s)he will have enormous power over the partner who is desperate that they stay together. Equally, if an employer can dismiss you and effortlessly replace you with someone at half the price tomorrow then he will not feel so pressed to negotiate at all. Conversely, an essential employee who can pick and choose his employer, and who cannot easily be replaced, will have substantial leverage over his boss even if the latter is part of a large multi-national concern. The large company may dwarf the employee in resources, but it is the company that will want the agreement more than the employee, and so the latter will have the whip-hand.

This takes us on to another way in which principled negotiation can fall down. When the other side has muscle, and little reason to find an agreement, they may not be much bothered about prin- ciple!. Skilled negotiators (whether honourable or dishonourable in their methods) can often use their skill to make up for other disadvantages they may have; but there are limits. And therefore there may be times when we might do best to work on our own alternatives to agreement and make these as attractive as possible.

Finally, let us remember that, however assertive we may learn to become, there are other virtues; and the practice of just one at the expense of all the others can itself become vicious. For example, shall I assertively command the bar-tender's eye? Or tactfully indi- cate that the small compliant person next to me has been waiting longer than I? Sometimes, surely, it is right for us to forgo our own possibilities of assertive trail-blazing in order to give other people a chance. This, after all, is what is meant by Good Manners, and if any society is to be regarded as civilised then it must surely be possible for us to be able to get what we want, need and have a right to without always having to be asserting ourselves!

In other words, assertiveness is fine and necessary, up to a point; but human relationships are not going to amount to much if we have to assert everything in order to get through to each other. Better, surely, for us to be more sensitive to, and respectful of, the needs and rights of others and to allow them their place without their always having to assert their right to it.

Questions and Exercises:

1. Take another look at the kinds of verbal punishments and rewards listed earlier in this chapter. See if you can become more aware of the particular punishments you inflict, and rewards you offer, to others. How do they reward and punish you? Could you discuss this with anyone? What might be the benefits and risks of doing so?

2. Would you (really) like to increase the rewards you offer? And decrease the punishments you inflict? When, where and how will you do this? What will you do about it today? What might you gain? What do you fear you might lose?

3. Do you consider that you need a 'permit' before you can give your views? Who is/are your permit-holder(s)?

4. Do you think it is possible for you to say what you want without injuring others? How could you do this? Are you trying to spare the feelings of particular individuals? What do you, and they, gain from this? What do you, and they, lose?

5. Do you wish that you were more assertive?
   ... In order to get *through* to others?
   ... In order to get *the better of* others?

6. In what situations do you find it difficult to assert yourself? What do you think is the cause of the trouble and what do you need to do differently?
   ... Can you speak up for yourself?
   ... Can you express anger without using it as a weapon?
   ... Can you speak up for yourself while allowing others to 'save face'?

7. Can you think of occasions where you have been ... aggressive? ... defensive? And occasions where others have been aggressive or defensive towards you? What might happen if you tried to talk about this to the person concerned? Would they have the same interpretation as you? Would such a conversation be helpful or counter-productive? Would you both become aggressive, manipulative or defensive even as you were trying to talk about all this? Or could you be genuinely helpful to each other?

8. What could you learn from your enemies? What criticisms do they make of you? What have they said about you that you can (privately) admit to as valid?

9. Can you get a glimpse of what your enemy looks like behind his arms and armour? How is (s)he feeling? What interpretations is (s)he making of you and her circumstances?

10. What are the biggest sticks that others can use to beat you? Are these weapons that you use against yourself? What is it that you really dislike about yourself? Do others dislike you for this as well? Do they use this against you? Are you willing to face yourself a little more? With compassion and forgiveness? Or will 'facing yourself' just mean that you 'beat yourself up' all the harder?

11. Do you tend to be the compliant or the aggressive type? Perhaps you are compliant with some people and aggressive with others? Are you willing to try a more principled approach to disagreement? Look again at the methods of 'principled bargaining'. Are you willing to try to put some of these methods into practice? When? With whom? What might you gain? What do you fear you will lose? Could you discuss this with anyone?

12. (If you are employed): how are disagreements and conflicts generally dealt with at work? In what respects is your management – macho? manipulative? honourable?

13. You are an advisor at Disarmament Talks between the 'Superpowers'. What advice can you offer?

14. Can you think of occasions where non-agreement has been almost as attractive, or more attractive, to you than agreement? What has been the result of this? Have you ever been in the opposite situation? i.e. where others are not much bothered about coming to an agreement with you? How did you deal with this? What else could you have done?

15. Can you think of occasions where your quarrelling has become simply a *ritual* or a *pastime*? . . .
    • Do you sometimes forget what you are trying to achieve when you quarrel?
    • Are you genuinely trying to communicate something about yourself?
    • Or are you merely trying to score points?
    • Or gathering evidence to support a conclusion you've already drawn?
    • Do you have a practical, achievable, purpose when you quarrel?

• Or are you merely defending a much cherished cause – on principle – and regardless of the practical consequences?

16. Next time you quarrel see if you can:

a) Put yourself in their shoes.
b) Avoid assuming that what you fear is what they intend.
c) Avoid blame and accusation.
d) Discuss each others perceptions and interpretations (with good-will!).
e) Behave in a way that is an improvement on their (low?) expectations of you.
f) Avoid cornering them; allow them to 'save face'. If they have difficult decisions to make, see if you can help to make things easier for them.
g) Look for solutions where you both can gain.
h) Recognise and understand emotions – yours and theirs.
i) Be explicit about emotions.
j) Accept the fact that it is legitimate for people to feel their emotions.
k) Allow each other to 'let off steam' without malice.
l) Avoid reacting when others let off steam.
m) Make a few positive gestures of good-will.
n) State your interests first and suggest lots of ways of meeting these rather than locking yourself up into one option.
o) Allow that they have legitimate interests too that need to be met if a wise and amicable solution is to be found.
p) Look forwards into possible solutions rather than backwards at previous problems.
q) Be specific, but flexible.
r) Invent your options first. And see if you can do this together. Judge them later.
s) Take a positive attitude. Remember that there may be options that are 'low cost' to one party and 'high benefit' to the other. Search for such options for each of you.

17. Next time you want to assert yourself see if you can repeat what you want to say if the person doesn't hear first time. See if you can go on repeating it until the other person has heard you. See if you can do this with tact and good-will.

18. In the following sentence there are two different ways being used to communicate a similar message. The first takes the form "You . . . (blame)". The second is in the form "I . . . (responsibility)":

a) *"You shouldn't go on and on at me like this."*
b) *"I think you're nagging, and I'm finding it very hard to cope with it."*

Can you 'translate' the following "You . . . (blame)" messages into the form "I . . . (responsibility)"? (There are many different ways of doing this):

"You should feel disgusted with yourself."
"You are an absolute bitch"
"Why can't you be more loving and affectionate?"
"Your work is everything, I mean nothing to you."
"How can you be so cruel and selfish?"
"You have failed to make the grade in this department."
"You simply haven't provided us with an adequate service."
"You just don't behave like a mature adult."

19. Look again at the different kinds of verbal punishment (and the corresponding verbal rewards) listed earlier in this chapter. Below are examples of these various forms of punishment. See if you can recognise each one; and then 'translate' it so that it rewards rather than punishes: ('answers' are provided at the back of the book!)

    i *"You stupid fool!"*

    ii *"Just get out of my sight!"*
    iii *"Just look at the state of you!"*
    iv *"I'll do what I can to help you but, knowing you, that's going to be an uphill struggle."*
    v *"You never say anything worth listening to, and you are the most insensitive clod that walked the Earth!"*
    vi *"You only said that in order to get at me."*
    vii *"I think you ought to know that many people have been laughing at you behind your back recently."*
    viii *"It's all your fault; and, if you don't change, I'm going to leave!"*
    ix *"You need to make a much better job of this; the work so far just won't do."*
    x *"You must realise that the way you've been behaving lately is simply awful. You've treated me terribly badly, and I just can't stand it anymore!"*
    xi *"Go and buy yourself a shirt and make sure it is a blue one so that it matches your trousers."*
    xii *"I hope you're not about to start another one of your tantrums are you?"*
    xiii *"You're not exactly the biggest stud in town are you?"*
    xiv *"Just think about what you've just said. Can't you see how it makes me feel? I'm at my wits end."*

xv *"Don't come near me. I don't want you to touch me."*
xvi *"You've really been very good to me lately (and God knows it's about time!)"*
xvii *"It's been good to see you and I hope we meet again soon. You're nothing like as gauche and clumsy as they said you are."*
xviii *"Well, it's not really been the way I wanted it to be this evening."*
xix *"Look, everyone in this room can see that you have made a complete hash of this job. It's about time you faced up to the facts."*
xx *"When I think of the way you have been for all these years; and you expect me to be nice to you now!"*
xxi *"Don't come to me now with your apologies; it's too late! The damage is done!"*

20. Do you expect that, as a result of learning to be more assertive, you will be able to live a 'hassle free' life?

21. Do you think it is worth trying to assert something when it seems fairly clear that a person is neither ready, willing nor able to hear?

22. Can you think of occasions when it would be ill-mannered to be powerfully assertive?

6. Getting through without Words.

This girl approached me and placed this flower in my rifle. She didn't even look me in the eye. I might have been anyone. Then she stepped back, and everyone applauded and congratulated her, and she looked pretty pleased with herself. And they had this "Make Love, Not War" poster, but it didn't feel like love to me. It was like I wasn't even there. But of course I was. Turned out there was a picture to prove it. Right on the front page of the paper, with me standing there looking like a stiff and her all angelic. The Associated Press got hold of it and it went out all over the world. I felt used. Thing is, I'd been coming around to feeling the war was wrong. But that experience just pushed me back. There was nothing among those people in front of me that felt like they were inviting me in. If anything, quite the contrary.

Quoted in Ram Dass and Paul Gorman *How Can I Help?* (Rider 1985)

I remember the photograph in question, which is a classic, taken over twenty years ago at a demonstration against the Vietnam War. I had been using it for years as a very clear (and tragic) example of an incongruent message; i.e. where the verbal and non-verbal components are inconsistent with each other. And so I was particularly interested to discover, more recently, the above passage with the soldier's view of the whole business. His expression in the photograph made it obvious that he was unhappy with what was being done at his expense. The flower may have seemed like a symbol of peace to the superficial observer, but it was being used as a weapon. And the smug and superior expression on the girl's face was a picture of unlovingness.

We are all familiar (aren't we?), with the way in which we can say one thing and mean something quite different. What we say and what we do are not necessarily in line with each other and the non-verbal aspects of our communication (movements, posture, gestures, expression, tone of voice) may often 'say' more than the words themselves.

Take, for example, a simple sentence like:

"What are you doing?"

When it is merely written on a page and there is no context of words or circumstances to go on then we are likely to interpret it as a neutral request for information. But when we actually hear the question being put to us we are likely to interpret it in a variety of ways simply depending on the tone of voice in which the question is put. The questioner may sound neutral, critical, superior, haughty, furious, desperate, irritable, terrified, malicious, provocative, flabbergasted, vaguely curious, interested, sarcastic, condescending, loving, outraged, affectionate, indifferent (etc.).

Many arguments can develop as a result of what we may believe a person did or didn't say. The classic, and most degenerate, sometimes laughable, form of this is:

"You said . . ."
"No I didn't."
"Yes you did."
"Didn't!"
"Did!"
"Didn't!". And so on.

But another, perhaps even more common, form of dispute concerns the *tone* in which a person did or didn't say something. For example:

"What are you doing?"
"Do you have to ask in that condescending tone of voice?"
"I wasn't being condescending, I was simply asking!"
"Well you sounded condescending."
"No I didn't!"
"And now you're sounding irritable too!"
"For goodness sake I'm not irritable."
"Oh yes you are."
"Well, if I'm irritable, who can blame me? You sound like you're trying to cause trouble."
"No I'm not, I'm feeling hurt!"
"You sound revengeful to me.". And so on.

Our tone of voice can be a powerful weapon when we want to hurt or undermine someone while pretending to be innocent. For example, the sentence *"I think you've done really well!"* can sound like praise and reward and it could easily be said in a warm and friendly tone that is congruent with the words. Equally, though, it could be said in a tone of sarcasm and ridicule.

When the tone and content of what someone says are clashing with each other, we tend to believe the tone and disbelieve the content. In other words, we rightly suspect that non-verbal components provide a more honest and accurate insight into a speaker's thoughts and feelings than the words themselves!

Why does the non-verbal tend to be nearer to the truth than language itself? The answer is fairly simple: liars have to control what they present to people around them; but before you can control something you have to be aware of its existence. Just about everyone is sufficiently awake to be conscious of what they are saying; but surprisingly few people are aware of what they are doing and the way they are doing it. Consequently, their words may be designed to deceive yet, through lack of awareness and conscious control, their tone and posture may give them away.

The really skilled liar, therefore, learns how to consciously control all his non-verbal behaviour as well as his words. Eventually, his skill may be such that he can afford to become unconscious once again. In other words lying through your teeth first requires conscious effort and awareness of what you are doing with your teeth. With sufficient practice, it just comes 'naturally'.

Every actor and actress knows that, in order to be convincing, you have got to do far more than know the words. You've got to know how to say them, how to move around, how to hold yourself in the style of your character. You have got to 'inhabit' the part without understating or over-acting it. It has got to look as though you really are this person.

Similarly, if we wish to hide our fears for example, it is not enough that we use brave words. We have also got to put on a brave face, and make brave movements with a brave posture and brave tone. Sometimes, the pretence may actually create the reality, so that, for example, we successfully overcome our fear. Maybe this can happen occasionally when we pretend to be benevolent and caring?

With sufficient skill, we will be able to deceive all but the shrewdest observers. In other words, it is a fallacy to pretend that, say, the tone of voice always gives you away. It doesn't if you've spent enough time working on your tone of voice!

The more skilled you are as a communicator, the more you will be able to get through to others and get to the heart of a situation as you see it. Good communicators, in other words, are able, because of their skills, to tell the truth more profoundly and more effectively than the rest of us. But there is a dark side to this that we now have to face: the more skilled you are as a communicator the more you will have it in your power to be able to *lie* more profoundly, more cleverly and more successfully than anyone else around you! Indeed, you may even be able to fool yourself!

Some of our greatest communicators take us to the heart of things, beneath mere appearances, distractions and superficialities. Others, however, become experts in *not* communicating! They take us ever further away from ourselves and from each other, and leave us ever more lost within a dross of deception, illusion and fantasy. Our most professional manipulators would be most offended, however, if we accused them of lying. And their skills may be so developed that they have little need to descend to such disreputable measures.

Outright lying is, in fact, a sign of an unskilled communicator. As you develop more professional skill and finesse, new options become available to you. For example, you learn:

- How to avoid telling lies without revealing the truth.
- How to tell the truth in such a way that the effect is the same as if you'd lied.
- How to be selective and *economical* with the truth so as to guide and manipulate the outcome to suit yourself.
- How to bombard people with so many facts that they are incapable of seeing the truth.
- How to tell the truth in such a way that it won't be believed.
- How to tell the truth in such a way that the wrong conclusions will be drawn.
- How to select your facts so that they will support your own particular *fiction.*
- How to hint at, and imply, something without actually saying it at all.
- How to proclaim one truth in order to draw a veil over another.
- How to tell the truth – at the right time.
- How to be honest 'to the letter' and dishonest 'in spirit'.
- How to ensure that the truth you tell will not be heard or spotted.

The brilliant, hilarious and much celebrated series on BBC, *Yes Minister*, provided, among other things, one of the finest and most sustained training programmes in manipulation and distortion. It is of most immediate value to civil servants and politicians; though most of these are already skilled enough at such black arts. But the principles are of equal value to people working within any organisation or grouping, large or small, formal or informal. This is indeed an Age of Instant Communication; perhaps more accurately, it is an era of '*Dis*-information' and 'Opinion Management'.

It would be wrong, though, to imply that such deception is only to be found among the sophisticated; and it must not be assumed that dishonesty is 'unnatural'. It may well be that many animals that know something about communication also know quite a bit about deception. Camouflage, for example, is a form of deception; and many animals practice this. Among our nearer neighbours, various species of monkeys have been shown to practice deception in many ways; through facial expressions, posture and deliberate efforts to hide their real intentions and behaviour.

The shrewd communicator, learns how to appear to reveal a great deal while revealing nothing. Conversely, the shrewd observer may discover far more about you than you want them to know; and far more, even, than you are aware of yourself. Faced with such an observer, you may try to lie and manipulate, but fail to notice that your tone and movements are giving you away.

Many politicians these days employ public-relations specialists who 'groom' them so that they present themselves in a way that will attract and convince the voter. Such training is becoming ever more detailed and thorough; and no aspect of non-verbal presentation is ignored. But voters vary of course, and so the really skilled operator has to learn to become like a chameleon and present a different *persona* to different audiences. I suspect that sometimes this presentation and control of appearances is taken to such lengths that the celebrity figure actually forgets who he or she really is. When asked, *"What are you really feeling now? What do you actually think and genuinely want?"* – their immediate response might be, *"What do you mean? What do you want? What's your game?"* More likely than not, though, this itself will be a reaction that they will skilfully hide.

Please bear all this in mind as we explore (below) the subtleties of non-verbal communication. As you go deeper into this topic you will discover new possibilities – to get through to others; and/or to get the better of them. As I try to communicate with you now I can use only words. There is no non-verbal component that I can put across to you; and you can only make (shrewd?) guesses at the sort of tone I would be using if I was reading this out loud. Consequently, there are very real difficulties in exploring the non-verbal side of communication when all we have available are words. Non-verbal messages are generally very subtle, and they are best described when they are also being shown. Also, the whole topic of non-verbal communication is one that most comes alive when you become more aware of the nature and meaning of your own postures, movements, gestures, clothes, accessories and tone of voice.

You can do this on your own to just a very limited extent. Really, though, you need to be able to view yourself from the outside; and this is best done by getting feedback from other people about the ways in which you present yourself. Second best, is to see yourself on a video recording and hear a playback of your tone of voice. It can be very difficult to hear the latter because we, uniquely, hear our own voice through the bones in our head and this gives the sound a different quality from the way others hear it. Also, we become so habituated to our voice that we find it difficult to hear it afresh. That is why it can come as quite a shock when you hear it, as if for the first time, played back through a tape recorder. Perhaps an even bigger shock is to see yourself on television, as others see you – though through your eyes.

Having said all that, there is a variety of questions you can ask yourself, and exercises that you can try out, that will throw light on the non-verbal side of communication, and I want to begin with the matter of clothing.

The clothes we wear do not serve simply a utilitarian function, however much some of us may pretend otherwise. They are a statement of the kind of personality we want to present to the world and, whatever clothes we wear, we will be making a statement, either deliberately or by default.

To some, considerable, extent we can't actually avoid communicating! After all, if I say nothing and withdraw from the company of others then that is in itself a statement to the effect that I am, quite probably, a rather shy, withdrawn sort of person. And if I take no trouble about the clothes I wear then that too will tell people something about my reluctance to make a conscious and high profile statement about myself. Even the person who takes little trouble and who says that he wears 'just anything', will in fact be unlikely to wear a leotard, or blanket, or leopard skin, or Red Indian Head-dress! He will in fact, 'just carelessly' find that he wears precisely the sort of clothes that the people of his own particular social class, personality and sub-culture are presently wearing . . .

Exercises:

1. If the clothes you are wearing could speak, what would they say about the sort of clothes they are, the way they are treated, and the person wearing them?

2. How do you want people to react to your clothes? (Note: if you don't want anyone to notice what you are wearing then that in itself is indicative of the low profile way in which you wish to relate to others. Withdrawal from society is in itself a form of relationship with society and it has consequences for all of us. In other words we cannot avoid a relationship of some sort with the world around us.)

3. Is/are there any person(s) in particular that you would like to have notice you and what you are wearing?

4. If you ever decided to try to make a stronger statement about yourself to the people around you what effect would this have on the clothes you wear?

5. Think of occasions when you changed your style of dress. Were these changes small and subtle, or large and dramatic? Why did you do this? What new impression were you trying to make? What impression were you trying to avoid?

6. What do you like and dislike about the way you dress? What would you like to change? Would it be possible, and desirable, for you to change?

7. When do you think you will make some changes (however small) in the way you dress? Do you believe you will wear exactly the same style of clothing for the rest of your life? Would you like to do this? What, do you think, will lead you to change your style?

8. What do other people think about the way you dress? Do you know this or are you merely speculating? What if you were to ask people? What do you think you might gain (or lose) if you did this?

It is fashionable, among some people, to say that "clothes don't matter, it's the person inside that really counts". Obviously, we can become too obsessed with mere appearances, and it would be absurd to say that an endless preoccupation with high fashion is essential if you are to 'find yourself' and communicate effectively with others. We can no doubt become too preoccupied with what we wear; and some wealthy people spend a degree of time and money on their appearance that is essentially immoral, given the poverty and suffering that exists in this world!

Having said that, if we take no interest at all in what we wear then that in itself is a sign that we are probably not bothering sufficiently (for our own good) with the people around us. And, given that we are essentially social animals, if we don't bother much with others, it is likely that we are not much bothering about ourselves either!

Thus, for example, a classic symptom of depression is a lack of concern about one's appearance. The depressed individual withdraws from the people around her, and thus no longer cares about how she appears to others since she does not wish to appear at all. Alternatively, it may on occasions be that she is still deliberately making a sort of statement; i.e. *"Look at me! Look at the state I am getting into! For God's sake help me!"*

And so some concern about our clothes and overall appearance is a sign that we still want to engage, and communicate, with others. Most people wish to do this and that is why most people spend a 'reasonable' amount of time and money on the clothes they wear, within the constraints of what they can sensibly afford.

It is not just a matter of clothes. To the extent that we have any options, then everything we own is a statement to the World about the sort of person we are, or would like to be. If I choose (even use) one sort of butter dish rather than another then that may reveal a little about me. If I use margarine instead of butter, that too is another small piece of information that others will use in order to build up a picture of who I am. The brands I use, also, may provide a few clues; and advertisers spend enormous sums of money in their efforts to give products a 'personality' that will be attractive to potential customers!

It is a contemporary cliche', though none the less (all the more?) true for that, to say that we live in a materialistic society. But people can mistakenly conclude from this that we are obsessed with material goods for their own sake. Nothing could be further from the truth. Generally speaking, we are interested in material things because we hope that they will help us to make statements about our (non-material) self and, even more, that they will help to bring us a whole host of non-material benefits; like love, sex, attention, respect, peace of mind, excitement, adventure, security, or a sense of belonging, or pride, or fulfilment, or achievement. In other words, we hope that, through our material goods we may be able to meet many of our various non-material needs. We assume that

I own, therefore I can give out of myself and receive from others. Or "I own, therefore I exist".

As regards communication, most of the things we own nowadays declare, or reveal, something about who we are. In Western society, at least, there is a growing range of choices when you are buying even the simplest and cheapest of goods. And the choices you make are not random or arbitrary; how can they be?

A stranger can walk into a room, look around, choose a chair and sit down, and it may take only six seconds to do all this. Even in this tiny amount of time we will all of us have received a considerable amount of information about the sort of person this is. His clothes, the way he comes in, the way he walks, chooses a chair, sits, the chair he sits on, the way he speaks (or stays silent). If all this information could be translated into machine code and programmed into a computer then it would take up an substantial slice of the machine's memory.

Even within such a short time you could distribute a questionnaire and ask people, via the answers they give, to speculate about the sort of person who has just come in. Almost everyone will have begun to form tentative hypotheses (and even fairly firm conclusions!) about the stranger's personality, likely opinions and background. They will also, quite likely, have made up their minds as to whether or not they would like to get to know this person more (and, even, whether they would like to go to bed with him or her!)

The fact that he has come into *this* room at this particular time for this likely purpose will in itself tell us something about the new stranger. And if *we* are coming into his room (an office say) then that too will quickly be used by us as a means of determining his status, his roles and the kind of behaviour we will probably expect of each other. It will be still more revealing if he shows us his car (or if we find out that he hasn't got one).

Most revealing of all will be if he invites us home and we walk into his living room, kitchen, bathroom etc. Immediately, we will take in an overall impression of everything that is around us. We will then rapidly size up one object after another, and the overall effect it has, in order to get more of an idea of the sort of person we are with. We will, all of us, consider that such a stranger 'comes over to us' far more quickly when we get even a glimpse of his home and the way he is within it. (Another whole vista of possibility is revealed when we see how he relates to his spouse and family, and how the latter behave towards him! You can fool many of the people much of the time; but not when your spouse and children are standing right by and having interesting responses of their own!)

Questions (1):

1. If the objects you own could speak, what would they say about the sort of person you are and are trying to be?

2. If you had a little more money, what would you spend it on? What do you think this would reveal about the sort of person you are?

3. Do you think the stuff you own successfully communicates the real you? Does it portray an image that is not really you? What impression does your property make on other people? Are you guessing or do you have reasonable evidence? Are you happy/unhappy about the reaction your property sometimes promotes in some people? Which people react in a way that causes you difficulties?

4. Are you getting ahead of others with the property you own? Or are others leaving you behind? Have you ever lost or gained contacts with people because you couldn't keep up with each other materially? How do you each feel about this?

5. If you lost all your goods overnight how well do you think you would cope? And if your insurance company paid in full would you replace them with much the same sort of possessions? Or would you try to present a slightly different image? If so, what?

6. If you could suddenly start a new life in a new place amongst new people, would you keep your present lifestyle and image? Or try something different? If so, what? Does such a prospect excite you? Terrify you? Both?

7. How do you respond to other people's property? Are you envious? Superior? Condescending? What? Do you think they make the impression they are intending to make? How far do you know?

8. Do the people you know present the same sort of image with similar goods to you? How far are they different? The same? How do you feel about this? Would you prefer to see a greater

variety of life-styles in your 'network'? What differences would you like to see? Or would you prefer people to be more conforming?

Next, of course, there is the matter of what we communicate with our actual bodies rather than our accessories. Much of this, again, can best be explored by means of questions; (and if you have difficulty answering them you might find it useful to see who you could talk to about all this).

1. Look at your body overall. How do you feel when you do this; (a) with your clothes on? (b) without clothes? Which bits do you like the best? The least? Would you change any parts if you could and, if so, why?

2. What does your body reveal about the sort of person you are? What does it hide?

3. What changes would you like to make in yourself? What effects, if any, would this have on your body?

4. Which bits of your body do you most like to show? . . . and to hide? . . . Why?

5. What range of expressions will people most frequently observe in your face? What is the expression on your face right now?

6. What does your face tell you about the way you have lived your life so far? What does it reveal about your most habitual emotions and attitudes?

7. What do your eyes reveal to an outside observer? How much eye contact do you tend to make with others? Do others find you withdrawn, with no eye contact? Or invasive, with too much?

8. How do you feel about the physical features of your face? Do they seem like an asset? A liability? Would you change any of them if you could? Would you change some of the habitual expressions on your face?

9. Does your face tend to reveal or hide the way you are really feeling? When? Why? How do you feel about this?

10. How do you feel about your hair and hairstyle? What does it tell others about the sort of person you are? Would you like to change it? Have you changed it very much in the past? Why? Do you think you will do so again? If so, what do you think you will do with it next?

11. Is your face generally tense or relaxed? When it is tense which particular muscles hold the tension? Your eyes? Forehead? Cheeks, Mouth? Jaw? Tongue? Do you grind your teeth? Do you bite the inside of your face?

12. Where else do you hold excess tension in your body? Neck? Shoulders? Upper and lower arms? Hands? Chest? Stomach? Back? Pelvis? Upper and lower legs? Feet?

13. Can you be aware of any tension in any of these places – right now?

14. And, right now, is your breathing: shallow? deep? regular? irregular? agitated? relaxed? Are you breathing by using your rib-cage and/or lower down through the use of your abdomen?

15. Do you have any noticeable mannerisms or gestures? What are they? What do they reveal? Are they broad and expansive? Constrained and limited? What?

16. Are your movements generally relaxed, confident and flowing? Or tense, uneasy and jerky? Do you rush or dawdle?

17. What about your habitual posture? Are you rigidly erect? Slouching? Hunched? Upright in a relaxed and easy way?

18. When we are tense it sometimes feels as though we are holding on and holding in. What are you trying to hold onto? What are you trying to hold out against? What are you trying to hold in? Is chronic tension the best way of dealing with these matters? What could you do to deal with the sources of the tension?

19. Do you occupy a lot of space as you move around? Or do you try to take up as little room as possible?

20. How do you walk? Stand? Sit?

21. How do you talk? Fast? Slow? Loud? Soft?

22. What is your most habitual tone of voice? Angry? Friendly? Haughty? Kind? Indifferent? Hostile? Aggressive? Apologetic? Deferential? Defiant? Provocative? . . . ? With whom? When? Why?

23. What is the most habitual pitch of your voice? Low monotone? High and squeaky? Sing-song? Shrill? Soft? Harsh? Does your voice seem to come mainly from your chest, throat? nose? Does the air come from low down inside you when you speak? From high up? Do you cut off much of the air to your voice? How?

24. How far have these various non-verbal features changed over the years? What changes have taken place? How far were they the result of a conscious effort on your part? What further changes would you like to see/make? What changes do you expect to see?

25. Imagine you are an old person coming to the very end of your days. What will your body and non-verbal behaviour tell others about the way you have lived your life?

26. Consider all the above questions in relation to people you are close to you. What can you learn? How far would it ever be possible for you to discuss any of this with others? What might you each gain? What could you lose?

27. Consider tones, tensions, expressions, gestures and movements that are of particular interest/concern to you. If each could speak what would it say? What would it reveal about the sort of person you are? What would you like to say to it?

28. Make a list of the five most important non-verbal behaviours that reveal who you are. How far do you like/dislike these non-verbal cues you give? How far would you like to change them?

29. (In pairs) Give a running commentary on what you are aware of within and about you right now. (Thoughts, feelings, sensations, non-verbal behaviour). Ask for feedback – was any of this noticed by the other person? What were they noticing?

30. (In pairs) Try having a conversation without words for five minutes. What can you reveal to each other? What can you observe in each other? How do each of you feel? How far do you know what's going on with the other person? How can you tell? What do you notice? Have a discussion about all this afterwards.

We have considered our accessories and our bodies; there is just one other topic that is not quite one nor the other, yet maybe it is both! I am referring to the food we eat! This, too, reveals something about the sort of person we are; both in terms of how much we eat; what we eat and the way we eat it.

1. What do you think you reveal about yourself as a result of what, when, how and how much you eat? How do you feel about all this? What, if anything, would you like to change?

2. If you over-eat or under-eat what is that all about? If your dietary habits could speak what would they tell you about the sort of person you are? What would a wise dietary expert advise you to do about your eating habits? How do you know? Have you ever checked?

3. Do you taste your food and savour it? Or do you 'stoke it down' carelessly while attending to something else? Do you gobble? Nibble? Pick? Shovel?

4. Are table manners important to you? What are they? What do they signify?

5. Is eating a symbolic event you look forward to or a chore to be got out of the way? Do you eat with others or alone? Is eating with others important to you? What does it signify to you?

There is one more important means of non-verbal communication which we have yet to consider; and that is touch. As new-born babies, our earliest and most important contacts with the outside world come to us through the tone of voice of our mother and, even more important, in the way in which she touches us. Parental tension and anxiety (or confidence and peace of mind) are communicated to the infant depending on the way in which (s)he is touched, cuddled, and handled generally. Such early contacts may be a solid foundation from which we can move out into the world or, at the other extreme, they may be a traumatic hell from which it may take us years to recover (if we ever do). Most childhood experiences, needless to say, are neither so 'perfect' nor so terrible and, fortunately, children can be surprisingly resilient!

It is difficult, though not impossible, to lie with our tone of voice; and it is even more difficult to do so with the way we touch. In other words, when (if) we touch someone we may be able to get a deeper sense of who they are and what they are all about than any number of words and gestures will reveal. Hence the expression *"I was really touched by what you did"* means, *"you got really close to me"*.

However, I don't want to pretend that people can never deceive each other once they have made bodily contact. That, clearly, would be an absurd delusion. It is worth pointing out, though, that if we are deceived by the touch of another, it may very well be because we are deceiving ourselves. We may well be choosing to ignore the messages that are coming to us through physical contact.

Touch, obviously, can take many forms; and different varieties
of bodily contact, of course, are considered appropriate, or inappropriate, between different individuals and in different cultures.
Touch can be affectionate, hostile, controlling, condescending,
punishing, sensual, erotic or reassuring. If we are never touched,
nor ever touch, we may well be limited in the extent of our meeting.
But it is also true that we may fail to make real contact with another
if all we can do is 'grind against' each other through full sexual
contact.

The most intimate form of tactile contact, obviously, is likely to
be full penetration and sexual orgasm. Some couples may not get
close to each other because sexual contact is a barrier for one reason
or another. But, let us not forget it, there may be quite a few
partners who engage in sexual relations in order to avoid their
failure to communicate intimately in other important respects. We
may get through to each other through sexual contact; equally
likely, though, we may be lost within our own fantasies and preoccupations even in the most intimate sexual embrace. The sex may
be very satisfying erotically and yet there may be little emotional
intimacy and human contact. Indeed, there are some for whom
satisfying sexual connection is only possible if we are not *too* close
to each other. The thought of sexual intimacy combined with, and
as a form of, real close human encounter can, for some people,
seem too scary and overwhelming. Sex, then, can be a means of
intimacy; yet it can also be a substitute for intimacy!

There is plenty of evidence to show that the health and well-being
of adults, quite as much as children, is greatly enhanced by an
abundant quality, quantity and variety of touch. Human touch is
best, and I suspect that many of us look with envy when we see
monkeys in a zoo, or better still in the wild, sitting and lying
together in a close-knit group, taking in the sun, and idly picking,
stroking and grooming each other! Such primitive and 'uncivilised'
behaviour certainly strikes me as one form of bliss that I sorely
envy! I know that I am not alone in this; particularly among the
relatively untouchable English with our collective 'stiff upper lip'.

But if humans are too touchy about being touched we can at
least make do with a pet and, again, the evidence suggests that
people living alone who have a cat or dog to stroke and care for
are likely to remain happier and healthier than those who have
nothing. Even young monkeys, deprived of their mother, will do
better if they have some sort of 'teddy bear' substitute-mother that
they can run and cling to. The real mother is best of all, of course,
but a soft, inanimate mother figure will be better than nothing at all.

We sense the importance of something to cuddle when we give children soft toys. Most young children like to have something soft and familiar to cuddle at night and many build up these toys into full-blooded pretend friends. Psychologists call such toys 'transitional objects' since they form part of the transition from the clinging on to a mother figure to a more independent existence. The danger, of course, is that for children whose development has been traumatised for one reason or another, they can become too much a substitute for real human contact.

The vast majority of the adults that I have met in courses on Communication Skills (and other topics) believe that, in England at least, nearly all of us would like to touch and be touched far more than we actually do and are. There is a great degree of quiet envy of Latin cultures where, (perhaps because of the sunshine?), there is more of a street culture; more communal getting-together; more open expression of emotion; and more physical contact. Just possibly, this Latin sensuality envied within Anglo-Saxon cultures may be more of a myth than a reality. But, if so, it is a powerful, and revealing, one.

I hope it is clear that I am not talking primarily about sexual contact. (We will come to that in a later chapter). Rather, I am referring to the ordinary 'common-or-garden' (yet rare) touch of reassurance, recognition and simple friendship. Men, in particular, (as we shall later see in more detail) find touch-as-friendship very difficult to handle, since so many of us are so terrified that this will signify that we are homosexual. And so, insofar as men ever touch each other at all, it will be touch-as-control or touch-as-eroticism. Sadly, so much of this erotic touching is somewhat deficient in ordinary sensuality and, even, basic friendship.

I see no simple escape from the frozen, bloodless, 'untouched-by-human-hand' existence that so many of us presently lead. The revolution in information technology, and other forms of technical progress keep us ever more easily in touch with each other, except that we never actually touch. Indeed, we no longer have to have any physical contact at all, nor even see each other face to face.

Growing numbers of people in advanced Western society live alone:

- We can travel in a hermetically sealed motor car, or on a train or bus which has no conductor and soon will have no driver.
- We can be crowded close together yet each staring into our own private infinity or our own newspaper; and this to 'put us in touch with' the outside world.

- We can shop in a supermarket where we pick up all our goods directly for ourselves.
- These goods will be vacuum wrapped and sealed, in plastic or metal, and may never have been touched by a human hand at any stage during planting, growth, harvesting, packing and delivery.
- We can take our goods to the check-out counter and avoid any contact or conversation with the sales assistant. She will be too busy ringing up prices and we will be busy stacking our trolley.
- We can 'keep in touch' with the world around us through TV, video, film, telephone, Fax, computer terminals, cable and who knows what next? Yet none of these contacts involve physical contact.
- We live in increasingly controlled environments where not even the wind, sun and rain can touch us. Instead, 'for our comfort and convenience', we inspire a conditioned air at constant temperature and humidity that is generally somewhat stale, though deodorised! It is not inspiring!

And then we wonder why we may feel stale and anxious. The wonder is, I sometimes think, that we survive at all!

I myself, in the 1970s and early 1980s, experimented with many forms of 'Encounter Group' culture where, generally for a weekend, people would get together with a group leader using one or other of a variety of psycho-technologies. With these we would seek to 'really meet'; 'really face ourselves as we really are'; really try to release, learn and move on from our various 'hang-ups' and traumas. The quality of these experiences varied enormously. Some were inspiring, uplifting and unforgettable. Others were destructive, unprofessional, and sterile. Some substituted 'new games for old' or were constrained by a tyranny of *fun*. Most, as you might expect, were somewhere in between. I learnt a great deal both from very good and very bad group experiences. In particular I learned that, even if we want so much to meet and touch, we may not easily succeed, and there is no simple methodology or technique that will help us to do so. We may touch each other (and 'group-gropes' were a part of some of these experiences), but even then we may not really be touched!

At some such groups I also learned about phoney touch, phoney smiles, phoney 'intimacy', as well as more genuine encounters. I learned, too, that we can only meet each other if we can find the distance between us that feels right and real, neither too close nor too far away. If I avoid touching you when touch would be appropriate, then I am missing an opportunity to meet. But if we touch when one or both of us are not really ready, willing or able to do so then our touch will feel forced, false and intrusive.

Through touch, perhaps more than through any other medium of communication, we may seek to avoid the fact that we are basically, each of us, alone. As we cling to each other it can seem as though we may perhaps be able to merge. But such union is only temporary, fleeting and limited. Moreover, if we touch in order to run away from our aloneness then our touching will have a desperate, fugitive quality to it. We will not be at peace with it since our aloneness will loom up from behind and haunt us.

Therefore, if we are really to meet, and to touch as mature adults, we must do so through, and from within, our experience of separateness, independence and aloneness. You and I can meet, if it is meet to do so, when we each of us know that you are you, that I am I, and that there *is* a boundary between us. Thus the paradox: it can be exquisite when boundaries between us are blurred and we seem to fuse together as one. But, mainly, it is exquisite when the points of contact between us hover lightly and delicately, so that they are neither forced nor evaded. Then we can really celebrate the mystery of ourselves, each other and our (genuine) encounter.

If the only touch available is forced and phoney, then I'd (sometimes) rather we keep our hands to ourselves! But, even when we are being genuine, there is a risk in reaching out to others: we may, after all, be rejected, or we may discover that this person does not have the 'feel' to them that we thought, and hoped, they might. Alternatively, we may be misunderstood, or drawn in to a greater degree of intimacy than we actually want.

Through touch we may make ourselves vulnerable, and the 'touchy' person is uneasy about being touched, vulnerable and intruded upon. Such defensiveness has its place since, after all, there are plenty of times when people are indeed trying to get at us, get the better of us or exploit us in one way or another. In particular, the fear of sexual exploitation, particularly for women, can often prevent us from touching and being touched. We may be so scared that we will slip, or be forced into, sexual contact that we will avoid any form of touch altogether in case our intentions are misunderstood or the situation gets 'out of hand' (or beyond the stage of mere hands!).

Men, in particular, seem to be limited in the number of touch-

skills and 'touch strategies' (sic) that they are able to use. For
example, any form of touch whatever between men is often taboo,
apart perhaps from a (somewhat too firm) handshake or the (somewhat too rough) slap on the back. And even the touch between
men and women is, in the view of many women, somewhat limited
in quality and variety.

Women quite often complain, when given the chance, that men
will touch them only if they are in the role of:

The Boss (showing his power over subordinates);
The Little Boy (being 'mothered' by his wife);
The Father or SuperHero (nurturing his 'daughter' or 'little
woman');
The Sex Stud ('scoring' another woman; celebrating his enormous virility, 'overwhelming' a female with his sexual
prowess).

There is a place for these roles from time to time; but women
increasingly, and understandably, complain that they would
also like an 'adult-adult' touch relationship with men; where
there was a flexible interchange of giving and receiving, and
where both parties could risk being vulnerable and open without
having always to regress to a childlike dependency. It sometimes
seems as though men make a fetish of sexuality in an ultimately
futile attempt to compensate for a fear of sensuality. This im-
poverishes the sex and doesn't provide a substitute for intimate
talk and touch.

Such a macho stereotype is, just possibly, losing its hold over
men, at least in some sub-cultures. And so, for example, we are
witnessing the emergence of the 'New Man' in advertising; who
sensually contemplates his forearm – in advertisements at least if
not in the world. Changes are, undeniably, taking place. But I
suspect that they are likely to be slow; and it is hard to predict
where they will lead.

It is generally frustrating when we force or falsify the nature of
our touch; though let's not go to the other extreme and avoid all
touch just because it might not be the 'right' sort! Such avoidance
might shield us from our own defensiveness and vulnerability, but
it would also keep us out of touch with each other. This brings me
to what I think is the 'bottom line' on the matter of touch; which
is that we can more easily touch others to the extent to which we
are in touch with ourselves! Moreover, when I am really touched
by you I am awakened not just to you; but to myself; and to
us.

Questions (2):

1. Think about your last week: Who have you touched and been touched by? How? Where? When? Why? Was it pleasant or unpleasant? How did you feel about it? How did the other person feel about it? How do you know?

2. Think of the touching that occurs (or doesn't!) between you and particular individuals: would you like more? less? different forms of touching? If so, what changes would you like to see?

3. Have you ever talked about 'touch' with particular individuals? Who? What would happen if you tried?

4. Are you 'better-than-average' in your ability and willingness to touch? Or worse?

5. Imagine that you had as much of the right sort of touching that you wanted from as many people as you preferred: What would this be like? How many people are involved? How are you touching each other? How would you, and they, feel about this?

6. Are your touch fantasies purely sexual? erotic? . . . or do you imagine other forms of contact?

7. Could you use your fantasies to develop and work towards a realistic ideal? Or are they quite unrealistic, impractical and unworkable? (If the latter, why not recast some of them so that they are practical and realistic?)

8. Do you think that the people concerned would actually enjoy your 'touch paradise' as much as you? Or would they feel exploited, or threatened, or repulsed or abused? What evidence do you have?

9. How well, or badly, were you touched as a child? Where? By whom? In what way? How did you feel about it?

10. Are you still influenced by what you learned, or didn't learn, about touch as a child? What can you do about it?

11. (For Groups): Where are you on the continuum:
    Touch very little . . . Touch a lot? Stand in the appropriate position in the room.
    Where would you like to be on this continuum? Move to this position in the room.

12. (For Groups): Where are you on the continuum:
    Touch the most in this group . . . Touch the least in this group? Stand
    in the appropriate position in the room.

13. (In pairs): Stand, or sit, facing each other and hold out the
    palms of your hands so that they are flat and almost touching
    the palms of your partner.
    • Imagine that there is an invisible glass between you and
      your partner.
    • Imagine that an invisible force joins your hands with those
      of your partner; so that your palms remain close, but not
      touching.
    • Imagine that your hands have a life of their own. Watch
      them as they gently 'dance' with the hands of your partner,
      palm to palm.
    • See which hands lead and which follow. Take your time.
      Don't rush. Don't 'try' to do anything. Just see what
      happens.
    • See how far you wish to 'get through' to each other.
    • See how far you can.

14. (For Anglo-Saxon Men): Do you ever find it possible to touch
    other men? Are you restricted to hand-shakes and a rough and
    ready 'back-slapping' style with other men? Could you ever
    touch another man in a supportive or affectionate way? Or
    would this scare you, or others, into thinking you were homo-
    sexual?

15. How far are you able to allow your partner to touch people of
    the opposite sex? What rules do you have about this? How do
    you each feel about this? (This 'harmless little question' could
    keep you occupied for hours!)

7.   Getting through the Sex Barrier

Boys will be Boys – And Girls will be Women.
(Graffiti)

Women are never stronger than when they arm themselves with their weaknesses.
Marquise du Deffand, *Letters to Voltaire* (1759-75)

God created man and, finding him not sufficiently alone, gave him a companion to make him feel his solitude more keenly.
Paul Valéry, *Tel quel* (1943)

As a male, I sense that, among some feminist circles at least, I am to be viewed (and read?) with suspicion. It is rather painful to have people respond to you as though you might be concealing a tail and horns as well as a phallus, and although I find female wariness of men quite understandable, that does not make the hurt any less intense.

Some women seem to have more or less given up on, or 'fired' (dismissed), men, and not just those who would describe themselves as feminist. I suspect that there are numerous women, from many different walks of life, who are not conscious of how despairing they are about the possibility of ever being able to communicate seriously except with other women. Quite a few women, it seems, take the view that "It's useless to try to get through to a man," and some are quite 'matter of fact' about it.

For (what I hope is) a minority of women, men have already been tried, found guilty and sentenced to permanent exile from the Human Race. For others, men are, as it were, on probation; and decisions will be taken depending on whether or not they can 'shape up' in the not too distant future.

I have discussed this subject within a large number of (mixed) groups (where women have generally outnumbered men by three or four to one) and it is very distressing to witness the degree of frustration that so many women feel about men, and the degree of bafflement and surprise that so many men evince in response!

Female complaints about 'maleness', as it presently exists, have been so much discussed and written about in the last twenty years that you might wonder if there is anything else that needs saying. Some people, perhaps, have discussed the subject into the ground. Others, probably a majority, continue to give little thought to the matter. Certainly, it appears that the vast majority of men still give scant, or nil, consideration to the question of what it is to be male. Men rarely, if ever, ask whether some of the assumptions and expectations made of them are oppressive to themselves as well as to women.

But what are the common complaints that women have of men? Some of you will be so familiar with these that the following will be in no way new. Other readers, however, will be unaware of all this, and so a brief background is necessary before we move on to what seems to me to be relatively uncharted territory.

A good starting place, still, is to look at the toys that girls and boys play with. Girls have dolls and teddy bears, and many of the games they play involve nurturing relationships; with 'mothers', 'fathers', and 'children' going on relatively safe adventures of one sort or another. Boys, too, have teddy bears; though they have to relinquish them sooner than the girls, and they can only have a doll if it carries a gun! You might think that this is a rather extreme statement. It is not. It is, almost without exception, the simple truth of the matter. Boys play with space monsters and animals that transform into machines, tanks and battle cruisers. All of these tend to be very heavily armed and armoured.

- Boys, still, are encouraged to "boldly go where no man has been before" (to quote the opening of *Startrek*, the cult space soap opera).
- Girls learn to dress up, imitate their favourite pop star and play with make-up.
- Boys seek to *go*, and *look* and *want*.
- Girls learn to *be*, and *be looked at* and *be wanted*.

All this may be changing just a little. But not very much; and some of the differences in male and female roles and behaviour are not merely slight, they are vast and profound in the extreme.

For example, next time you are in a pub or restaurant or any social situation, listen unobtrusively to the sort of conversations that are going on. Over and over again, when women are talking to each other, you will find them sharing, and discussing, personal experiences, feelings and relationships. Men seldom share their emotions or talk about their own personal relationships. Instead, they will be giving their opinions or talking about what they have done or plan to do next. Alternatively, they will be engaging in more superficial kinds of banter and time-filling pastimes and pleasantries.

Such differences, I want to stress, are not small and marginal, they are vast and fundamental. It can be very difficult to get a man to say what he is feeling; and this is often because he doesn't actually know! Conversely, it may be very difficult to convince a woman that her present feelings are not of much relevance to the job in hand! Ask a man what he feels and he will assume that you are asking for his opinions. And so he will answer you by telling you what he thinks. More than one woman has suggested to me that men generally don't know what they are feeling; consequently, they have to ask a woman to tell them. I have seen many cases where the man has been baffled about what is going on and the woman says "This has been building up, and you have been feeling like this for the past six months!"

This is not to say that women are paragons of insight, openness and maturity. Far from it! But there is no denying that women are generally more expressive of, and sensitive to, emotion than men. We don't really know how far this is due to differences in temperament that are innate, invariable and written in to our genes. What we do know, though, is that a very great deal of these gender differences can be attributed to upbringing.

From the earliest years girls are encouraged to pay attention to their own feelings and to the feelings of others. They are encouraged to disclose information about themselves to friends and they receive more personal disclosure from people around them. They are encouraged to be comforting; to be sensitive rather than demanding; to co-operate; to be open; to have awareness of, and insight into, the motives, needs and behaviour of others.

With boys, the opposite is the case. They are encouraged to be adventurous, to go and do, to get on with the job, or the game and to make their demands known. They are told that "big boys don't cry", and even as babies they are handled more vigorously than the girls. They are asked for their opinions and preferences and told that they must stand up for themselves and not let their feelings run away with them.

Compare the way in which boys and girls spend time together:

- Girls will 'gossip' (as men see it); they will talk about themselves and each other; they will share their feelings, compare experiences, and ask about the feelings of others. Their games will often involve animals who will be assumed to have feelings, hopes and fears and these will be consulted and reassured in their turn.

- Boys' games, on the other hand, will more likely involve objects (trucks, cars, aeroplanes etc.) rather than 'living' animals (dolls, care-bears, nurses).

My own daughter has always had both 'boys' and 'girls' toys to play with, but the dolls and animals were always far more popular than the trains and lorries. I remember one occasion when she was playing with another little girl in the garden. One was pulling a large wooden train behind her, the other had a large tip-up truck (the sort that I had worshipped as a child). I was very struck by this since my daughter had almost never played with these before. I listened in unobtrusively to their conversation and found . . . that the lorry was being used as a 'dog' and the train was a 'cat'!

I doubt that this shows that my daughter has an innate interest in cats and dogs and none whatever in trains and lorries. More likely, I suspect that her parents unwittingly communicate a set of assumptions and expectations that are quite different from their conscious, and stated, intentions. Moreover, regardless of parental influence, my daughter, like all children, faces an outside world where deep-seated assumptions about what 'proper little girls' do continue to be made and change only slowly. Such expectations are all the stronger because they are rarely stated explicitly, but merely assumed as 'the way things are'. Consequently, they are all the more difficult to challenge.

After years of practice, then, boys learn to be 'businesslike'. Their approach to people and situations generally begins with such questions as: "What do I want to do? What needs to be done here? How can I get on and get things moving?" Girls, on the other hand, tend to operate out of a very different set of questions: for example, "What are our reactions to this situation? What are my feelings about this? What kind of meeting is possible here?"

Of course, I am not saying that women are never businesslike and men never aware of emotions. Indeed, on the all-important domestic front, with chores and children, it is the woman who is infinitely more businesslike, competent, practical, resourceful, responsible and efficient than the man. Moreover, there is probably some truth in the claim that the female executive will have to prove that she is more 'driving' and efficient than her male counterpart if she is to achieve promotion.

Nonetheless, the differences in stereotypes remain considerable; their influence substantial; and old attitudes and influences die hard. For example:

> *Women are always eagerly on the lookout for any emotion.*
>> Stendhal, *On Love* (1822)

> *Womankind*
> *Is ever a fickle and changeful thing.*
>> Virgil, *Aenid* (30-19BC)

> *Women are a decorative sex. They never have anything to say, but they say it charmingly.*
>> Oscar Wilde, *The Picture of Dorian Gray* (1891)

> *The only way to behave to a woman is to make love to her, if she is pretty, and to someone else if she is plain.*
>> Oscar Wilde, *The Importance of Being Earnest* (1895)

> *Man is the hunter; woman is his game.*
> *The sleek and shining creatures of the chase,*
> *We hunt them for the beauty of their skins;*
> *They love us for it, and we ride them down.*
>> Alfred, Lord Tennyson, *The Princess; A Medley* (1851)

Many men, including myself, would never dare any longer to make such sexist remarks. But, given that such things have been said by so many for so long, we are not entirely free of their influence; and neither are women. Nor have we yet worked out just what differences we want to celebrate – or to diminish!

As a result of all this, there are certain kinds of communication problems that recur over and over again between men and women. Both sexes, for example, will tend to the view that the other party has "essentially missed the point of what I'm trying to say". For the woman, this will be because "He simply hasn't grasped the way I feel about this, and he's quite unaware of his own feelings". For the man, the problem will be that "She takes everything so personally and behaves quite irrationally".

To the male, 'rationality' consists in putting emotions entirely to one side as just so much 'noise' and 'static'. Rather than 'wallowing' in one's feelings, the 'rational' man analyses the problem, considers his opinions, marshals his arguments, clarifies his goals and methods; and debates the relative merits of the other man's view of the matter. Being 'rational', the rational man is not interested in the individual personalities and feelings of other rational men. All that matters are the opinions and plans themselves, their logical coherence and the evidence that can be assembled to support them.

Consequently, the rational man assumes an 'I-it' relationship with the world and other people. He relates impersonally to others, as objects rather than persons, and is far more interested in getting things done than in making an intimate, individual and personal contact. To his frequent despair, he finds that women either can't or won't accept such impersonal relationships. Even in formal and official contexts they go on and on taking their own 'pulse' and that of the people around them; and they insist on including personal experiences and emotions onto what the rational man considers to be an impersonal agenda.

Women frequently react angrily and impatiently against such 'rationality' since they see it as mechanical, inhumane and insensitively ignorant of what really matters. This leads (some of) them to subscribe to the ancient myth that they do not operate according to rational principles at all but, instead, are guided by their 'intuition'.

The myth of intuition requires that we distinguish between analysing with the mind and 'seeing with the heart'. Men, we are told, are lost in their minds. The woman, on the other hand, merely senses rather than analyses and, for some, her intuition is almost like a 'sixth sense'. Apparently, we need this 'magical' power of intuition if we are really to see into the heart of things. Through intuition we will 'know' but we will not know why we know! Nor will we attempt to find out, since the intuitive approach recognises that much must always remain mysterious and unknowable. In particular, little can be known about how and why we know anything at all.

Rational men and intuitive women are both, I believe, mythical figures. I find them equally frustrating and they are each an obstacle rather than an aid to understanding and communication. Consider first, the intuitive woman:

It is one thing to allow for a proper sense of awe at the underlying mystery and enigma of being alive. And we certainly cannot be explicit and coherent about everything we do and see around us. But it is quite another matter to suggest that we have some ghostly faculty or intuitive sense that women more than men can utilise – to their eternal credit and our eternal cost. Such mumbo-jumbo does nothing to help us get to grips with the problems of communication between men and women; rather it generates ever more fog and mutual frustration.

We can, and should, be much more explicit about the nature of (so-called) 'intuition'; and we need to get away from the view that it is a superior faculty that exists in opposition to (so-called) 'rationality'. Such a view is destructive because it encourages irrationality and blind prejudice. The intuitive individual is not being illogical or irrational, rather she is responding to perceptions, emotions and a logic that she cannot quite explicitly describe or explain.

Over and over again, when we come to examine the work of intuition we find, not magic, but a simple lack of awareness of the processes that are going on. In other words, a woman who describes her response as intuitive will in fact be picking up, and interpreting, cues from within herself and in others of which she is unaware. Her 'intuition', for example, might produce within her a sense of fear and uncertainty about a particular person in a particular situation. She may well not have noticed precisely what she has observed that makes her feel as she does; and so she may say "My intuition tells me that I need to be careful with you". It would be less pretentious and misleading, though, and more honest, if she merely said "I feel uneasy about you, but I'm not sure why. I suspect that there is something suspicious about your behaviour but I can't quite pin down what it is."

We simply don't need to postulate a sixth sense when we are at present so ignorant about what is coming to us through the other five! We gain, and process, far more information from within and outside ourselves than we are ever consciously aware of. But rather than call this intuition let's just call it what it is, namely information gathering and reasoning processes that lie outside our conscious awareness. As a consequence, we will then see that so-called 'feminine logic' is the same as any other logic, except that much of it operates outside the spotlight of our own introspection.

Equally, we will then appreciate why women might sometimes be impatient with (so-called) 'male logic'. The objection, and I have observed this endlessly, is not that males are being overly logical; rather it is that men tend to be logical about 'half-truths' while blithely ignoring at least half of what the woman would consider to be admissible evidence. Thus, for example, they will treat a personal matter as though it was an impersonal one; or they will talk abstractly about an issue in order to avoid their own particular specific desires and emotions about the matter.

The man who ignores his own emotions may never discover that his feelings are ruling his life and shaping all his seemingly independent and dispassionate thinking. His feelings may well shape his 'objectivity', though, since emotions that are overlooked can become all the more influential.

Similarly, the woman who disregards, or undervalues, her own thinking and reasoning processes may have an emotional life that is governed by shallow reasoning, faulty interpretation and a careless neglect of the evidence. She may well not be aware of this; instead, she may attempt to dress up and dignify her sloppy thinking by describing it as 'intuition'.

If intuition really was a magic power, then all those who claim to use it ought to have been coming to similar conclusions. In fact people have, for centuries, claimed that they have direct, intuitive, access to Absolute Certainty, and they have, with equal certainty, come to quite contrary, various and contradictory results. We all have times when we feel 'intuitive' (i.e. confident but unsure why), and sometimes our hunches will turn out to be correct. Such intuitions are worth attending to since, sometimes at least, we really may know; without knowing how, or why, we know. Our certainty will not be because of any sixth sense; rather, we will have been picking up on cues and evidence from our five basic senses without being able to pin down where these cues are coming from. In other words, a supposedly magical intuitive sense ought to encourage us to look for the common-or-garden evidence we are actually drawing on. In any case, let us not forget that, despite our 'intuition', we might still turn out to be quite mistaken. We tend to forget this (error prone) side of our intuitive skill; others, perhaps more accurately, may be inclined to call it blind prejudice and dogma!

So much for the myth about female intuition. Females do not have magic powers; but they may well be better than men at picking up cues about the feelings of others; simply as a result of long practice. Let's not forget, though, the equally absurd myth about male logic and objectivity! If men really were so good at abstract and dispassionate enquiry, and could totally disregard personality, feelings and prejudice; then there are many matters about which they ought by now to have made more progress. They ought to have been able to transcend all personal ambition, passion and partiality in a co-operative search for truth, freed of ego-centric competitiveness and display. Self-evidently, neither men nor women have achieved any such Olympian detachment and impartiality! This is not merely due to faulty reasoning and inadequate evidence. It is because the who and what of our own individual personality and emotion often shapes what we see, what we value and what we think ought to be done.

In conclusion, I suggest that male and female styles of being-in-the-world need a deeper integration in each of us. We all exhibit both sets of characteristics; and so, for example, the stereotypical female might be wiser if she was more willing to accept that her feelings don't exist in a vacuum; nor do they well-up spontaneously through 'intuition'.

It is not enough to say "This is the way I *feel* about it", as though that was the last word on the subject. We are right to ask why we feel as we do and attempt to place our feelings in some context of (relatively) dispassionate thought and impersonal enquiry. Feelings are not necessarily 'the bottom line' on anything. For example, we may be feeling as we do because we are not thinking about and interpreting the situation correctly. We may be ascribing motives and intentions to people that they don't have. We may have got 'the wrong end of the stick' in our understanding of what is going on. We may have expectations, demands, beliefs and values that could, and should, be reappraised. And we should not ignore all these considerations by stubbornly and childishly clinging on to the observation that "This is simply the way I *feel* about it! (So there!)".

Whether male or female, we need to be serious about the evidence and the coherence of our reasons even if we can't always be clear about what motivates us to see things as we do. In other words, we need to think about what we feel; think why we feel as we do; and consider, as dispassionately as we can, just what we can do about it.

Equally, the stereotypical male needs to accept that human emotions (including his own) are in fact part of the evidence and often determine the way in which we think. Moreover, they will do this all the more powerfully and destructively if we try to repress and ignore personalities and feelings. In other words, we need to accept that our feelings both affect, and are affected by, our thoughts and interpretations. We cannot pretend to be merely 'talking heads'. We do not sit, in disembodied form, in some Cloud Nine existence above the weather of our own personality and emotion. Consequently, if we ignore our own, and other people's, feelings, we will find that our logic leads us to sterile and absurd conclusions.

Neither arid intellect nor indulgent emotion serve us well; and perhaps of greater importance than either is the underlying 'spirit' with which we communicate our thoughts and feelings. For example, if our underlying spirit, or intention, is one of good-will, then this will provide a context within which we will learn to cope with whatever tricky emotions or uncomfortable opinions may happen to arise (in ourselves or others). Whereas, if emotion and intellect feed off each other within an underlying spirit of malevolence, then even our seemingly most positive emotions and opinions might be co-opted as weapons to score a point against our adversary.

One interesting consequence of these myths about male logic and female intuition is that when we are being childish, as we are all bound to be at times, we tend to do it in a different way depending on whether we are male or female. Male childishness and naivety will be evident when men pontificate about some abstract matter and it is clear, to most female observers, that they are quite unaware of their own feelings and everyone else's. Such ignorance is a form of irresponsibility and women commonly complain that, at home in particular, men simply don't bother to be aware of, or take responsibility for, the domestic needs of children and social and family matters generally. Instead, at best, they 'help out', even when both partners are in full time paid work. This, too, is changing, but the change is very slow.

Often, male vanity is protected because the woman pretends that the man is in charge; and so she serves him with the major decisions to be taken – in much the same way that Sir Humphrey Appleby served his Minister in the TV series mentioned earlier. In other words, real power is firmly in the hands of the 'servant', but the apparent 'boss', posturing and deluded as he is, goes through the motions of being aware and in command. In many households, perhaps, the man of the house is given a paper crown to wear and a throne to sit on, but is in fact seen and treated by his wife like a little boy! (How many personal secretaries and assistants adopt a similar role with their chief executive?)

Female childishness, on the other hand, is more likely to take the form of a petulant disregard for facts and arguments and a somewhat indulgent wallowing in raw emotion; whether of a sulky or hysterical variety. Of course, men, too, can sulk and indulge their feelings in one way or another, but they tend to disguise this by trying to be 'logical' and 'right'; while failing to see that they are being merely argumentative.

So often, male and female stereotypes will tend to drive each side into an ever more unhelpful polarisation. The 'rational' man will try to stick to the facts, yet will disregard the most important of these, namely his own and his partner's feelings. This will lead the woman to feel increasingly frustrated and ever more tempted to say "away with all your logic, it's how we *feel* that counts". The male, in response to this, will cling on more stubbornly to his presentation of the argument so that, in a very short time, each may be driven into his and her own corner. The male in an arid world of pseudo-logic; the female in a raw pit of emotion; and both of them cut off from their underlying intentions which, by this stage, are likely to be competitive and malevolent.

The tragedy is that each could be giving the other something of value if each was willing to be more open. The woman could help the man to pay more attention to his own and other people's feelings; thus providing a 'feeling-perspective' on his thoughts. The man, on the other hand, could help the woman by providing a 'thinking-perspective' on her feelings. That way we might get a little more of a perspective on ourselves and our lives . . . fuelled, rather than clouded, by passion; and guided, rather than guarded, by thought.

Fifteen years experience in leading mixed groups has taught me a great deal about the different styles of communication adopted by men and women. It has been well documented that, whenever abstract matters and opinions are being debated, the men tend to dominate such discussions, and women tend to be much quieter and less confident and demanding. This is not the case, though, when the group agenda consists in sharing and exploring personal feelings and experiences. On such occasions it is the women who dominate, who are more open, more clear about what they want to say; and the men who tend to be defensive, uncertain of their ground, unclear about their feelings and unsure about how to talk about them. Instead they often try to shift the discussion into more abstract areas, but will dry up again when they are brought back to the matter of feelings and the present-moment activity of the group. Again, I want to stress, such differences are large and fundamental; they go very deep.

Male lack of awareness of feeling is particularly noticeable in relation to feelings of insecurity, fear and vulnerability. Men are not supposed to have such feelings; indeed, I sometimes think that anger, aggression and a stiff jaw are the only emotions that are permissible among 'real', macho, men. The fear has to go somewhere, of course, and it may be observed among many men in the way they carry themselves around:

Thus the macho man may be observed to walk around with a rigid, wary, defiant, armoured posture. He is forever on his guard. Everyone around him is looked upon with suspicion. He moves as though he was expecting to be ambushed at any moment. His shoulders are rigid, his chest is inflated, his arms and hands are flexed, his face is determined, his eyes are cold and hard, his entire musculature is tense and like a form of armour. He is 'boldly going where no man has been before' even when he's walking down the High Street that he's known all his life. He's on the look out for potential trouble and the more he and others get themselves into this posture, the more likely it is that their attitude will become self-fulfilling.

Needless to say, therefore, male aggression tends to be on the surface and 'up front'. It is 'manly' to be aggressive and assertively demanding; it is the male style to take a loud high profile approach. And so, it is scarcely surprising to find that men adopt such a style far more readily than women.

However, women are human too, and being human they are bound to be aggressive at times. Yet women are not supposed to be aggressive. They are supposed to be sensitive, passive, nurturing, 'at one' with Nature and with themselves. Sometimes, no doubt, they are, and more so, probably, than men. But they can't conceivably manage this all the time! What, then, do they do about aggression?

The answer, needless to say, is that female aggression tends to 'go underground' in one way or another. It is more likely to be covert and manipulative. When a man is punishing he will tend to do it by being 'right' in his logical arguments or by being deliberately threatening and angry; up to and including physical violence! The woman, more often, will withdraw into passive aggression, or skilful vindictiveness and subterfuge of various kinds. There are many ways of punishing people, and most of us, let's be honest, use quite a number of different strategies as earlier discussions have shown. Yet men do tend to differ from women in the punishment regimes they most prefer simply because cultural norms tend to encourage such specialisation!

> *"In the sex-war thoughtlessness is the weapon of the male, vindictiveness of the female."*
>
> Cyril Connolly, *The Unquiet Grace* (1945)

. . . Both sides use far more than one weapon; yet there is some truth in the above quotation.

. . recent years, feminism has produced a whole industry of literature that explores male failings and inadequacies. This is all very well; the criticisms have often been trenchant, deep, and substantially valid. Men do have a case to answer and profound changes do need to be made that would, I think, be of equal benefit to both themselves and women.

Yet, I suppose in the nature of things, such criticisms have sometimes been careless, self-righteous, pious and lacking in basic humanity and respect. It is no sign of progress when women abandon all hope and desire ever to communicate with men. And it is a poor state of affairs when women descend to stereotyping and the kind of abuse that, if made of ethnic minorities or women, would rightly be seen as offensive and gratuitous. There is no doubt in my mind that men need to be more willing to find and express their own compassion for others and take women's dissatisfaction with men far more seriously than they generally do. But let's hope that no more than a few women ever come to the conclusion that compassion is for fools and weaklings or should be preserved for members of one's own sex alone.

Let's not forget that men can have dissatisfactions too and that male withdrawal from feeling can be just as much of a purgatory as female exclusion from power – even if many men are too deadened to realise this. And, within such a spirit, let me share with you some more personal writing, that draws from my experience of what is, thank goodness, a *minority* of feminist women:

Feminists:

Parading, advancing, manoeuvring with their 'femininity';
Implying, not quite saying, . . . "I'm more sensitive *than thou;*
more loving, caring, supportive, vulnerable.

Feminist? Feminine? or Feminine-guile?
How senseless, hurtful, careless, destructive, armoured.
How masculine *(beneath it all!)*

With words of love
their game, like ours, is Power
Hypocrisy unmatched, unmasked!

To the 'New Woman':
Oppressed by Your Oppression

Look, I know you're oppressed and all.
I've read the books
I've tried to raise my consciousness
I may be irredeemable.
You know, 'product of patriarchy' etc.
And so are you!

But do you have to
make a career out of
being 'right' and 'right on'?
and indulging your hurt
and exulting in your anger?
and playing one up-personship games?

What about some good old good-will?
and (just a bit of) trust?
You're hurt inside
And so am I
Let's try.
Shall we?

No longer mice
You've grown and joined the Rat Race
As the Rats
We're trained to be.
Let's burrow to the bottom line
To truth or truce or peace.

We each of us have a 'shadow' consisting in all those aspects of our personality that shame and horrify us. Much of the male shadow consists of all those 'feminine' characteristics that 'real men' are not supposed to have: for example vulnerability, tenderness, compassion, fear and other, 'irrational', emotion. Similarly, a large part of the female shadow consists in all those supposedly 'male' qualities that even progressive women are supposed to avoid: e.g. aggression, domination, vengefulness, violence and the urge to control and achieve 'mastery' over others. Rather than face these unwanted features of our own personalities, it is so tempting to project them onto others. And so, for example, my contempt for your irrationality and emotionalism may be very much fuelled by the fear and rejection of my own tempestuous temperament, that I so carefully hide away in my talk about rationality. Similarly, your disgust with my aggression, and your demand that I try to be a gentle caring creature like you, may have a lot to do with the fact that you are unwilling to come to terms with your own aggression and vindictiveness, and with the sly dishonest ways in which you express these feelings.

I suspect that women may have even more trouble with their 'shadow' than men because Society expects women to be altogether 'nicer' than men. It is expected that men will sometimes 'cut up rough' and hit below the belt since it is acknowledged that men must boldly go out into the wider world and battle for survival. However, until recently, the stereotypical woman was expected to stay in the nurturing role by the hearth, with the family, mopping wounds and propping up battered egos; encouraging others to grow and learn. She was not supposed to have an ego of her own and she was not supposed to be 'bitchy', since this was seen as a betrayal of her benign femininity. (Compare this with 'irritability' and impatience in males which tends to be seen as a positive sign of the energy, power and restless drive of a truly manly male!)

Consequently, many women may have particular difficulties in acknowledging their own powers of violence, provocation, vindictiveness and all the various dirty tricks that all human beings carry with them. This problem is compounded for feminists who see the opportunity of occupying the 'moral high ground' in their campaign against patriarchal injustice and oppression. We all of us have trouble when we are sure that right is on our side since, if we are honest, we will look at the crusaders gathering around our holy flag, and find that they are sullied with most, if not all, of the human failings that we are seeking to root out in our enemies! Whenever we seek to promote a good cause, which involves highlighting the *motes* in the eyes of others, we need to be aware of the *beam* in our own. It is a difficult path to travel. We try to make a better world and encourage others to change for the better, yet there is so much that could be better within each of us!

In addition, let us remember some of the observations made in Chapter Four concerning Personal Identity. On the one hand I will have plans for you and will want you to change. Yet on the other, my view of myself may presuppose a view of you that will discourage change. For example, the 'fatherly' male protector and rescuer may say that he wants to help his 'helpless little wife' to grow and change and become more self sufficient. But does he really? What would he do with his much cherished role of fatherly protector if he had no one left to protect? Similarly, the poor oppressed woman may wish that her man would become more progressive, sensitive and caring. But does she really? What would she do with her comfortable role as virtuous, outraged victim? How would she feel if she could no longer occupy the moral high ground, and no longer had a licence to be sanctimonious, superior, 'holier-than thou', and covertly punishing and revengeful?

This is a serious problem. Oppressors, rescuers and victims can get locked in a macabre dance from which no one finds it easy to extract themselves since it provides significant, ghastly, 'pay-offs' for all parties! If nothing else, familiar roles become a comfortable habit; a known quantity. We may all wish that we could be more liberated in one way or another and yet freedom of any sort is both prized and greatly feared! Our prison may confine us; yet it can become a comfortable enough home that is more appealing than the terrors of open spaces, uncertainty and genuine choice!

It follows from all this that the women I really respect are those who simply *assume* an equal place in the corridors of power without having to whinge or whine or be uppity and self-righteous about it. This, admittedly, is an awesomely difficult task; yet more and more women are managing to achieve it, and they do so without losing their 'femininity'. The woman can take a senior position in management without having to prove that she is still a woman and, likewise, the man can do the dishes at home without having to prove that he is a man. This, surely, is the ideal; but, with the years of conditioning that we all have to overcome, it is easier said than done!

In Western societies male-female relationships are at a crossroads. We are in a state of crisis, where many of the old certainties about how 'proper' men and women should live are being questioned. It is difficult to know where all this should, and will, lead us. There are, surely, more than simply anatomical differences between us; but it is much less clear than ever it was just what these differences are and should be. Whatever the outcome, let us hope that the crisis will lead, ultimately, to a break-*through* in relationships rather than an ever deeper break-*down*!

Having said all that, it is worth remembering that we have so far discussed male-female relationships purely as a gender issue, without mentioning the dreaded topic of sex even once. This is quite appropriate, since many of the issues between men and women do not concern sexuality first and foremost. But many others do, of course, and so it really is time that we considered the matter of male and female sexuality and the ways in which it can help (or hinder) us in our efforts to 'get through'.

At one level, sex is a simple physical, biological act that we are driven to engage in as a result of our genetic make up, in the same way as other animals. Obviously, it is fundamental to the survival of any species that sufficient numbers are driven to the act of copulation. Furthermore, given that the young of the higher mammals take a long time to develop and need a good deal of parental care, it is essential too that such animals are 'wired up' so that the sight of their helpless young will elicit protective and nurturing behaviour. The female of many species is more urgently required to fulfil this role than the male. She, after all, must carry, give birth to, and suckle the young and it is scarcely surprising that, as a result of this, she will become more quickly bonded to her offspring than the father; whose basic biological function is completed with conception.

Of course, it is not just the young of *homo sapiens* that thrive best with both male and female parental support. Many species seem to do better if the male can be persuaded to be sexually faithful and domestically responsible; though there are plenty of others where the 'ideal' practice varies according to circumstances.

The more sophisticated the species the more likely it is that male and female will co-operate as the length of time required to bring up baby increases. However, there are lots of exceptions. Undeniably, and unsurprisingly, child-care is a larger task for the female of most species than it is for the male; and this, surely, is a simple consequence of biology rather than a 'patriarchal plot'!

For the potential mother, then, the sexual act may very well bring with it awesome consequences and responsibilities that she is unlikely to forget about even in the moments of wildest erotic passion. It is easier for the man to disregard the consequences since it is not his body that will well-up with child. For him, orgasmic release and biological function are completed in the moment of ejaculation. For the woman the lifetime task may only then be beginning.

The man releases, or plants, his 'seed'; and, if he wishes, can walk away. The woman receives his sperm and she cannot then withdraw easily from the consequences. Of course this has changed just a little with contraception and abortion. But the latter is not the straightforward mechanical exercise that some modernists imagined it could be. It is a major emotional, human and spiritual matter of great import. Contraception, too, is no simple and entirely reliable decision. And so it is not as easy as we may think to uncouple sex and procreation as though the latter was an optional extra. They have gone together, profoundly and inevitably, for millions of years; so let us not imagine that we can easily pull them apart like separate courses on a menu!

On a crowded planet, it seems clear to me that contraception and abortion have an important role to play. But we really ought not to delude ourselves into thinking that these are simple, material, matters devoid of deep emotional consequences and implications.

For the man, commitment to his pregnant woman, involves the shouldering of perhaps his greatest ever responsibility. For the woman, the commitment of the man involves a reduction in her overall responsibility. This is because the woman, having carried and given birth to the child, will not generally see any real alternative to motherhood. The woman, in other words, knows very deeply that she is a mother as she feels the child grow inside her. (She may sometimes, of course, be more terrified than overjoyed in this knowledge!) The man observes that she is a mother and infers that he is, presumably, a father. Given these biological realities, it takes longer for the knowledge that *"I am now a parent"* to sink in to the man. The woman, more than the man, is asking for support in a task that she has already accepted. It is not surprising, therefore, that men may be rather less reliable than women in making the necessary act of parental and emotional commitment.

Needless to say, all this affects the (differing) ways in which men and women approach sex. For the man, sex can be more easily confinable as an erotic experience and no more. For the woman the eroticism will be more difficult if she fears that she may get pregnant by a man who is not committed, or able, to support her and bring up his child. The woman, more than the man, therefore, is more likely to be reluctant to engage in sexual relations unless she feels that the man is affectionate, supportive, caring, sensitive and loving. The woman, rather than the man, will more likely say:

"Do you love me?" "You only want me because of my body." "You are only after one thing."

The woman, more often, is the seduced rather than the active sexual seducer. The man declares his (undying?) love and affection, either because he genuinely means it or, cynically, because he hopes that the right words and gestures will constitute the 'key' with which he can unlock his way in to the female's secret places.

Given that the man can more easily confine himself to the sexual act, he may allow himself to be attracted merely to the physical attributes of a woman. Conversely, given that the woman is looking for a partner who would stand firm if she became pregnant, she will look more deeply into the overall personality of the man in addition to mere physical appearance.

The man, if you like, can carry his sexuality, with his genitals, 'on the outside'. He may indeed want a committed relationship but, if this is not available, a good time in bed will do fine, at least for the time being! The woman's sexuality, on the other hand, is embedded deep inside her and is likely to mean far more to her than just a physical act.

Consequently, when it comes to sex, it tends to be the man who goes after it more quickly, more often and more actively than the woman. Man is the 'actor'; woman the 'attractor'. Man requests the hand (and more) of the woman; woman grants or refuses his request. This process may be more disguised now that there are fewer balls, ballgowns, and twirling moustaches, and more unisex jeans and singles bars. But I would argue that the underlying pattern remains intact since, to some considerable extent, it is biologically rooted.

Most people see love and intimacy as part of the agenda in a sexual relationship – in addition, that is, to the sex! Sometimes, of course, the 'love' and closeness are little more than skin deep; and, in addition, there are often other agendas. For example, sex can be used as a way of *avoiding* intimacy (e.g. "Do we have to talk and hold hands, why don't we just go to bed?"). Alternatively, sex may be a means of pretending that there is more intimacy between us than is really the case.

People may be physically close, with the male literally inside the female, but that doesn't mean that they are necessarily close in any other way. They may each be lost in their own fantasies with little awareness of, or interest in, the experience and behaviour of their partner. Sex may be a substitute for intimacy; or the only form of intimacy we can deal with. For some, it will be possible only if we are not intimate since, otherwise, it would be just too overwhelming. And sex, too, far from being a place where we are really naked, may be "yet another area in which I have to put on a show!"

Sex may be used in an effort to gain love; "to prove I love you", "to prove you love me", "to make you love me", "to prove that we are intimate". It may be a substitute for sensuality. It may be exciting only if there is real emotional commitment; conversely, there may be excitement only if it is forbidden! It may be a source of great tension, or used as a simple release from our tensions! It may be impossible without love ("because it makes me too vulnerable"); or impossible *with* it ("because it makes me too vulnerable!") It may be a release from, or a Royal Road to, struggle, suffering, neurotic clinging and neediness! Either way, it is likely to provide us, if we are willing to look, with clues as to the nature of our relationship.

Sex can be a brief and peaceful interlude in the interminable battle between the sexes. Alternatively it can be the place where some of the biggest battles are fought! We like to think that love and sex go together, at least most of the time. Very often, though, let's face it, the sex goes together with power and becomes yet another means by which we try to gain power and 'leverage' over others. Thus, for example, the male may seek to 'score'; as though he was notching up a body count in the way that a fighter pilot marks up the number of killings he has achieved on the side of his plane. The female, on the other hand, may be 'casting her spell' over the hapless male like some carnivorous spider!

We may rarely say, though often we might think:

- "Now that we've made love, you are mine. I *own* you. You are my property".
- "I will *punish* you; there will be no sex for you tonight."
- "I will *reward* you, or try to make amends by giving you a good time this evening."
- "I will let you make love to me, but you are going to have to work hard at it because I'm going to play very *hard to get* as a result of your terrible behaviour today."

In other words, many meanings, intentions and interpretations are possible when people 'make love'. Furthermore, many games and performances may be operating regardless of whether or not people are clothed or undressed. Indeed, it is probably much easier, these days at least, to be nude in body than naked in spirit. The sexual act may, in itself, be simple enough; but once it has been drawn in to our dreams, schemes, fears, hopes and fantasies it becomes anything but a simple, biological, act! We can make almost anything we like of it: a trivial release; an earth shattering glimpse of infinity; a dissolving of two souls into one; an ever deeper discovery of my own aloneness; a chance to score a point; a place to 'swagger', or cringe with guilt and self doubt; a small comfort; a fumbling, awkward, absurd or tedious routine; a simple habit. Indeed, at different times it is likely to be all these things and more.

It can be very difficult for partners to talk about sex and what it means to them since there are (absurd) pressures on males to imagine always that "I'm such a stud" and on females to pretend that "the earth really moved when you did that to me!"Furthermore, it is difficult for *non*-partners to talk about sex because, with our puritan inheritance, we still feel a tremendous amount of guilt and insecurity about the subject. Also, there is the understandable suspicion that, were we to talk about sex, this talk would itself get mixed up with the light sexual flirtation, play, mutual awareness and celebration of sexuality that generally goes on among most groups of people.

In other words, sexuality almost inevitably influences any efforts we make to talk about it; the very effort to clear away the fog of our understanding – creates more fog! Our sexuality gives rise to many contrary and contradictory feelings; yet talking about all this produces still more feelings faster than we have a chance to get some insight into them. For example, even in the very process of talking about sexual games, we may well find ourselves playing some of them!

As a consequence of all this, whatever talk we may manage is often less than honest, and our realisation of this difficulty increase our reluctance to talk. In short, our passion, (or the lack of it), makes it difficult for us to be dispassionate!

Self-esteem is greatly influenced by the image we have of ourselves as sexual beings; and so guilt is never likely to be far away. In the Victorian past, the guilt arose with the dreadful discovery that "I am a sexual animal with sexual thoughts and fantasies." These days, the guilt is more likely to arise because "I am not sexual enough!"

The person who feels uneasy and insecure about his or her sexuality may find that the very unease makes matters worse. We may get into the habit of checking up and observing ourselves to ensure that we are 'doing it right'. We become nervous spectators of our own sexual performance and this in itself can dampen, or kill, our arousal. The more uncertain and tense we are, the more fumbling and asexual we are likely to become; and this can easily become a vicious spiral. Consequently, sex therapy, far from focusing too much on methods and performance, seeks to take the pressure off partners by giving them 'homework assignments' where, initially, they have to *refrain* from sexual intercourse, avoid genital contact, and abandon any attempt to 'achieve' something. Instead they are invited to take a holiday from the need to achieve; and simply, without pressure, see if they can find straightforward and undemanding ways of giving and receiving pleasure.

A person who is overly anxious about sexual performance finds that the anxiety itself destroys the erotic mood. Some things, and sex is one of them, work better when we stop trying to do anything or get anywhere. In other words, sex is more likely to go well when we really don't mind if it goes badly or doesn't go at all! When we stop trying to get anywhere we have more of a chance of discovering what we like about where we are right now. Furthermore, by accepting where we are right now we are more likely to relax and be at peace. That way, an erotic mood may develop all on its own and, if it doesn't, that's okay too!

One of the greatest sources of sex education, I think, can come from the comedian. We've had rather too many people who have told us that sex is dirty and that we should feel ashamed. In more recent years, there have been too many, rather over-earnest, folk who reassure us, somewhat clinically, that sex is a very fine thing between properly committed people and that we shouldn't feel ashamed when the circumstances are right. What too few of these people make clear is that it is actually O.K. if it is pleasurable and exciting, that it can be done in all kinds of ways, for many reasons and with many results and that, given that we make a mess of most things, we are bound to 'screw things up' with sex as well at times. That's okay, though, because it's simply part of the Human Condition!

I like, for example, several of Woody Allen's 'one-liners' about sex: for example, when co-star Diane Keaton complemented him on his sexual prowess in a torrid bedroom scene, he responded by explaining that "I put in a lot of practice on my own!"

I remember the enormous release of tension that went up in the cinema audience when we heard this. Such a laugh of recognition. And no one had hairs on the palms of their hands as far as I could make out as we left the cinema. Of masturbation? Well, it's better than nothing; and it's sometimes better than, or indistinguishable from, sex with a partner! But mental images and pictures are no real substitute for flesh and blood reality – at its best, and even when it's only third-best!

However, let's not let anyone try to take away our sexual fantasies, and let's not worry ourselves about them (unless they are just systematically and unendingly violent and sadistic!). After all, fantasy can help us to lift our reality into something more charming, erotic, sensual, romantic, caring or whatever. Fantasy can provide us with the vision to make something of our lives.

Equally, fantasy can become a substitute for, and escape from, our reality and although this is okay up to a point there may come a time when we would do better if we paid more attention to what is here and now and possible. Some partners, certainly would get through to each other if they spent less time in their own respective fantasy worlds, paid more attention to each other and were more willing to communicate sensitively about what they wanted and didn't want.

It is a cliché, of course, to say that sexuality, like anything else, involves a certain amount of 'give and take'; but it's true all the same. Some, clearly, are quite selfish about sex and seek their own enjoyment without any real regard for their partner's pleasure. Others, and not infrequently, have a different problem; which is that they are too 'giving'; and too exclusively concerned about the needs of their partner. As a result, they are not sufficiently assertive about their own needs. Moreover, they can be something of a disappointment for their partner. After all, it's a bit of a 'turn-off' if your partner is merely 'thinking of England' or compassionately making sure you are enjoying yourself. You would find it still more exciting if you could believe that (s)he was also actively enjoying, demanding and taking for herself! (In this case, I suspect we are talking more often of 'she' than 'he').

Sex, usually, is likely to be one of our most private activities, given the degree of personal commitment and intimacy that is so often involved. And, given all that has been said about the difficulties we have with intimacy and relationship, it is scarcely surprising that we may experience a good deal of turmoil, uncertainty, jealousy, insecurity and internal conflict about sexuality. Furthermore, there is likely to remain a substantial degree of tentativeness and doubt about the *boundaries* between what is appropriate to share, and with whom, about sex; and what is, and ought to be, private. Everyone is talking about the way that everyone is talking about sex; but in actual fact, I don't think there are all that many people who actually do talk about it, in any serious way!

Women more than men, I am sure, confide in each other about it very occasionally. Men will brag and banter of course, but this is no serious discussion; and most men would find it impossible to confide in another man about their fears, doubts and insecurity about sex. Men, in fact, tend to find it difficult to confide to anyone about anything of a personal nature, except perhaps to their wives or girlfriends. This can put a tremendous strain on the woman who knows that she is the sole confessor figure; and she may try to relieve the pressure a little by herself confiding in a woman friend. (She will, though, be most unlikely to tell her boyfriend or spouse that she has done so!) As a consequence, it is perhaps unsurprising that the average man claims to have a number of acquaintances, but very few close friends (or none at all).

In other respects, though, sexuality is a highly public activity in the sense that, for a large part of our lives at least, we are often conscious of being physically attracted (and/or attrac*tive*) to some of the people around us.

A great deal of excitement comes just from being around with people who are mutually attracted to each other sexually, even though it may be quite clear to all that no one is going to do anything about it. A good deal of non-verbal (and verbal) communication may be the means by which we dance and sparkle for each other, and, goodness knows, there's nothing wrong with any of that!

In a (male dominated) society, it tends to be the woman who is

the desirable object to be observed and admired, and the man who
does the looking. (The female looks, too, of course, but she is
generally much more surreptitious about it). Indeed, the differences
between the sexes go very deep in this respect, with females experiencing themselves as beings-to-be-looked-at, while males see
themselves as beings-who-look. This, let us hope, may be changing;
though *very* slowly. It might be healthier, both for men and women,
if women did not have to be so very furtive when they looked at
men, and if the 'new male' could sit back into his own sensuality
and enjoy being admired! The trouble is, though, that the woman
who shows even a flirtatious interest rightly fears that this will be
misconstrued and exploited. The man, conversely, tends to be
locked into a macho domineering style or, if he is of the clean
liberal sort, is almost afraid to flirt at all in case he suffers the scorn
and disapproval of the nearest puritanical feminist. None of this
gives anyone much room to breathe!

Meeting Place

*Man and woman
eyes catch each other
seeking, not quite, to hide
that billowing, growing, attention.
Extended gaze, lingering
trying not to lock
reveals mutual interest.
We meet*

*Words and gestures hovering, a space between
tentative, exploratory, testing
We move closer*

*Surveying, tracking each other, sharing and mirroring
seeking our game, set, rule and match-making.
We parade and perform a subtle dance.
Revealing just a little
We make more commitment.*

*The surprise and expectation of that first touch
Holding out against a swirling dash
for more.
Impatient eagerness to reach in
to (folded) secrecies.*

Do we meet?

Or malinger in misty fantasy?

Self-Defeating Attitudes about Sexuality
(adapted from Albert Ellis)

1. I must always perform well and win approval from my partner.

2. I must be loved and lusted after all the time.

3. I must be outstanding as a sexual partner.

4. I must never be anxious or depressed about sex. I must always be in the mood for sex.

5. I must be completely 'normal' in my sexual behaviour.

6. Others must serve me sexually and do exactly what I want. If they don't then they are awkward, mean, sexless and therefore utterly damnable and horrible.

7. Others must read my mind and know what I want sexually – without my having to tell them.

8. Others must follow the right rules about sex (the ones I believe in) or else they are stupid, weird, cussed, unco-operative and damnable.

9. Others must achieve their full sexual potential (like I have). Otherwise they are frigid, cold, retarded, useless, no fun at all.

10. Conditions must be so arranged that all my sexual desires are easily and completely fulfilled.

11. Everything should go the way I want it to go when we make love; it is just awful and terrible when things don't go my way.

12. There must not be any problems or difficulties for me in relation to sex. If there are, then I must obsessively go on and on about them and try desperately to get everything just right. I must get myself into a terrible state when faced with sexual problems. I must tell myself that it is all too hard and that it shouldn't be as bad as this.

13. When there are problems about sex, I must hide my head (and genitals) in the sand, and do all I can to deny that they are there and avoid facing them.

14. I should not have to work for sexual pleasure. It should always come spontaneously and easily, damn it!

15. There must be a perfect solution to all my sex problems. Otherwise I can't bear it, and I must feel terrible forever.

16. Fairness and justice in relation to sex must exist – particularly for me! Otherwise life is totally unfair, miserable and awful beyond belief.

17. Other people and circumstances are to blame for my sexual unhappiness. I am a totally innocent victim who has been most unjustly treated. I have no control whatsoever over my feelings, options and behaviour. Poor victim, I!

18. My sex life must continue forever without any loss of impetus. The *earth must move* every time I want it too! I must not die impotent or inorgasmic – or ever die at all!

19. The universe must guarantee that sex will always be totally enjoyable – otherwise I'm not playing.

20. I must never feel any discomfort about my sex problems and never have any anxiety. Otherwise I just can't stand it!

Questions:

1. In what respects do you find it easier or more difficult to communicate with people of the opposite sex?

2. Are there particular 'no go' areas that you would find it impossible to talk about to people of: a) the opposite sex? b) the same sex? Why is this? Do you wish it could be different?

3. How far do the following apply to the men in your family?

   a) They/we don't do enough work in the house or take enough responsibility for what goes on.
   b) They/we are not sufficiently expressive of emotion or aware of feelings generally.

4. How far do the men and women in your family fit the stereotype of the 'typical' male/female?

5. How far could you discuss the benefits and frustrations of roles in your family?

6. If relationships between men and women were better . . . what would that be like?

7. How far do you agree with the following? "Men very rarely confide in each other. Women frequently do. There is a vast difference between men and women in this respect."

8. How far do you agree with the following statement? "Women often seem to use power covertly rather than openly. The relationship between some husbands and wives is the same as that between the minister and the civil servant as portrayed in *Yes Minister*. She pretends that he is in charge and defers to him. But she is the one who is in close touch with everything that is going on and she can often make the decisions while making it appear as though he is the one in charge. He, on the other hand, postures with power but is essentially naive and ignorant."

9. How far do you agree with the following? "Given their naivety about their own and other people's feelings and their failure to take responsibility for much of day-to-day living, it can be argued that some men never really grow up."

10. In what respects do you find the expectations that others have of you, and the various roles you have as a man/woman, are
    a) fulfilling?
    b) frustrating?

11. How far have you ever been able to confide to another concerning your hopes, fears and fantasies about your sexuality? What might you *gain* if you could confide in another? What might you *lose*

Exercises:

1. Dialogue with my genitals, (and other erogenous zones); i.e. if they could talk, what would they say? And what would you want to say to them?!

2. Complete the following sentences: "As a (mother, daughter, wife, father, son, husband) . . .
   I'm expected to . . ."
   I feel . . . "

3. Complete the following:
   "The trouble with too many men/women is . . ."
   "What I admire about many men/women is . . ."
   "What I envy about many men/women is . . ."

4. Discuss:
   "Is sex 'dirty'? – if it's any good it is!"
   "Sex between two partners can be wonderful; though it depends on which two partners you come between."

8. Getting through with Manipulation

A truth that's told with bad intent
Beats all the lies you can invent.

William Blake, *"Auguries of Innocence"* (1800–1810)

One likes people much better when they're battered down by a prodigious
siege of misfortune than when they triumph.

Virginia Woolf, *"A Writer's Diary"*, 13 August 1921

Most people have seen worse things in private than they pretend to be
shocked at in public.

Edgar Watson Howe, *"Country Town Sayings"* (1911)

Compare the following:

"I was very *touched* by what you said"
"I felt *manipulated* by you."

The first statement, clearly, is quite different in meaning from the second. We all like to be 'touched'; we none of us like to be manipulated; whether in body, mind or spirit. To feel touched – in body or soul – is human, humane and respectful, and preserves the integrity of all of us. Manipulation, on the other hand, describes one person as the malleable victim of another and shows that the communication is unscrupulous and dishonourable.

Yet when does touch turn into manipulation? Am I being manipulated when I'm skilfully managed, handled and dealt with by a politician, advertiser, manager or other professional communicator? I may very well be, yet how can I tell? When does the constructive management of a situation turn into the cynical use (and abuse) of the people being managed? And who decides? There are no clear answers to such questions and no clear boundaries either. Honourable contact moves, through many shades of grey, into dishonourable manipulation, and there is a large borderline area in between where it is difficult to make clear judgements about what is going on.

We have seen, in previous chapters, that the fundamental spirit of what we do is not always as benevolent as we might like to pretend. This is of crucial importance, since it is our underlying spirit, or intention, that is of greatest significance. After all, it is the spirit with which we communicate our thoughts and feelings, our fundamental intention, that determines the outcome; more so, even, than the emotions and intellect themselves. For example, we sometimes may say that we are trying to get *through* – with our feelings or our opinions – when what we really want to do is to get *control*. The latter, in other words, is our real intention, and everything we do is done within the spirit, however much we protest that we are really operating according to the principle of honest communication.

Our efforts to control others are generally anything but honest, since control is the strongest when it is most disguised. For example, I may best get you into a vice-like grip if I can make it look as though I have no hold on you at all. I may best control the agenda if I can convince you that you are in charge of your own affairs. And I may best do all of this if you have no inkling that I am doing any such thing.

Overt uses of power, threats and domination are not the best ways to get round and get the better of people; and our political and economic leaders are becoming increasingly aware of this. Consequently, many of the humanistic methods of empowering people and helping them to 'actualise' themselves are being bought-up wholesale by interest groups who already have too much power. Such psycho-technology is then used to establish the powerful ever more firmly in their positions of authority and influence.

We have seen some examples of this already in previous chapters. The sophisticated authority tries to avoid crude forms of control; and so (s)he eschews commands, threats and an imperious, domineering style. Instead, (s)he listens, shows concern and empathy, asks questions, provides rewards and quietly steers her people into making the 'right' choices. The sophisticated boss, nowadays, wants you to know that he cares about you; he is concerned for your welfare and personal development; he wants you to be happy and fulfilled; make positive choices and take responsibility for yourself and your work. To some extent all these concerns are quite genuine, since there is a growing body of evidence that points to the fact that rewards, empathy and genuine commitment produce better outcomes than punishments, threats and sullen obedience.

However, the new progressive manager may not want you to know about some of the tricks he gets up to. He may not want you to know how he can set the agenda while appearing to keep it open; how he can be 'economical' with the truth; provide rewards at little cost to himself and generally create an illusion of freedom and individual autonomy that is very different from the actual reality.

In our democratic society it is generally considered wrong for one person to impose on another. Instead, we try to induce each other to do what we want, and some are far more skilled in these oily arts than others. The most skilful of all will nowadays tend to present themselves as simple, ordinary honest Joe's; 'one of the people', just like you and me. They will not want you to see how cleverly they can operate, since that would put you on your guard and make you all the more difficult to persuade and convince.

I don't want to underestimate the (relatively recent) achievement of democracy in Western Society. It really does matter that we can vote our politicians in and out of power, and that there is far more freedom of speech and action than there has generally been in the past. But there are certain inevitable features of democracy that deserve attention:

- When you give 'power to the people' it becomes more and more important that you stay quiet about the (possibly far greater) power that you have kept for yourself.

- When there is 'freedom of speech' you have to keep a very low profile about those things that you don't wish to be talked about.

- When there is freedom of information you need to become very skilled about how secrets are kept, facts are 'massaged' and 'news' is 'managed'.

- When everyone has a vote you need to become an expert in 'shaping' your answers, questions and agendas.

- When there is freedom of choice you need to employ ever growing numbers of sophisticated communicators and professional hidden persuaders if you are to ensure that people make the 'right choices'.

- And, finally, when the leadership is accountable to public opinion you need to become highly skilled at appearing open and open minded if you are to keep some of the facts to yourself.

It is not surprising, then, that many who wish to achieve mastery over others nowadays take a great interest in communication and presentation skills. Democracy is the inevitable father of Hypocrisy in Public Life, and the more we operate an 'open door' policy, the more is becomes necessary to stay quiet about those places where the doors remain firmly closed. Moreover, the more we open up the 'corridors of power' to the general public the more the focus of real power shifts away elsewhere, leaving Joe Public with 'insider information' about antique relics, 'fine old traditions' and empty charades.

Little of this takes place as a result of a conspiracy; it is simply that new conditions require the acquisition of new skills and these are learned by the new generation of leaders who wish to 'get on'. Thus, for example, as soon as ordinary people were given the vote the greatest rewards went to politicians who could sway 'the Mob' with the power of their oratory. And, in our own generation, the advent of television means that greater rewards are now available to those who know how to present themselves in this new medium.

All this may sound overly cynical. It is not meant to. I really do think that it is a sign of real progress when any leadership is forced to be hypocritical; since it shows that we, 'the people', have more power than we had before. After all, when you really are completely helpless, your leaders have no need whatever to pretend about anything. But let us not exaggerate the effects of the emancipation that has taken place in the last one hundred years. There is still a long way to go before what people currently pretend exists (e.g. justice, equality of opportunity, democratic freedom) really do so to the extent that Governments would have us believe.

In previous chapters we have seen how some of these communication skills are put to work; and I have said more than once that there is no useful tool or method in existence that cannot be used for destructive and manipulative uses as well as for more honourable purposes. Additionally, though, there are specific skills of manipulation, bamboozlement and hypnosis that we have not examined elsewhere and which deserve more careful consideration.

Most books about communication skills talk about the importance of clarity if we are to get through to others. It is so easy to be misunderstood, so easy to misinterpret what others say and mean; surely, therefore, it is a virtue if we can be as clear and unambiguous as we can about what we are thinking, feeling and wanting? Well, yes it is if all we really want to do is let someone know our views. But clarity may not be so useful if we actually want to influence the other person. If this is our purpose, then a studied vagueness might best serve us on occasions; particularly if we don't mind using a few shady (if not downright dirty) tricks.

Vagueness can take a variety of forms; and a skilled communicator will know most of them. For example, we can use nouns and verbs with very broad and vague meanings, where it is not at all clear what particular objects or activities are being referred to. We can use abstract nouns denoting concepts that cannot be seen, touched, heard, tasted or smelled and which cannot, therefore, be 'loaded onto the back of a lorry' as it were. Such nouns, generally, denote processes rather than entities and they can have any number of specific meanings. The shrewd communicator may, however, be deliberately vague about what he precisely means and what he is talking about. As a result, the listener has to add his own specific meanings in order to make much sense of what is being said. Take for example the two party political speeches given below:

"My friends, in the light of present day developments let me say right away that I am more than sensible of the precise issues that are, at this very moment, of concern to us all. We must build, but we must build surely. I put it to you like this: if any part of what I am saying is challenged, then I am more than ready to meet such a challenge. For I have no doubt whatsoever that whatever I may have said in the past, or what I am saying now, is the precise, literal and absolute truth as to the state of the case. I cannot offer you vague promises of better things to come; for if I were to convey to you a spirit of false optimism then I would be neither clear to you nor true to myself. But does this mean, I hear you cry, that we can no longer look forward to the future that is to come? Certainly not!"

("What about the workers?")

"What about the workers indeed, sir? Grasp I beseech you with both hands (I'm so sorry madam, I beg your pardon) the opportunities that are offered. Let us put on a bold front and go forward together. Let us take the fight against ignorance to the far corners of the Earth; for it is a fight that concerns us all. And now finally my friends, in conclusion, let me say just this . . ."

(Peter Sellers; c.1957)

"It is a very great pleasure to be here with you all today. You know, things are changing fast. We live in a world of change. The silicon chip is changing our lives. The quality of life is becoming more important: the environment, conservation, the problem of pollution, the future of our children and our children's children, these are today's issues."

(*Yes Minister* Volume Two, BBC 1982)

These are both, of course, deliberate caricatures and spoofs of the real thing; yet, like any good caricature, they are sufficiently similar to leave us uneasy and concerned. They are full of 'hurrah' words; i.e. words or phrases whose specific meanings are very vague, but which encourage us to respond in an emotionally positive way. ('Boo' words and phrases, like 'extremist', 'threat to our democratic society', 'politically motivated' do the opposite).

A skilled use of vagueness allows the listener to 'fill in the gaps' as he pleases. For example, many of the verbs used above specify nothing in particular, yet may be interpreted so as to specify almost anything. If the overall tone and style of what is said has a positive ring to it then the listener will be inclined to fill in his own details in a positive way. He will then like the sound of what he hears and hear far more than was actually said.

Such skill is not confined merely to politicians. The following, could quite easily be programmed into a counsellor/computer:

"I can hear that you are having a number of difficult *problems* in your life right now, Jean, and that you would like to find some workable *solutions*. Having heard you, I am confident that you have the *skills* and *abilities* needed to come to grips with your *troubles*. You may not know this, Jean, but if you use the power of your *unconscious* you could select from your *experience* exactly those *talents* latent inside you that would see you through."

The nouns are all extremely vague and general, yet any listener who has faith in the powers of the speaker will select her own personal meanings and 'hear' them as though they were coming from outside herself. She will then feel extremely impressed with the 'mind reading' powers of her counsellor, and his (seemingly) specific and clear advice! She may even take the advice, inspired to go off and make genuinely positive changes in her own life.

The astrological guides in popular magazines are full of such carefully formed vagueness. They take such a general and abstract form that there is no risk that they will say anything that runs counter to the reader's personal experience. The reader will then project his own specific wisdom and insight onto this general framework and feel duly grateful for all the help he has received!

The sophisticated communicator can easily make himself sound like a skilled and sensitive mind reader even if he knows nothing about the people he is addressing. For example, the charismatic guru might address his vast audience with something along the following lines:

"You are all gathered here this evening, silent, shuffling a little, expectant, preoccupied, resistant, hopeful, on your guard, facing an inner turmoil of hidden joy and nagging doubt. You look up and wonder what I am going to say next and whether it will be of use to you. You are almost too afraid

to ask whether this time, at last, you have come home to a place of peace, love, and understanding. My friends, I want to welcome you; I want to reach out and embrace you all. I want you to know that this can be your home and that here you are known and loved and accepted as you are. I want you to shed your doubts and fears and open yourself to what is available to you here. Notice, right now, a certain strange sensation from within. Breath in the air of this place. Let it fill you and heal you. Breath out all your troubles and woes. Let them fall away lightly in their own time. Be courageous; but be patient. I know it has been hard for you all. I know that the journey has been long and arduous and that you still have a long way to go. But you arrived here. You have taken the first real step, though you may not know this yet. I honour you. I salute you. And I see in the eyes of you all the eternal love of . . . Humanity, Christ, Buddha, Bhagwan, Mohammed, Snow White, Father Christmas, Micky Mouse)"

Such a speech can have a hypnotic effect and indeed it is a form of mass hypnosis. The hypnotist, in order to 'enter the mind' of his subject and leave her more open to his own suggestions, first begins with a calm slow repetitive 'patter' of observations that are so vague that they can mean anything and yet can be given a specific reference by the listener. Indeed, the best suggestions not only can be given a specific meaning, they have to be, if they are to be understood. For example:

" . . . *you can hear the sound of my voice."*
" . . . *you may notice the sensation of your elbow resting against the chair."*
" . . . *feel your fingers lightly touching your arm."*
" . . . *the experience of your feet resting on the floor."*
" . . . *and you begin to relax . . ."*

In order to understand vague statements like this you will find yourself paying attention, probably for the first time, to the specific, personal, private experience to which the statement refers. It is easy then to think to yourself, "Goodness, how could he know about that experience that I hadn't even noticed myself; yet which is now so vivid and so strong!" In fact, of course, the hypnotic communicator has no access to your experience at all; but he is highly skilled in using vague language that will help *you* access your experience. Nothing will be said that can actually be contradicted by what you see, hear and feel; but a lot can be suggested that may, bit by bit, shift the nature of your experience. For example, *"you begin to relax"* doesn't require you to be relaxed right now; it is 'merely' an optimistic interpretation of whatever you are presently experiencing. It will have a seductive appeal, of course, since you are very likely to be predisposed to accept it!

Vagueness alone, however, is not enough. A second important
skill for the Machiavellian communicator is mastery of the power of
presupposition. If I assert something directly and openly, you may
very well decide that you disagree with what I am saying; and you
will be likely, then, to resist it. Thus, by sending you a message that
is 'above board' and clearly 'on the table', you may reject it however
much you hear it. Indeed, the more clearly and explicitly you get the
message, the more determined you may be to keep it at a distance.

But what if I implicitly presuppose that my message is already
your view of the matter? And what if I do so in such a skilful way
that you remain quite unaware that I have presupposed anything at
all? You may then slowly 'discover' that this really is your own personal view buried away inside you. And I will have stealthily
planted my own opinion within you and crept away without your
ever realising what has occurred. There are many ways of doing
this: for example, I might imply that there is a causal relationship
between what's real and what I want to make real in your mind. I
will presuppose the linkage and you will remain unconscious of
what I have done. Thus:

> "*You can hear me* and *you begin to feel more at peace.*"
> "*We come along here this evening* and *we begin to see a way forward for
> our once Great Party.*"
> " *As you sit back in your chair* you can begin to go into a trance."
> "While *we prepare for the next election* we renew our commitment once
> again to our finest traditions."
> "*The outflow of your breath* makes *you feel ever more relaxed.*"
> "*The tension in this hall this evening* forces *us to ask some fundamental
> questions.*"
> "*The zingy taste of new blue 'Octane'* gives *you energy and
> confidence.*"

The first assertion in each of the above statements is undoubtedly
true if only because, in some cases, it is so vague that it could not
be false. When a speaker makes statements that are clearly true
we tend to form a 'mental set' wherein we expect that the next
statement will be equally true. Furthermore, we tend to accept that
'A' causes 'B' if A and B are skilfully bracketed together and if the
speaker has established some credibility for us. There are, of course,
limits. If I presuppose something that clearly runs counter to your
experience then you will more likely snap out of your trance. For
example:

> "*As you notice the clean state of your kitchen floor* you conclude that
> the pigs in this area must indeed be able to fly."

Another way of making presuppositions that can be successfully 'planted' on the unwary listener is to make an evaluation, yet disguise the fact that you have done so. The honest and assertive communicator will be 'above board' when he makes evaluations. He will use sentences of the form: "I think...", "I feel...", "I want...", "I expect...", "I believe . . .". The sharp operator who wants to 'tag' you in a more subliminal way will avoid such words. Most often, he will use the form *"It's . . ."* For example, compare the following:

> I believe *that you can relax and be at peace."*
> "It is *good that you can begin to relax so easily."*

To say that I *believe* something is to acknowledge that this is just my opinion, which may or may not be shared with others. When, on the other hand, I say that something *is* the case, I give it an objectivity and solidity that, though spurious, may be nonetheless effective when skilfully presented.

Thus, for example, notice how 'begin to' allows you to suggest almost anything since how can we be sure that we have not begun to do something new? To say: "You are now flying round the room" will run counter to most people's experience. But to suggest that "You are beginning to feel a little more light as you move towards the first major step in a whole new world of flight . . ." – will be rather easier to swallow!

> *"I want you to listen."*
> "It is *ever more clear that you are beginning now really to listen."*
> *"I think the Jews, Blacks, Trade Unionists, Bosses (etc.) are the cause of all our troubles."*
> *"There is the cause of the trouble! Look at them! Look at what they've done! A clean-up is needed, that's clear!"*

There are other key words that can do a similar job in the seductive arts of presupposition. For example should, must, got to, have to, can't, won't etc. are all very handy ways of avoiding an explicit statement of my views and preferences. Consequently, they are also useful if we want to avoid responsibility for our own feelings and opinions. For example:

> *"This is important; you* must *listen."*
> *"They should all be exterminated!"*
> *"We can't go on like this."*
> *"This has to be done by tomorrow."*
> *"You won't be able to resist Squire – in the flip top box."*

The art of over-generalisation, similarly, provides us with a handy
vehicle for planting our presuppositions, using words like Always,
never, all, nothing, no one, every. Thus compare:

"We think you'll like this product.". . . in contrast with:
"Every *mother's son loves a* Wallbanger!"
"Never *be without a spare pack of* Glitz!"
"Always *use* Bimbo *for that personal touch!*"
"No one *gets anywhere who votes Labour!*"

"I think this may be the time to take a risk." . . . compared with:
"Nothing *ventured,* nothing *gained."*

Other key words to practice for planting presuppositions are those
that deal with time. Thus: when, while, once, before, after, during,
since, prior, as, begin, end, proceed, start, stop, continue, already,
anymore, first, last, second, another. Any of these can be used to
provide a fake link between a true statement and the one you wish
to presuppose. Alternatively, the presupposition can be made directly. For example:

"When *did you last beat your wife?*"
"Before *you sign, I want you to choose the colour scheme.*"
"Once *you've tasted this, you'll want nothing else.*"
"There *has been nothing but trouble ever* since the Government bet-
rayed us."
"We *cannot tolerate this Government* anymore!"
"When *will this nightmare* ever *end?*"
"We *must* stop *this nonsense for we cannot* continue *like this any-
more.*"
"Let's begin *afresh with a new* start."
"There *is a way to* proceed *with dignity from now on.*"
"I *hope that the* end *of all these troubles is now in sight and that it's*
not *already too late to make some positive changes!*"
"You'll *have* another *chance to play in our competition while you* enjoy
what's on offer in our showrooms."

The latter example introduces yet another category of words that
can be designed to presuppose. These are the 'consciousness verbs'
that plant in your mind an 'awareness' of something you were not
in fact aware of at all and which may not have existed at all prior
to the suggestion being made. Thus: 'feel', 'notice', 'enjoy', 'know',
'realise', 'aware', 'think', 'see', 'hear', 'smell'.

Notice *the new 'big car sound' of the doors.*"
"Feel *the velvety touch of the Dacron blouse.*"

"*Do you* realise *that you've stepped into the Future with New World Gaz?*"

"*Can you be* aware *of the profound love all around you?*"

"Smell *the success of a* Sapphire."

"*Do you* realise *how much damage this government has inflicted on manufacturing industry?*"

"*Can you* think *of a more absurd way of running the department?*"

"*I can* see *now just how useful you have been.*"

Finally, on the matter of presuppositions, we can use qualifying remarks, with adverbs and adjectives, in order to take the listener's attention away from the statement that is being presupposed. For example: the statement "*We can help you master the art of communicating*" is very 'bald' as it stands and is therefore wide open to being challenged. It can be disguised by the use of qualifying remarks like "*Fortunately . . .*" "*Luckily . . .*" "*Amazingly . . .*", each of which presupposes everything that comes after them.

In all these ways, then, we can submerge our assertions so that they creep up on our victim without his knowledge. Instead of saying "*Let us suppose that . . .*" or "*I want to you accept that . . .*", we simply assume it, presuppose it, and bury it deeply within the structure of what we are saying. And, in order to be even more successful, we launch our presuppositions out in droves so that, even if one or two are spotted, the others can successfully get through. Furthermore, if one assumption is of particular importance to us, we can insinuate it upon the other person in a dozen or so different ways. He will be unlikely to be able to shake them all off!

No language is possible without presupposing all kinds of 'facts'. In order to think and communicate at all we all have to make scores of prior assumptions about how the world is, who we are, what sort of person we are talking to and what kind of situation and transaction is involved. The difference between the communicator who plays 'with a straight bat' and the less scrupulous operator is that the latter will bury the controversial and contentious parts of his message, while the former will be open and honest about these and seek to negotiate about them.

Two final examples: the use of 'or' and 'we'. For example, a mother might say to a young child – "*Do you want to clean your teeth before or after I comb your hair*". Similarly: "*Would you prefer to clean your room; help with the dishes; or put away some of the shopping?*". This gives the child some real choices, but it presupposes what the range of choices are going to be! Better still, might be to say

"Shall we *do the dishes now or later?"* 'We' is a terribly seductive word much favoured by politicians who want to quietly dissolve any sense of separation between leaders and led. It seems so humble and unassuming; yet, once it slips successfully without challenge in a conversation, the battle-lines for future conflicts might have been quietly drawn. Instead of saying: *"I want you to be on my side against . . . ."* the subtle operator will say "We *must do something about . . .".* With use of the 'simple' word 'we', then, a very great deal may have been quietly presupposed.

'Suggestion' in all its various forms is the third major manipulative hook. This, like Presupposition and Vagueness, can be used on its own or, better still, in subtle combination with the latter. Best of all, the three can be employed together in a steady barrage; where Vagueness, Presupposition and Suggestion all rain down on the hapless innocent who may lack the perceptiveness and skill needed to ward off very much of it.

An asserted message is one that travels above the surface of our consciousness for all to see and hear. Both listener and speaker are aware of what is going on, and awareness on the part of both may be at a high level. The listener is thus free to make a conscious and explicit assessment of what he has heard; and hence respond actively, freely and deliberately. A suggested message, on the other hand, is a kind of linguistic (or non-verbal) submarine. It takes a very sharp observer to spot any trace of it. It creeps up on you without your realising it and, at its best, it structures the way you think and respond without your having any idea that such colonisation of your mind has occurred.

Like submarines, suggestions need to be sunk deeply into the structure of our communication; and the deeper they are embedded the less likely it is that they will be spotted. However, they need to have power if they are to have any effect; and one way of adding to their power is to find a non-verbal means of *stressing* them, so that they can come across forcefully while remaining invisible. Such non-verbal support, most likely, will be a change in tone of voice, a pause, a facial gesture or movement of the arms.

We can quietly suggest questions, opinions; even commands to the unwitting listener and the command may be all the more effective because the person is unconscious of receiving it. Some examples:

"With these tablets, Mr. Johnson, you will feel better in the next few days." (Subliminal command; could be stressed by a louder, firmer tone and/or a forward lean of the head and/or eye contact).

"It seems that you are not as happy *as you used to be in this job Mr. Smith."* This contains a subliminal question: (*"Are you happy in this job?"*) along with a subliminal presupposition (*"You used to be happy in this job"*). Depending on the tone of voice, it could also be a subliminal command (*"You are definitely not happy here and therefore you should leave"*).

"Once you become a part of us, here at the 'Cloud Nine Institute', you will discover *a degree of peace and freedom beyond your wildest dreams."* This contains a subliminal command along with vagueness (concerning the nature of 'peace', 'freedom' and 'wild dreams'); also various presuppositions (. . . You *will* join; there is an 'us' that you can be part of).

The real art of this kind of hypnotic communication involves confusing and overwhelming the victim with more vagueness, presupposition and suggestion than he can cope with, while at the same time avoiding anything that violates his own experience of what is 'right' and 'sensible'. Sometimes we will unwittingly and unconsciously suggest something while, on the surface, we will appear to be wanting the opposite. We can make such suggestions even to ourselves, without realising what we are doing. Often, we will do this in the form of a negative command. For example: the chronic insomniac might hypnotise herself into staying awake, for all that she dearly wants to get to sleep by saying to herself:

"I absolutely must not sit up all night worrying *about what I've got to do tomorrow!"*. In order to understand this statement she must form a conception of sitting up all night and worrying; and this very conception will in itself be likely to produce the result. Similarly:

"I must not allow myself to get tense and wound up *about every little thing that happens in my life!"*. Here, again, there is, in effect, an embedded command that is quite the opposite to what may be consciously desired. Finally:

"I have got to stop being down and depressed *about everything."*

If I say *"for goodness sake don't think of pink elephants for the next five minutes"* then, the harder you try *not* to think about them the more you will find they fill your consciousness. This is because the only way you can consciously check on the fact that there are 'no elephants here' is to think of an elephant!

All the various means of manipulation described above can best operate using (hints of) rewards rather than threats and punish-

ment. In other words, the manipulative individual does not have
to threaten or undermine others in order to get what he wants.
Indeed, (s)he may be a master at helping others to feel good about
themselves even as they continue to hand him their money, votes,
goods or services! He will be a master, too, in the use both of
language and all the various non-verbal aspects of communication
described in these pages. Moreover, let us remember that language
does not have to take the form of dry prose or a rambling unstruc-
tured and informal conversation. At its best it will use rhythm,
metre, even loose rhyme and 'chime' in the language in order to
make a more forceful, yet subliminal, impact. Thus, compare:

"Friends, Romans, Countrymen . . . lend me your ears!" with . . . *"I've
got something I want to tell you."*

Listen to the recorded speeches of any successful demagogue.
At their best they are masterpieces of the use of timing and every
other feature of communication; with just the same degree of intensity employed by a poet! Think of Martin Luther King, Adolf Hitler
or any other major leader. Whether for good or for ill, you will
find that their powers of suggestion, presupposition and strategic,
purposeful vagueness are often abnormally great, and all the more
so because of the vigour, subtlety and style of their language and
gestures.

The most powerful communicators can have a hypnotic effect
on their audiences; and this may often be because they are using
precisely the same methods that are used by a professional hypnotist! They may, as a result produce a set of followers who blindly
obey and who are no longer able to think for themselves. On the
other hand, they may, by the power of their oratory, inspire us to
draw on strengths within ourselves that we never knew we had;
so that we become far more self-determining than we had ever
been before. Such powerful leaders may take a very 'high profile'
approach to leadership or, alternatively, they may appear to be
quite unassuming. Nonetheless, their hold on others may be very
great indeed; for all that they might pretend that they never impose
and are merely trying to facilitate, empower and use non-directive
methods. The latter, in the hands of a powerful communicator, is
generally a covertly directive approach!

As a general rule, indeed, the so called 'non-directive' communicator is the one who often needs to be most watched. The
person who acknowledges that he is directive in approach will
tend to use control strategies that are visible to all. He is like the
aircraft carrier that can be observed from a great distance. The

'non-directive facilitator', on the other hand, is more likely to use subliminal control strategies of the form outlined in this chapter and elsewhere. Consequently, I am quite fundamentally dubious about the whole notion of 'non-directiveness'! It seems to me that our non-directive apologists are either very naive about the subtlety of communication (if they really believe what they say); or else they are very sharp operators whose propaganda about being non-directive is just part of their sophisticated stratagem to achieve control.

The fact of the matter is that in the very act of communicating at all we are bound to influence and change the 'consciousness' of the people we are addressing. If you are to understand what I say then what is going on inside your head is going to have to be different from what was happening before I began to speak. And the more fundamental and important the message, the more profound and elemental are the changes likely to be. Someone communicates to me and I say to them, *"I see; I get it"* and, if this is the case, then I do indeed see the world and myself in some slightly or profoundly different way. We are influencing each other all the time, whether we do so deliberately or not. This is not to say, of course, that every stratagem is as honourable as every other! As we have seen, some styles of communication are rather dubious; particularly when we try to covertly induce and insinuate our own perceptions on others when we know perfectly well that they would wish to resist us if our approach was more direct and open.

Some styles of communication are generally perceived as being inherently more authoritative than others. For example, in the U.S.A. the business executive will get nowhere if he has a squeaky, high pitched voice. Indeed he has to learn how to speak from a deep place in the chest as though, for European ears, he was speaking through a layer of gravel! In the U.K., class-ridden as it continues to be, the voice of authority must be that of BBC 'received pronunciation'. This is changing; and so there are some younger City whiz-kids who affect, or were born with, a fast, slick, go-getting Cockney accent that they hang on to, or cultivate, as though it was a valuable investment. (Which it may yet turn out to be.) A voice that is too 'hoighty toighty' will be seen as too much of a sound from the past; no longer the authority that it once was; the province of backwoods Tory squires of the old school.

This matter of accent is of profound importance however much it is fashionable nowadays to pretend otherwise. Every U.K. newsreading 'anchorman' speaks with 'received pronunciation', since only this is considered to be sufficiently authoritative for the serious

news. Regional stories can be presented via a token regional accent,
(though many such accents are still off-limits): sport can be reported
with chummy informality, and weathermen have a variety of
friendly provincial twangs. This is okay because the weather is a
specialist, technical matter that is seen as the preserve of people
lower down in the social pecking order.

Certain U.K. politicians who wish to be seen as a 'man (or woman)
of the people' have in post-war years quietly dropped the clipped,
authoritative Voice of the Establishment and taken up a more
chummy, avuncular, even regional, style to show that *"I'm an
'honest-Joe' just like you!"* (These seemingly trivial matters are not
trivial at all; they make all the difference in the world if you want
people to take you seriously about serious affairs!)

Yet despite politician's efforts at a relative chumminess, it
remains the case that people who are brought up within the
Establishment, with the expectation that they will become the
leaders of tomorrow, will indeed, by and large, achieve these key
positions of leadership. (And thus, generally, take over smoothly
from similar positions occupied by their parents.) Such elitism is
less in evidence in the U.S.A., but the differences ought not to be
exaggerated!

A minority of youngsters are brought up in a climate of assumption wherein it is simply taken for granted that, as they get older,
they will be listened to, obeyed and moved to the very highest
positions of power and influence. Their whole attitude to themselves and others; their style and demeanour; their expectations;
their assumptions about their own talents and rights; all this leads
them to presuppose that they are 'officer material'. Their belief,
moreover, is the potent father to the reality!

Others, with less favoured and elitist origins can overcome their
handicap with time, talent and effort. But it can be an uphill job
and, for many, their accent, origin (and race!) simply excludes them
forever from the highest (and even the lower) positions of authority.
However, whether placed on the inside track, or way behind with
a fatal handicap; the unscrupulous competitor will make constant
use of a studied vagueness; a deeply layered and entrenched
presumption; and a subtle and persistent pattern of suggestion.
All these, however immoral, can be an important means of 'getting
on'.

Clearly, whenever we are trying, less than honestly, to steal
an advantage over others, it is important that we are less
than open about some of our presumptions and expectations. For
example, just suppose that, when you went for your first job inter-

view, you were assertively and explicitly to state something as follows:

"I have been to Eton, my father is very rich and powerful and, although I am only averagely bright, I take it for granted that there are big dinners available to me."

Such an open, direct and honest approach would be highly offensive and embarrassing and would get you nowhere. Instead, you simply assume all these things, your presumptuousness is quiet, covert yet unrelenting, and, with deep-seated confidence, you affect a matter-of-fact style which convinces all around you. That, in its turn, convinces you that you are indeed made of the 'right stuff'; you are 'one of us'. (I wonder what accent you have been assuming I speak with? . . . And what would be the effect if I told you?)

There are other manipulative methods of achieving control that deserve a mention. For example, a great deal of supposedly authoritative writing these days is infested with a dense, pseudo-scientific, jargon-ridden style. This is difficult to disentangle for the lay reader, and unpleasant to read for anyone. Yet people have somehow been sold the idea that dull, cumbersome prose is an authoritative form of communication. In social science in particular a great deal of simple personal prejudice and sloppy thinking is disguised in a pseudo-abstract and supposedly value-free style. Such work tends to be full of pretentious multi-syllabic nouns with Latin roots. The polysyllables, so often, could be pruned and translated into simple Anglo-Saxon verbs with no loss of meaning and a vast gain in clarity. All that would be lost would be the pretensions and pretentiousness of the prose, which would then tend to come across as much more ordinary. That, of course, is the trouble. Seekers of self-promotion shy-away from making ordinary observations in an ordinary language. That would make them sound like ordinary people who, quite possibly, have nothing very much that is extraordinary to say! In a world where so many of us are trying to show that we have something special to offer, deserving of special status and attention, such honesty is anathema!

If I am to get on, therefore, it is no good for me to say that *"I'll think about"* a suggestion you have made to me. Instead, I will *"take it on board"*. I won't say, *"I've got time to listen now,"* rather I'll inform you that *"I have a time slot"* or that *"I can organise the time resources"*. If you have a good idea, it really won't do just to say so in ordinary English; I will say that there has been some very useful 'Cross-fertilisation'. Alternatively, if I feel less certain, I'll tell you that I'm rather agnostic about your proposal. And when I start to run out of time I won't just say that I need to end the session. Rather, I'll suggest that we 'operate a guillotine'!

Another important self-promoting device in academe is to quote an excessive number of sources in order to further lend authority to the status-seeker's claim to fame. These are offered in quantities that are way beyond what is needed to give a responsible account. Instead the academic sources and footnotes become a means of deluging the reader, as if to say, *"Look at all the hundreds of books and learned articles I've read on this tiny aspect of a part of this subject. Obviously, then, with such a weight of quoted publications, what I have to say must be weighty and authoritative in the extreme. How on earth could it be pretentious or trivial nonsense?"*

I, too, have read, or skimmed, hundreds (thousands!) of books on psychology and related subjects. And if this book purported to be an academic presentation, I might have to quote a dozen or more close packed pages of these; just so that you could be reassured that here was an authoritative writer! As it is, I have quoted just a few, related, books that you may find useful. There are plenty of others. They move on and off bookshelves at an ever faster rate and each of them will quote many more titles. More important, I hope that what I have to say in these pages stands, or falls, on its own merits. You will have to be the judge of how far I am getting through to you; and I hope that I can be a useful influence without puffing up my words.

Finally, there are all the devices of rhetoric, wit, manipulative humour, emotional loading, special pleading, pseudo-reasoning, dishonest appeals to authority, selective presentation of facts, diversionary tactics, disguised question-begging, subtle condescension, 'snide' personal attack and simple repetitive propaganda. These do *not* merit a thorough exploration here since I fear that to do so would merely add to people's 'armouries' rather than make a positive contribution to effective and productive communication. We know enough about these various dirty tricks; they cannot be used productively and honourably; let us just see if we can avoid them as far as possible.

Wherever we look, then, we will find plenty of examples of manipulation, posturing and pretentiousness of one sort or another. In the academic world, in business, commerce, in advertising and, in different ways, among friends and family. Increasingly we seem to be under pressure to promote and present ourselves as a desirable commodity, rather than be ourselves and be with other people. Any such simple authenticity is, among the cynical, regarded as just yet another game. Perhaps most ominously of all, politics itself has become yet another arena where the public relations specialist is king. In a world of mirrors and fantasy, our candidate leaders are served up and promoted to us in much the same way that any other commodity is packaged. Here is an example from a disillusioned advertising man who was involved in selling President Nixon:

"*When all the commercials were finally made, Jim Sage put them together on a single reel. . . . Sage was suffering. Eighteen commercials had been too much. He was blinded by rosy sunsets, choking on the smoke from America's bustling factories, and sick to death of towheaded little kids romping in the sun. 'The script', (he told the men from the Museum of Modern Art), 'is in most cases very, very basic. We try to create an atmosphere through our selection of pictures . . . which create an image without actually saying anything.'*

The museum men made no comment until the reel was done. Until all of the steel girders, sunsets, mountain peaks and bare-assed little kids had passed.

Then the first museum man spoke: 'I'll say one thing. It's easy to tell the good guys from the bad guys.'

'What do you mean?'

'The good guys are either children, soldiers or over fifty years old.'

The second museum man was shaking his head.

'I don't believe it,' he said. 'This is incredible. Every goddamned cliché in the book. There's not one – not one – you've missed.'

'Insidious isn't it?' Jim Sage said.

'No, it's not insidious,' the museum man said. It's just trite'. Then they picked up their umbrellas and left.

'Asses', Jim Sage said. 'They've missed the whole point.' The point was that the commercials were supposed to be trite. They had to be to move the audience they would reach. Their message was intended for people who had triteness oozing from every pore. Persons . . . who had never made an original observation in their lives.

'What are you going to do when all this is over?' I said.

'Move out.' . . . 'I've bought myself some land in the Caribbean – on the island of Montserrat – and that's where I'm going as soon as this is over.'

'Permanently?'

'Yes, permanently,' he said. And then he talked about the direct plane service . . . and about how America was no place to bring up kids anymore. And all this against the background of the commercials he had made: with the laughing, playing children and the green grass and the sunsets and Richard Nixon saying over and over again what wonderful people we all were and what a wonderful place we lived in."

from The Selling of the President, Joe McGinniss, (Penguin).

Questions:

1. Can you think of an occasion when you were being skilfully managed, handled and dealt with? How was it done? How did you feel about it?

2. Can you think of an occasion when you were being skilfully manipulated? How was it done? How did you feel about this? In what ways did this experience differ from '1' above?

3. Can you think of occasions when you were the manager (or manipulator) of others? How did you do it? Were others aware of what you were doing? How did they feel about it?

4. What if we said what we meant and meant what we said, giving our words due weight, no more, no less? (Over time, our words might be like a reliable currency; instead of the debased and devalued version we presently employ.)

5. What if our words, being reliable, carried their own force? (Then, maybe, we would have less need to be forceful and to force our words!)

6. What if we could 'speak from the heart' rather than 'give a presentation'?

7. What if we spoke from the centre of our being rather than from one of our many fronts? What if we were sincere rather than seductive?

8. What if our word was our credit rather than a means to secure credit? (With all the current cleverness with words and money – the value of both is debased. The 'glitz' communication becomes, so easily, a 'tinsel' message).

9. What if we could say, like some fabled Indian Chief: "I have spoken, and I have given you my word."

10. What are we to say to our children who, via their daily dose of advertising, see that people are, albeit cleverly and entertainingly, distorting, deceiving and seducing them – for a fee?

11. What are we to do now that, through advertising, we see that the 'Word' of humanity can be bought for a fee so that it is, ultimately, valueless?

12. When will we see that our words have value only if they have no price? (Words are be empty whose contents can be bought).

Exercises:

1. Next time you watch an advertisement or listen to a professional speaker see if you can be aware of any manipulative devices; e.g. vagueness, presupposition, suggestion.

2. Can you spot the manipulative techniques used in the following?

a) *"When you consider the appalling mess made by the Opposition and you look at the turmoil they are presently in, you cannot help but conclude that they can never make any headway as a credible alternative. We know what the real issues are and we know how to tackle them. Everyone who is listening now can see for themselves the ways in which we have begun to pull Britain out of its tired old rut. You have to face the facts, and the British economy has been allowed to avoid these unpalatable truths for far too long!"*

b) *"As you look into the new world of Anglo-Fizz Investment, you can see what's on offer for the person who cares about financial security. We offer you reassurance that, in a fast changing world, your money will be safe as it earns you a return others will envy. While visiting your nearest friendly Cash Counter take a look at our special free flight offers for the holiday of a lifetime and let us take your breath away. There's fun for children, too, at the Kiddi-counter, with a surprise each month for the young tycoon. Anglo-Fizz Investment. We'll put life in your lolly!"*

c) *"I simply cannot put up with the way you treat me anymore. You may not realise the way I've been feeling but you must accept that I have rights too and that nothing can justify this present mess. Even as you look at me now I can see that you are feeling resistant, defensive and uneasy. I don't want to attack you but we've got to work together more and make a new start. Fortunately, I understand the way you feel and I know you are bound to feel irritated and insecure yourself at times. But as you come to trust me more you will feel more at peace."*

d) *"Here at High Gloss Hype we offer you a two week turnover at a fraction of the price of other major consultancies. With Top-down-turn-around overhaul we can facilitate in-house re-structuring to suit you. Our Senile Personnel Ejection Schemes remain flexible but pack a punch. As a manager on the leading edge in your field we know that you need a training plan that is guaranteed to yield high-quality outcomes while allowing, even within the initial scaffold, for your own managerial flair awareness. Our TEMPO team provides multi-modal, multi-disciplinary action-research profiles, with tight targeting in a crisp package. Add-ons include quality circles, block-moduling and frame-arrangement survey methods. Talk to Gillian on 099 665 233 who will be happy to arrange an early appointment."*

e) *"Going round the groups and listening to the hum of activity, it's obvious to the facilitators that everyone has found the discussion very useful."*

9.   Getting Through Despite It All

Perseverance: A lowly virtue whereby mediocrity achieves an inglorious success.

Ambrose Bierce, *The Devil's Dictionary* (1881-1911)

A pessimist is a man who has been compelled to live with an optimist.

Elbert Hubbard, *The Note Book*, (1927)

Look round the habitable world: how few
Know their own good, or knowing it, pursue.

Juvenal, *Satires* (c. AD 100)

In earlier chapters we have explored cycles of destructiveness; various kinds of competitive struggle; defensiveness; and all manner of ways in which we can misunderstand each other. We have also considered ways in which we might more effectively 'get through' to each other; and we've examined some of the skills that we can use to smooth and facilitate constructive relationships at home, at work and with friends. This is all very well, and is, I hope, of practical use. It is, as it were, a 'do-gooding' exercise, based on the assumption that we do quite enough harm to each other and that we would be helping both ourselves and others if we were less self-defeating in the ways we communicate.

'Do-goodery', though, can in itself become a harmful and destructive business. It can involve a kind of moral snobbery that is more irksome than mere social and material varieties. There is a whole industry, now, of people trying to help others towards more meaningful relationships, 'personal growth', 'transpersonal insight' and the realisation of our full potential as human beings. This can be wonderful – up to a point – and this book, after all, is one more contribution to that effort. But such do-goodery can also be smug, sanctimonious, holier-than-thou and very subtly condescending to

the laity who have not yet had their consciousness raised or their life-skills checklisted and developed; and who therefore need to be saved by duly accredited facilitators and communication specialists!

We need, as we have seen, to protect ourselves from defensive, aggressive, manipulative souls who would seek to do us harm. Less obviously, but just as urgently, we often need to be on our guard against those who have our best interests at heart and are trying to help us and do good. It is easy for the helper to create dependency needs in the person being 'helped', so that the latter's self esteem and competence actually fall rather than increase. It is easy to set the agenda while pretending to be open and non-manipulative. Furthermore, there is a danger that, even when we really are being 'nice', and helping a person to feel better, we are not actually being of much use.

> *"I got very upset at a Quaker Meeting and after seventeen years of membership never went back. I felt that there had been a good deal of dishonesty and repressed emotion at a time which called for emotional expression and authenticity. That was my crude and angry judgement and on the way to the car park after the meeting I felt violent with passion. An elderly Quakeress pulled at my arm.*
> *'Why are you so depressed David?'*
> *'I'm not depressed. Not at all. I am feeling absolutely bloody furious with you all.'*
> *'Come and have some coffee with me and talk it over. You'll soon feel better.'*
> *'I do not want to feel better. Thank you for the offer. I will have coffee with you some other time.'*
> *'Come and have coffee with me. It is very unchristian of you to refuse.'*
> *Unchristian or not, I walked off without looking back and was much too angry to be affected by the final twist of guilt until later.*
> *Clearly it was important that I had coffee with her – to her rather than me. I felt she wanted to pour sugared cream over all my emotions."*
>
> from David Brandon, *Zen in the Art of Helping* (RKP 1976)

'Social skills' experts may sometimes be in the business of subtle manipulation, as we have seen. But even when they are genuinely benign they may do more harm than good. For example, Social Skills Training programmes ('SST') (sic) advise that we should be polite and persuasive, rewarding, interesting, amusing, co-operative, friendly, empathetic and all the rest of it. (And, of course, we have explored all this in considerable detail in previous chapters.) But there is a danger that we will become so smooth and competent in the way we handle each other; so skilled in calming ruffled feathers; so competent in our ability to lubricate a sticky situation – that we glide right past each other and make no genuine, human (and therefore possibly painful) contact at all!

> *"Thus the marriage guidance counsellor tells us, the husband should 'understand' his wife and be helpful. He should comment favourably on her new dress, and on a tasty dish. She, in turn, should understand when he comes home tired and disgruntled, she should listen attentively when he talks about his business troubles, should not get angry but be understanding when he forgets her birthday. All this kind of relationship amounts to is the well-oiled relationship between two persons who remain strangers all their lives, who never arrive at a 'central relationship', but who treat each other with courtesy and who attempt to make each other feel better."*
>
> Erich Fromm, *The Art of Loving*

Cyra McFadden, whose excellent novel I have referred to earlier, makes a similar point (in Anthony Clare & Sally Thompson's *Let's Talk about ME*, BBC 1981). It is fine to be concerned about the overall health of our relationships. But:

> *"There is something dreadfully wrong with the notion of health as we define it here. You never get out of bed in the morning and say 'Today I feel reasonably okay. I think I might be able to bumble through. If I have a stiff drink at lunch, and go about my business, I might conceivably make it through till five in the afternoon.' One is too busy taking one's emotional pulse, all, all, all the time. It is a cumbersome preoccupation. It takes away a lot of time that one could spend more profitably, seeing friends and doing things that involve more gratification and far less earnest cumbersome endeavour."*

We can so easily become puritanical and neurotic in our quest for health, fulfilment, insight and (even) in our over-earnest search for fun. For example, 'knowing thyself' seems to me to be a virtuous enough ideal and, as I have indicated earlier, there really are limits on how we can get through to others when we have not even got through to ourselves. But the search for self awareness can itself become obsessive, sterile and perfectionistic. If we are ever to reach out to each other we had better not wait until we are paragons of insight and social competence; or else we'll wait forever! In any case, who could stomach, or believe in, a social scene where everyone was entirely competent, confident, insightful, mature and positive?

Being positive is generally seen as a virtue. But even this can be taken to excess. If we are to be remotely real we had better come to terms with, and live with, our bitchy, shadowy, violent, unreasonable, stupid, contradictory and defensive self; and, even, discover that all these negative features of our personality may have a place and a role to play. But let us not imagine that we can, or should, try to sort out each and every one of these mysteries. I believe that many people would be better off if they spent a little more time looking at the ways in which they interact with others and tried to change some of their self-defeating patterns. That, after all, is an assumption upon which this entire book rests. But, for goodness sake, let's not try to work on, sort out, discuss, dissect and analyse every last move we make. If we do, we'll spend more time analysing than living and doing and we will analyse and introspect ourselves out of existence!

> *"Here in the United States we have this obsession with perfection. One dare not have a wrong attitude around anyone else or you have to go through this incredibly complicated nonsense of 'working it out'".*
>
> John Maher, quoted in *Let's Talk about ME*

Ok . . . , so we want to be more mature, happier, wiser and more 'in touch with' the people around us. But:

- An obsession with mental health can itself become a form of mental illness;
- An over-zealous effort to be happy will make you miserable;
- A belief that we can abolish all our stupidities is itself stupid;
- A hope that we can always act with wisdom is yet another kind of folly!
- It is childish to imagine that we will ever be in some final sense, entirely mature!
- We will all need to run away from each other if we try too hard, and too earnestly, to 'get through'!

Even the search for fun can become a form of tyranny. I can think of several weekend 'personal growth' groups where we were all told that one of the aims was for us to 'have fun'. Immediately, I started to feel pressurised in a brand new way. Here was a new task that had to be achieved. Would I be up to it? Would I suffer forms of subtle disapproval and condescension from other groupies if I didn't show that I was having the requisite amount of fun, or, even worse, if I spoiled the fun of others? (The answer was, Yes, I would face a delicate and caring form of chastisement!) And if, far from having fun, I showed any sign of irritation and made a playful effort to wreck the proceedings, would this have to be 'worked upon' in some way, so that it could all be properly 'sorted out'? (The answer was, yes indeed, we would have to take a break from our 'fun' and do some 'work'.)

We are assailed by people who wish to harm others and wreck their efforts to build and work positively. But we are also set upon, from all sides, by well-meaning souls who want to help us in a way that doesn't help. Let's try to avoid some of our worst excesses; but let us remember, too, that it is possible to 'strive officiously to do good' in a way that irks and disrupts the real flow of life in all its mystery. Sometimes my belief in your 'progress', or our belief in the progress of society, are themselves unhelpful obsessions that do more harm than good. So many have died and have massacred others 'for the good of . . .' whatever personal and collective obsession is the order of the day. Maybe the greatest obstacle to progress is the belief that there are some people who are an obstacle to progress, and the greatest evil is the belief that we can, and should, abolish all evil on earth. For such beliefs lead us, seductively, down the ancient road to fanaticism.

Where do we think we are trying to go with our human relations skills and all the rest? One image that I have is of a bunch of keen middle management people on some human-relations-in-management programme. They are learning how to look at themselves, stand four-square on the ground, set their goals, polish their 'mission statement', facilitate the personal development of their staff, meet their targets, formulate their appraisal criteria, jog, keep fit, absail off a cliff face and, even, have the appropriate amount of 'fun'! They have their track suits for the outdoor activities, their suits for 'power lunches', and their sweaters for after hours socialising at the hotel.

Another image is of a mixed bunch of no one in particular; in a pub, diner, café or just taking in the sun: they're not trying to get anywhere in particular;

- Just being with where they are and who they are.
- Just tolerating others, or not, as the case may be.
- Bantering, withdrawing, feuding, laughing, looking lost or in despair.
- Enjoying a good lunch or cursing the lousy beer or rain.

The latter image feels like a (small) slice of life in all its richness, joy, pain, comfort and confusion. The former mentality, if taken to excess, feels hollow, sterile, false, forced, inhuman, inhumane and positively destructive in a perverse kind of way!

As I look out of my window, and watch the plastic bags flying around in the wind with the birds, I can often wish that this country, and this City, was a cleaner and better-ordered place. I can wish that the kids didn't spoil Municipal efforts at 'gentrification' with their graffiti, and that the car could be left alone for a few weeks without being broken into. Yet, I have visited foreign streets that were so aseptically clean that I felt inclined to do something outrageous with them; and I have visited houses where the decor was so impeccable and the diet so wholesome that I have wanted to install a garish plastic table, tuck in to a fat-burger and wash it down with a chocolate bar and fizzy drink!

Such demonic impulses can, of course, be counterproductive, unwholesome, malicious and hurtful to us all. They may also be necessary for our longer term survival and carry messages that deserve a hearing. Violence, for example, is generally seen as the ultimate failure of effective communication. And so it is – generally speaking. Having abused each other in subtle ways and failed to make a positive contact, one, or other, or both, or all, of us may take a swing at the next person, or we may try to claw each other's eyes out – with care and courtesy perhaps!

Violence, then, in our brave new world of sophisticated communicators, would presumably be entirely abolished or, more accurately, it would become extinct; since everyone would have more effective and productive means of communicating? In any case, we would all, supposedly, know how to take a perspective on our emotions and get them into a proper proportion. Or would we? And do we even want to?

The (infamous) 19th Century philosopher, Nietzsche, described contemporary Christianity, with its doctrines of submission and self-abnegation, as a religion for weaklings. He had nothing but contempt for the kind of 'keep your nose clean do-goodery' that he saw all around him and which he would, undoubtedly, castigate in its trendy twentieth century manifestations. For Nietzsche, a demoniacal assertiveness, and willingness to challenge the whole universe to combat, was a human, and superhuman quality, that had a seductive attractiveness. He urged it upon us as the way to achieve joy and transcendence if we had the guts to rise to the challenge. Such a philosophy can become an embodiment of evil and can lead those who travel on such a road to *hubris;* hell; nemesis on Earth. Thus Nietzsche is accused of being a pernicious influence who, arguably, was an inspiration for Hitler. He is, therefore, implicated by some as responsible for all the hellish consequences of Nazism. Maybe so. We can undoubtedly become intoxicated by the 'Mr Hyde' that inhabits us all, and we will do great harm if we allow our 'lesser self' to get the upper hand. Yet we also inflict perhaps more, damage on ourselves and others if we try too hard to abolish our own shadow and strive only to be good.

For, if we refuse to face up to the violent passions and impulses in ourselves, we will project these onto others, denounce them as abhorrent and intolerable and begin a crusade against them that may well wreak far more havoc than would have resulted in a less purist approach and a more tolerant attitude.

There is a 'demon' in all of us, and sometimes it can even be harnessed to do good. We will certainly do harm if we don't acknowledge its existence, or if we try too hard to root it out, in ourselves and others. Violence and hatred can, obviously, lead to appalling results. Yet an intolerance of these, and a lack of insight and understanding, will itself lead to hatred and violence. There is, then, no easy solution; and 'solutions' can, in any case, become another form of death (or, at least, can dissolve some of the much needed salt from our lives!)

There are some scary paradoxes that we need to face up to. For example, love-making and violence can sometimes look rather frighteningly similar. Lover's quarrels, not infrequently, end in sexual intercourse. Fighting can become a powerful form of intimacy that may have a seductive appeal. This may be, and often is, pernicious, neurotic, revolting and destructive. Yet it may also provide a break-through away from a staid, oppressive, smooth yet bloodless relationship from which both partners would wish to be, and need to be, released!

- If we are, finally and completely, cornered in some way;
- If our self-respect lies in tatters;
- If there seems to be no way in which we can negotiate a way out of our predicament – and if no one wants to help us to do so;
- If we feel that we have no recognition, no respect, no sense of significance, no place, nowhere to go;
- If we feel that we have our backs to the wall and we have nowhere to breathe and move;
- If our very survival, dignity and integrity are at stake and no recognition of this is offered . . .

. . then:

. . . We may need to fight our way out of it!
 . . . We may need to blast our way along whatever trail we can find!
 . . . We may try to destroy anyone who tries to stop us!
 . . . We may want to leave whatever destructive mark we can behind us, if only to prove that we still exist and deserve to be noticed!

. . . We may use violence if this is the only way left to us to have some kind of power and control and influence on the world around us.

Of course, all this can be glorified in a way that is thoroughly harmful; and the adrenalin of the primitive 'fight-flight' response that rouses us to do battle can itself become an addictive drug. Furthermore, the paranoid individual may be 'fighting for his survival' when every 'threat' he engages with is just a figment of his own fantasy! But let us not go to the other extreme and try to inhabit a clean and lifeless reasonableness about everything. Let us not run away altogether from the more shadowy facts of life. If we are to be even vaguely mature let us not pretend that we can retain our innocence. And if we are to tame, or come to terms with, the more hideous features of life, let us remember that every single quality out there that shocks, terrifies, outrages, revolts and sickens us can, also, be found . . . within! (and can never, finally, be exorcised!)

"No society is strong which does not acknowledge the protesting man; and no man is human who does not draw strength from the natural animal."

Jacob Bronowski, from *The Face of Violence*

If we are to grow 'higher' in the knowledge of our good, we will probably need to move deeper in the knowledge of our evil, and to accept that this shadow can never finally be left behind us. And, if we are to be able to hear Wordsworth's 'deeper music of humanity', let us remember that we will need to move out of innocence and away from the 'Garden of Eden'. Such a move does not constitute the Fall of Man; (whoever took that view was simply refusing to grow up!); it consists in our rising up and away from childhood innocence and ignorance and into a full adulthood.

Compassion is, indeed, a virtue; but there is a tendency to view it as soft and naive; to be practised by those who don't understand the real world and who are rather too good to be true. The compassionate person, we imagine, has very high ideals and it would be wonderful if we could all live like that. But, unfortunately, (s)he is not at all streetwise and realistic. Worse yet, (s)he has no real power or skill when it comes to making things happen in the Big Bad World. Compassion, then, tends to be seen as somewhat bloodless, clinical, prissy and, worst of all, totally ineffective! It is the prerogative of nice, good people who retain their purity by living out on the margins of society. They remain unsullied because they never even put so much as a foot into the murky, sordid, water of day-to-day power broking and compromise.

Such too-good-to-be-true compassion is of no real use to anyone. The only way we can be this good is to avoid doing anything; because as soon as we make a move in any direction we start to discover that there are moral dilemmas and compromises at every turn. Mistakes are inevitable; pain unavoidable; and, sometimes, we may even have to do a certain amount of harm in the process of pursuing what we hope to be a greater good! (Though the vicious streak in us all may often use this 'ends justify the means' argument as a rationalisation!)

There is a tendency to imagine that we must choose between two mutually exclusive paths: either we travel on a road towards Goodness, or else our interest lies in the acquisition of Power and influence. Thus we carry in our minds the image of good and ineffective people who retain, and try to practice, their ideals yet never become 'part of the System'. On the other hand, there is the stereotype of Mr Big who lies at the heart of the System but who has therefore entirely sold out all his values and ideals. He pulls all the strings because of personal greed, vanity and the sheer intoxication that can arise from the exercise of power. But people get crushed on the way and he deadens himself to these evil effects because he has abandoned Goodness in his worship of Power.

Such a distinction between Power and Virtue is, I think, very commonly made, and it is thoroughly pernicious. After all, what is the point of having, and trying to practice, ideals if we are not willing to gain the necessary power to put them into effect? And how can we expect to be able to exercise power if we are not willing to make mistakes, face unavoidable dilemmas and be forced into making necessary compromise? The wheels of day to day life are not kept turning by people who wish to be so pure that they are never willing to get their hands dirty. We don't need perfection or saintliness. But neither do we need cynicism and cruel indifference to humanity. Instead, a dose of humility, commitment, a willingness to make mistakes and acknowledge the evil in all of us – all this is a practical and workable ideal:

We cannot avoid
Using power,
Cannot escape the compulsion
To afflict the world,
So let us, cautious in diction
And mighty in contradiction,
Love powerfully.
Martin Buber, *Power and Love*

Trying too hard

I try too hard
I try not to try
I try to trust
I sometimes trust my trying
I often try myself.

I try to relax
I feel tried, but little trusted
I'm trying to tell you
Trying too hard's a very trying process.

If I tried less hard . . ?
If I tried harder . . ?
If I tried something else . . ?
If I stopped trying . . ?

Trying to avoid
Mere trial and error
Itself's an error
And a trial?

When I try myself
I usually find – I'm guilty.
I'm guilty about my guilt
And protest my innocence.

You, and I,
We try to trace our
trials, guilt and error
back to . . . who knows what?

We try to trust
We trust that we can try
Yet we feel tired
and trussed up tight.

I'm tired of trying
I trust that we just might
Untruss ourselves from this
Trying tangle.

10. Getting through to Us

I know where I'm coming from but I don't know where I'm going!
Archetypal comment from 'Awareness Movement' groupie.

The air is saturated with statements that are neither true nor false but merely credible. The important thing is not whether information accurately describes an objective situation but whether it sounds true.
Christopher Lasch, *The Culture of Narcissism* (Abacus 1980)

You can 'get through' to others with what you say; you can also get through with the way you say it; with all the various non-verbal gestures and signals that we are sending out all the time. Most important of all, though, you can get through as a result of what you do. For example, a parent shows love for a child not primarily through fine words or an appropriate tone of voice, important though these may be. What counts above all, surely, are the *actions*. I feed you, clothe you, pick you up from school. I can be (just about?) relied upon to keep the agreements that I make with you (more or less well enough!). If, in all these ways, I seem to be genuinely committed to your safety and well-being, then you may be right to conclude that I love you. If, on the other hand, I regularly let you down and show, in my actions, a carelessness, indifference and a lack of *reliability*, then you may eventually begin to have doubts about my eloquent apologies, supposedly honourable intentions and defensive explanations! Certainly you will conclude that, however much I may (potentially or theoretically) love you, I am not very good at expressing this love!

If a person's tone of voice is out of line with their words then, as we have seen in earlier chapters, we tend to believe the non-verbal part of the message more than the words themselves. But if a person's actions are not in keeping with the tone of voice, then we will take the actions themselves far more seriously than any amount of verbosity or non-verbal gesturing, eye contact and post-uring. In other words, to quote the phrase which, being true, has become a cliché:

"Actions speak louder than words!"

And, however unsophisticated we may be, however lacking in verbal skills and non-verbal communication, we can make up for this to a very great extent if we take the right action at the right moment.

There are times when, in order to get to the heart of the matter, it is useful if we can look deeply at our motives, and at the subtleties and complexities of conflict and communication. There are other times, though, when we can best get through, and get to the heart of the matter by looking at what needs to be done (and doing it!) rather than endlessly searching for words and signs. Our action may be a symbolic gesture (like a well-timed and well meant bunch of flowers) or it may simply be our willingness to carry out our day to day duties to the people around us. Either way, our actions very often speak for themselves, and people can more effectively find out who we are from what we do (and the way we do it) than from what we say (and the way we say it).

Actions have their own eloquence which will not be drowned out by fine speech-making, gesticulation and empty gestures. We may often be bamboozled by words, gestures, posture and hype; but sooner or later we feel a staleness and frustration inside as we begin to suspect that 'this is all just a load of talk' (or a heap of paper). Then we start to ask; *"What does it all amount to in the end? What does it all mean?"*

This matter of our actions is of particular importance when it comes to the question of 'getting through' to the wider community. We want to get through and feel some sort of connection, not just with our immediate friends and neighbours, but with the wider world beyond. Otherwise it can feel as though our own particular narrow neighbourhood exists in a vacuum, cut off and isolated from the broader movements of history and the larger world canvas with all its various cultures and forms of life.

Of course, we can't get through to the wider world in the way we can with our spouse, friends or colleagues. Nor would we want to. But we do have to have some sense of our relationship with the Big Wide World beyond us. Otherwise, however rooted we are in our own community, we will still feel that we are 'hanging in mid-air' since our community itself will seem to lack roots!

At present, we commonly view the world beyond our own

neighbourhood as a threatening place that could engulf us. In other words, our relationship with it is based on unease, fear and insecurity, often arising from our ignorance! Those who are fortunate enough to feel 'at home' in a neighbourhood or workplace community will still tend to experience an underlying unease since, so often, they will sense that this community is itself under some sort of siege from the hostile world outside. My corporation, however large, might be swallowed up and devoured by another and all the values and styles of doing things could be consequently demolished. My local neighbourhood might be destroyed by some road development and may seem to be under constant attack from thieves and vandals. Even my country might be threatened and outmanoeuvred by more competitive or more aggressive rivals such that my present standards and way of life were overturned.

Thus we must ask how do we get through to each other; not just individually, at work at home and with friends; but collectively, between neighbourhoods, organisations, classes, nations, races and creeds? And, when we look at this larger picture, we can see that the quality of communication leaves much to be desired, if only because the opportunities for ignorance (breeding fear and misunderstanding) are so much greater.

We get through to other classes, races, nations and species according to what we do more than what we say. (We may, after all, be in no position to say anything whatever to people we never actually meet!) In other words, at the collective level, more than anywhere else, it is the action that counts. And what is the nature of our action? What do we do in relation to the people around us in the wider world? Well, given half a chance, we exploit each other, whether intentionally or otherwise; and we exploit the land and its materials with such ferocity that it is showing signs of being unable to renew itself! We, in the West, for example, consume the world's resources to an extent that would be totally unsustainable by the planet if imitated by the rest of the world. We consume and consume with (until recently) little thought of what effect this has on the environment and on other people who provide us with our goods and services. A visiting Martian might well assume that the heart of Western religious belief is to be found in the Shopping Mall. Here our deepest values are made manifest. *"I buy, therefore I exist."* And the skill that really counts is that we learn how to shop 'wisely'; i.e. that we 'get a good price' for the things we purchase and sell.

The consequences of our exploitative attitudes on the world we live in are becoming increasingly horrendous to contemplate. Here, for example, are a few of my more gloomy reactions:

Hymn Number?

We plough the fields and scatter
our litter on the land
And it is fed and watered
By Mammon's poisoned hand.
He sends the snow in Summer
The warmth to spoil the grain
The Season's ruined our harvest
We're parched or drowned in rain.

All free gifts around us
Are sent by Direct Mail
Oh pray, my God
Oh pray, my God
For bargains at the Sale.

We only are the makers
Of all things trite and cruel
The ad slot and the PR hype
Our death our sloth; we're fools . . .

Sadness

Sad that I live am I
'Neath the sky's strange hue.
Sad with the acid rain
And the deadly dew.
After the sun the pain
After the rain the flood
This is the Way of Life
Now the Work's undone.

All that we need to do
Be we low or high
Is to see what still grows
'Neath a twisted sky.

Green Christmas

I'm dreaming of a Green Christmas
Not like the ones we used to know
Where the plant tops listen
To false Spring's glisten
And shoot to sunlight all aglow.
I'm dreaming of a Green Christmas

With every Winter tree in leaf
May your days be merry and bright
Though our Christmas and the Seasons'
come to grief.

A 'wise buy', I would suggest, is one where we know the real price
of the things we buy. This is the human price that others have
paid in order to produce it and the cost that the environment has
met in order to supply it. A wise buy, too, requires us to know the
real human 'value' of the goods or services we have bought. It
requires us to determine whether the value justifies the price, where
none of this is measurable in simple monetary terms, and certainly
not when money (and therefore power) is so unevenly and unjustly
distributed!

We cannot get through to others if we don't get through to the
way we inter-relate with each other, both locally and globally. And
we will not discover these inter-relations unless we face up to the
ways in which some gain more than they can ever use, and some
lose more than they can ever cope with, in the present operation
of the world's economy.

I don't, for one moment, want to pretend to be able to lift out
some simple blue-print that would transform international relations
into a utopia of peace, love, harmony, justice and equality of opportunity for all! Nor do I want to suggest that we can wave a magic
wand and abolish greed, selfishness, insecurity, conflict and other
vices! After all, the last chapter was about getting through despite
it all, and warned of the dangers (and potential evils) of perfec-
tionism and utopianism.

Up until quite recently it has been possible to take an exploitative
attitude towards the environment because we have only been powerful enough to make a mess of things at a local level. And so we
have managed to get away with throwing our rubbish into the
river and sending our smoke into the sunset. We have assumed
that the world around us is more or less infinite in size and so is
quite capable of absorbing the by-products of our 'progress'.

Similarly, it has been possible to take a competitive and exploitative approach to other people, either because we have been much
better armed than they, or because the arms and technology on
both sides have only been capable of killing a minority of our
respective populations. In the twentieth century, however, the
growth of our military power, made available to us by technological
advance, has meant that the last two world wars produced few, if
any, real winners. Moreover, any third world war looks certain to

be a disaster for everyone. Even more local wars become unprofitable when the Super-powers are determined to ensure that no one can be allowed too great, and therefore destabilising, a victory.

And so, for the first time in history, the age old virtue of co-operation, both with other people and the world around us, is becoming a basic necessity for our very survival rather than a 'holier-than-thou' luxury. We need to rediscover a sense of harmony with our environment, not because this can be a rather pleasant 'peak experience' for the New Age connoisseur, but because, if we don't, we shall destroy ourselves in our own foul and overheated air; poisoned water and ruined soils!

Equally, unless we can make more serious efforts to negotiate and compromise rather than threaten and blackmail each other, then our ever growing skill at killing each other (skills that are bound to be spread to even quite poor countries and terrorist groups) will make any kind of civilised life impossible. Even if we don't actually destroy ourselves completely, our constant fear of highly armed fanaticism will somewhat diminish the 'quality of life' for us all.

A 'global consciousness', then, with the sense that 'we are all brothers and sisters together', is fast becoming a necessity for survival rather than an esoteric preserve for a few 'spiritually advanced' souls. The North American Indians and many other (so-called) primitive tribes, took the view that they were *of* the earth rather than *on* it; and therefore if they damaged and defaced it in some way they were damaging and defacing themselves. This supposedly primitive belief is one that we desperately need to retrieve for ourselves. For, in the West at least, we have declared war on our environment for at least the past two hundred years. We have thought of Nature as something that has to be conquered, subdued, overcome and exploited; as a potentially hostile force which can be defeated by our own skill and cunning.

We simply cannot continue with this exploitative attitude because, in the last few years, and for the very first time in the history of Humankind, we have discovered that we are having an effect;

- not just on a local waste tip;
- or on one foul river;
- or on one mucky beach;
- or within one region of ruined soil.

Now, for the first time ever, we are changing the atmosphere, and the weather, of the entire planet and there is nowhere we can run to in order to escape and ignore the effects of this. And so, for the first time, we really are 'in the same boat' together. For the first time, the whole of humanity faces the same common threat, which is the destruction of the entire environment, and not just the bit that someone else has to live on.

This crisis is likely to get worse before it gets better. (And let us hope that we do not leave it too late before we take adequate remedial action!) And so, as technology advances still further, we are going to find that ever more sophisticated electronic gadgetry becomes available to us, just as the most basic products (uncontaminated air, water and food), become more scarce! Even now, the kinds of materials and facilities that primitive people may take for granted are becoming luxury items – leather, wood, fur, uncrowded surroundings with plenty of space and a good view from home!

Our ability to get through to each other using a vast network of information technology is growing at an enormous pace. But our capacity to get through the street congestion and feel safe as we do so is declining fast. Indeed, the average speed of travel in many big Western cities has not increased at all in the last one hundred years, despite (or because of) the motor car.

We are getting ever more able to observe, and become informed about, the Wonders of Nature on countless natural history documentaries and coffee-table supplements. But the countryside around us is becoming ever more despoiled and difficult to reach! And just as we take more interest in the animal kingdom, the forest and hillside, so we find that plant and animal species are being destroyed at a terrifying rate.

Primitive tribes seek to get through, not just to their neighbours, but to the forest, the river, the mountain, the sea coast! They imagine that there are 'spirits' in all of these and that we have to discover a right relationship with all of them. And they are right! And we need to realise this without relapsing into superstition, irrationalism, and dogma. Because, if we listen, the river, sea coast, mountain and all the rest do, as it were, speak to us; they do have something to say to us, though not, of course, in a literal sense! Similarly, all the objects, buildings and artefacts around us can 'speak' and offer us information about ourselves and our lives!

What on earth, you may be wondering, am I saying here? Perhaps you imagine I have taken leave of my senses and you are already tempted to skip this part in order to find something more sensible? Let me, therefore, hasten to add that I am not suggesting that forests, mountains and all the rest are sentient beings that have moods, opinions, intentions and skills at communication! That, I think, really *is* a primitive fallacy. What I am saying, rather, is that we ourselves discover moods and meanings in our relationship with such objects in the world around us. For example, just suppose that you were to ask, *"If that hillside, (forest, building or whatever) could speak, what would it say?"* Just suppose that you abandoned your self-consciousness for a while and waited to see what answer occurred to you. Were you to do this, you might be amazed to discover some very interesting and very useful answers!

For instance, we might go out into the countryside for rest and recreation, and we may be inclined to the view that such activity is not part of the serious business of living but merely an escapist means of getting away from it all. Re creation, though, is a fundamental need of profound importance. We re-create ourselves and our nature as we move within the Nature all around us . . .

- We find some peace or energy within ourselves as we listen to the peace or energy of the natural world.

- The wind can blow away the 'dust' and 'cobwebs' within each of us and not just the dust in the street.

- The sunrise can lift our own spirits and inner darkness and not just the darkness of the night.

- The sun-set can bring about a peace, joy and tranquillity within ourselves and not just within the evening all around us.

- The mountain can reach up into space and help inspire ourselves to reach up and above the day to day minutiae.

- The sea coast with its broad horizon can help us to reach out beyond our normal narrow confines and, like a river, we can empty our sense of confinement into the boundless ocean.

- The unpompous elegance/dignity/humility/clean lines, even of a chair or table can trigger moods within ourselves; because even the most functional of objects may have symbolic meanings and overtones that are of great significance to us.

The list is endless and the variety of messages and moods as great as the canvas of possibilities within the human soul. Even the most utilitarian and functional modern building, for example, may have something to 'say'. For example, I imagine that if (some) modern buildings could speak they would say:

"I am a large and brash affair, designed to tower over the rest of you. Yet I am essentially functional, too. I have no unnecessary adornments because the people who own me are concerned with power and money above all

*else. I loom over and intimidate you. And my few decorative additions are
crude and trite. Forgive me. I have little soul, since I was created by
soulless people in a soulless world!"*

Any sort of artist knows that every event, and object, is full of
metaphorical and symbolic meaning, and that therefore, all things
have, as it were, something to say! (S)he can watch and listen to
the messages and meanings on offer in everything around her,
and that is why she is moved to paint, sing, or write of what she
sees. If you see everything in purely functional and utilitarian terms
then what is there to say about anything really? If you see yourself
as no more than a functionary then there is nothing else in life for
you to do other than get on with your job and your function. You
may occasionally take time off in order to have a rest. But you will
not re-create yourself since mere functioning does not require creation and creativity. You will not breath in the world around you
and so you will not be inspired. All you will do is get your breath
back, throw your litter out of the car window, and read through
the Sunday paper maybe in order to find something of 'interest'.

Sadly, there are many whose sensibilities have been so blunted
by a soul-destroying world that they will not allow the world
around to get through to them. They are deaf, blind and numb
both to the natural world and the built environment; and unable
to understand what all this might say to them. Equally they remain
unaware of what we are saying and doing to the environment itself
and deaf to what, increasingly, it is saying in response. Eventually,
I am sure, the world around will get through to all of us. But how
much poison, waste and litter will it have to throw in our faces
before we wake up to the message it is trying to give us?

And so we might do well if we could put a little more artistry
into our lives and a little less graft, craft and craftiness. If we came
to our senses a little more, and paid more attention to what the
world and other people have to say to us and what, through our
actions, we are saying to them; we might all be the better for it.
Our lives then might be less of a dirge or a forced march and more
of a poem, or dance, or symphony!

In addition to their absurd delusion that the Natural world can
talk to them, primitive peoples tend to have another tradition that
we maybe ought to attend to. This is the notion that the Elders of
any tribe, while they may not always live up to it, have an important
role in that they can be, or ought to be, the carriers, protectors and
teachers of their culture's deepest insights, wisdom and values.

Now, obviously, not every 'elder' achieves maturity. Not
everyone who grows old manages to grow up. And the more we

refuse to learn from experience and change our self-defeating ways, the more grotesque and visible will our folly be as the years go by. But, let's be optimistic for a moment, people do quite often learn from experience; we do sometimes learn from our mistakes even if we may have to sink deeply into our folly before we wake up to it. Thus, as the years go by, we may begin to distinguish between what is of passing importance and what is of much more long term significance.

There are, in fact, certain more or less unavoidable stages in our lives which we all have to find a way of getting through in one way or another . . . Childhood, youth, the early years of our own children and their eventual departure; the establishment of our place in the wider world of work; the development of our powers and opportunities; and the discovery of our limitations, constraints and ultimate mortality. All these stages are unavoidable for most people. As we get older, we may survey the growth and development of our own children and grandchildren and of the younger people coming up in our own organisation. Inevitably, then, we begin to ask what all this amounts to; what our life has meant; where we fit in to the larger scheme of things; what we have learnt from the whole experience and what we can offer to others.

The younger person is less in a position to take the longer view. (S)he does not survey the world 'from the mountain-top' because, quite rightly, (s)he is trying to establish him or herself in the 'foothills'; in the day to day world of affairs, with the immediate pressures and the immediate needs of gaining competence and 'making a mark'. Thus, the North American Indians recognised that the young 'warrior' had to go out and prove himself and that this was an important stage in the growth of a person.

The trouble with our culture, however, is that we are, as it were, stuck at the 'warrior' stage of existence! Our elders foolishly cling on to the warrior role when they ought to relinquish it. Alternatively, when they do have more to offer us, we generally refuse to listen. Thus the archetypal ideal and value system in this culture is that of the up-and-coming, ever striving 'yuppie', who is anxious to make his mark, prove himself or herself, and lead us all bravely into the Future. Paradise on earth, then, we are to believe, takes the form of a BMW, a filofax, a town house, and a stylish 'busyness' and 'success' orientation where you get all you can and boldly go forwards on the leading edge of 'quality change' and innovation!

Not everyone can possibly make it as a successful go-getter, and Society needs people to fulfil many other important functions and roles. In any case, this kind of image of success, however appropriate it may be for someone in their twenties and thirties, is an increasingly juvenile ideal as we move into our forties, fifties and sixties. As we get older, regardless of whether or not we have made it as an ego-centred go-getter, we need to look more deeply at what we are all about. It is not that there is anything necessarily wrong with our youthful urge to strive and achieve. Indeed, every culture needs its warriors (male and female!) But it also needs its Elders.

There is something disturbingly immature about a culture whose values have not moved beyond the stage of persons in their twenties and thirties who, as I say, are inevitably trying to achieve a position and make a mark. In a mature society, to repeat, all this is regarded as just a stage of existence and not the whole of it. And so the elders of the tribe have traditionally been seen as those who (potentially and ideally) can look upon life from a broader, spiritual perspective and who are the carriers of the culture's deepest values, strivings, perceptions and understanding. The elders provide the context and the continuity. A culture where the elders have forgotten how to carry out this function and where the rest of the tribe have lost sight of this role, is a culture that has lost its soul or, rather, has sacrificed its soul to the spirit of Mammon.

There are some disturbing consequences of all this. When we can only see our lives from the point of view of the market place and never from the hillside or temple, then we tend to see ourselves as commodities to be bought, sold and invested like everything else.

Commercial relationships, let us remember, are based upon the exchange of goods and services for money. Nothing is done for free, there are no gifts; merely investments, surpluses, debts, contracts and payments. We 'give' in order to get. Money is a convenient way of transferring what we are owed from one person to services paid out by another. It allows us to barter collectively rather than between individuals; who may not be able to fully pay us back or offer what we want in return for the services we have rendered to them. This is all very well and I am not about to be so foolish as to suggest that it can, or should, be abolished so that we can all move back, post haste, into some Garden of Eden! But it is not the whole story. There is another kind of relationship that does not have to operate on such commercial principles at all. Let us call it a human relationship.

Human relationships, at their best (where there is love), are about giving and receiving rather than buying and selling. If I have really given you something then you don't owe me anything; and if I feel that you are now in my debt then I was not giving you anything in the first place, I was merely investing in you! With a real gift, then, there is nothing that has to be repaid. Similarly, if I allow myself to receive a gift from you, then I won't feel that anything is owed. Now, of course, we all like to receive as well as to give, and, when we really understand the process, we know that, either way, we gain. But if we give in order to receive, we have given nothing; and if we feel we owe when we are given, then we have rejected the gift!

The young warrior is more preoccupied with earning, borrowing and paying back what is owed than with the gift relationship. At least, this is bound to be so in the marketplace. But, in a mature culture, everyone in the economy knows that it would be blasphemous to turn the market into a shrine and to collapse all human relationship into a commercial relation. Everyone knows that there is, and has to be, a Temple, a hillside, a still place by the lake; and that the overall perspective on our lives is to be found there rather than in the day to day hurly-burly.

Because, if we are really to get through to each other, then it has to be in a place that lies beyond our struggles, efforts, strivings, hustlings and hasslings; and even beyond our 'story'. And, if we are really to understand and act wisely with all this day-to-day noise and clutter, we have to find a place where we can 'look in', or 'look over', it all; rather than always looking out from such a narrow perspective of striving and acquisitiveness. Then, perhaps:

- We could really begin to see and hear each other free of our preconceptions, plans and prejudices.

- We could look out at each other rather than watching out for each other!

- We could begin to see the face of Christ/Humanity/Buddha/ Mohammed in everyone? . . . Including, of course, ourselves!

- We might at last begin to see how everyone is a mirror for everyone else, and constitutes the ground in which others may live their lives; that the whole context of life is reflected and contained in the content of any one face or activity.

- We would see the shared mystery of living in all things and in all people?

- We might, at last, more fundamentally, and however briefly, have 'got through'!

But for as long as we run away from such a spiritual apprehension, we are cast adrift from our world and, therefore, ourselves. Then we find . . .

- That social class divisions sustained by wealth destroy the bonds of fellowship which should exist between us, and encourage even morally sensitive individuals to act badly.

- That anxious self-scrutiny is used as a poor substitute for critical self-examination.

- That our political activity is used as a means of avoiding the terrors of our inner life.

- That our self absorption becomes part of a determined effort to insulate ourselves from much of the horror around us.

- That social discontent is conveniently redefined as personal inadequacy.

- That 'peak experiences' and transpersonal vision are turned into yet another marketable commodity for the jaded Western consumer.

- That underneath our hedonism and striving for success is an insecurity, loneliness, emptiness and desperation.

- That, as our sense of society and social responsibility collapses we are faced with an ever more demanding war of all against all.

- That, beneath all our mania and our obsession with glitz, glamour and celebrity, we face an underlying pessimism, even terror, of the Future and what it might bring.

- That we would dearly love, just sometimes, to communicate beyond the level of mere ego with its hustle, hassle, striving, efforting and manoeuvring to secure a good 'position' and place. Just occasionally, we would love to meet each other 'heart to heart'.

In order to re-connect ourselves with others and with the world around us ('re-ligio' means 'I re-connect'!) we need to do more than go through some ritual every Sunday. Getting through to ourselves and others in a spiritual sense means that we get through, not only to our rights (which so preoccupy the shallow hedonist) but also to our duties and obligations. The juvenile 'yuppie' stereotype/ideal tends to regard duties and obligations as an unwanted encumbrance that slow him down as he accelerates up the

fast lane of his career. They are for 'suckers'; to be avoided as far
as this is decently (or indecently) possible.

But such a mentality is itself just a sign of our ignorance and
isolation that the Elders of the tribe, ideally, would be best placed
to put right. It is not just that we *ought* to consider what it is right
to do; we actually *need* to do so for the sake of our own long term
well-being. The hedonist believes that fulfilment and 'self actuali-
sation' come merely from doing what we like. This is simply false,
as plenty of distressed gluttons who have only ever done what
takes their fancy may eventually discover. Fulfilment comes not
just from chasing after what we like but, often more importantly,
from doing what we think is right. Sometimes such fulfilment of
our duties provides us with no more than a grim satisfaction. But
if we don't do what we know to be right we suffer all the more in
the end. And there is a very great deal of suffering within Western
Society arising from a dim, or not so dim, awareness that, as we
have seen, many of the ways in which we are presently living are
unsustainable and wrong.

We need, for our fulfilment and healing, to understand how we
need others and are needed by them, and many of our obligations
arise, inevitably, from such mutual needs.

Our hedonistic culture has thrown out the word 'duty' since it
has so often been used oppressively. But a person who really was
totally independent; without duties; needed by, and needing, no-
body – would feel meaningless and in despair. And let's not say
'would'; let's say 'do', because there are many people who are
already in precisely this position: old people who are thrown onto
a kind of human scrap heap; unemployed with no sense of dignity
and place; and the over-employed who are so ground-down by
day to day pressures that they can never extract themselves from
the market place and its values.

Our own immediate hopes and fears, successes and failures can
feel like a prison at times. Our own self-obsession becomes a trap
that allows no peace and no release. And thus we try to take
ourselves 'out of ourselves' from time to time, yet, too often, we
imagine that this can only be done through distraction and entertainment. In fact, the best way to do it is by sensing and acting
upon the consequences of our interconnectedness with others,
with the ways in which we need and are needed by them.

Of course, as we have seen, any sense we may have of communion with other people and the world around us does not last and
then we are forced back on communication, the quality of which
may itself be far from ideal. Yet we survive and we might even

prosper if the preservation of true prosperity could, once again, be seen as requiring wisdom rather than mere cleverness or aggression. Some may communicate with the world via their in-car telephone and computer modem; but we create a soul-destroying world if such a lifestyle is seen as the only road to heaven on earth. For then our only God is Mammon and we suffer – we are suffering – the consequences. Ideally, our best communicators (and never mind information technology) will communicate because they can see the sun-set; the birds; that old woman begging in the street; and all the rest of the life around them in all its mystery and complexity. The best communicators, then, might well be some of our best poets and other artists. It is a measure of our topsy turvy value system that such communicators are so badly rewarded, whereas the disciples of hype and glitz are seen as 'where it's at'.

All this, though, is lofty stuff (albeit important!) And, before ending this chapter, I want to come back down to more lowly considerations and end with something more concrete as a practical way of beginning the long journey towards getting through to 'us'.

Getting Through in Groups:

A Twenty-Question Checklist to Aid Observation

Non-Verbal Cues:

1. What were the seating arrangements?
2. Was there anything particularly noticeable about the physical movements, posture and tone of voice of particular members? What did you notice? What do you think it meant?

Talking:

3. Did the group leader do most of the talking? What proportion?
4. How many people spoke?
5. Was discussion dominated by a minority? How small?
6. Did the group leader encourage everyone to talk? How?

Listening:

7. Were people listening to each other? How could you tell?
8. How far did people's comments relate to what others had previously said? How far did people make pre-planned statements independently of what anyone else was saying?

Atmosphere:

9. What signs did you notice of competition/co-operation between members of the group? How far was this a help or hindrance to tasks being achieved?
10. What was the overall 'atmosphere' of the group? e.g. relaxed-tense? friendly-unfriendly? formal-informal? organised-chaotic? . . .
11. What was the overall 'hum', 'tone', 'sound' and 'rhythm' of the group?

Sub-Groups:

12. Was there a polarisation of opinion? What were the consequences?
13. Did cliques form (or pre-exist)? What were the consequences? What is your evidence?
14. Were there 'insiders' and 'outsiders' in the group? How could you tell?

Roles:

15. Did individuals take on particular roles within the group (formal or informal?) e.g. chair, secretary, tutor, leader, leader of

the opposition, maverick, rebel, jester, saboteur, follower, observer, rescuer, victim, martyr, expert, nurse, healer, patient, delinquent. Were they helpful/unhelpful?

Feelings:

16. How were people feeling during the group discussion/activity? What is your evidence for this? Did people's feeling influence what went on, and if so, in what ways? Was there a large variety of feeling?

17. How were people feeling at the beginning of the group session? How were they feeling when it ended?

Aims:

18. What did people want from this group? Did they get what they wanted? Who was satisfied? Who was dissatisfied? Why? How do you know?

19. How far was there agreement about what the group was trying to achieve? How far did the group succeed in doing what it set out to do? Did it wander from its agenda? Was this constructive or merely a distraction? Did it have a (formal/informal/hidden) agenda?

20. Were any decisions taken in the group? How were decisions made? Who made them? Were there any dissenters and how did they behave?

Getting Through In Organisations:

Questionnaire

1. *Trust:* do you have to 'put on a show' and 'cover your back', or can you turn to colleagues and supervisors for support and inspiration? When under pressure, does your heart rate increase or decrease if faced with colleagues or supervisors?

2. *Authenticity:* do your roles at work help you to express aspects of your personality? Or are they more of a hindrance to genuine self-expression?

3. *Autonomy:* are you left too much on your own without sufficient direction or support? Or do you feel overly controlled so that you have too little chance to determine the nature and pace of your work? Do you think you could do a better job for your

employer if you were given more/less autonomy? Or is the balance of control/support and autonomy about right for you?

4. *Support:* how far do you feel valued and respected as a person who can make a useful contribution at work? How far does management genuinely and actively listen to the opinions, suggestions and concerns of employees?

5. *Leadership:* what is the quality of leadership in your organisation? Authoritarian . . . Democratic? Competent . . . Incompetent? Flexible . . . Rigid? Energetic . . . Lazy? Radical . . . Conservative? Ruthless . . . Humanitarian? Fair . . . Unfair? Hierarchical . . . Egalitarian? High Morale . . . Low Morale?

6. *Context:* what kind of environment does your organisation operate in? Highly competitive . . . Very little competitive pressure? Growth sector? Static? Declining sector? Methods and markets changing faster than we can cope? Change is manageable? Little or no change – stultifying? frustrating? sleepy climate?

7. *Morale:* what is the overall morale in your organisation? High . . . Low?

8. *Meaning and Purpose:* how far do you value and prize what you are doing (over and above the financial rewards)? How far do others (within and outside the organisation) value what you are doing? How does your particular contribution relate to the overall purposes of the organisation? What positive (and/or negative) contribution do you and your organisation make to society as a whole? Is your work: High status . . . Low status? High pay . . . Low pay?

9. *Incentives:* does your organisation operate mainly by rewards or by punishments and threats? What are the rewards, punishments and threats? If you do well does anyone notice and show appreciation? What happens if you do badly? Are you supported, encouraged, re-trained? Or punished, blamed, ignored?

10. *Competition:* do colleagues compete with or against each other? How far do colleagues co-operate and work as a team?

11. Performance: overall, how do you rate your own performance and that of the organisation you work in? Are you overloaded? Under-loaded? Faced with the wrong load? Carrying a worthless load?

12. Overall: what are the most positive features of working in your organisation? What are the most negative?

And finally, a couple of efforts of my own on the matter of 'getting through':

Balancing Act

Please don't go on about your job, or Mid-Life Crisis,
or Faith in the Future.
Perhaps a walk, I need more exercise
A swim perhaps? I'm always talking about it, I know.

We over-work,
The kids are fine, and grown up now
She's well too; we're much better than we have been
With age, you appreciate the little things.

Something's missing, yes it's a cliché
Perhaps another dinner party
We wouldn't mention it
It'll be missing there.

Another cliché to lampoon dinner parties
And the moaning about jobs and the
Common complaints about people complaining of
Cut-backs, over-work, incompetence, is it all worth it?

Does anyone take any notice really? Notice of what?
Some are lazy enough; let's not hear about that again
Work isn't everything, tell me about something else.
'Balanced your social life? 'Got enough exercise? 'Seeing people?

Well, that's okay – isn't it?

A Guardian *reader's fashionable malaise?*
What's new? A tired joke.
Trying to get out, finding the words, avoiding the Cliché
It's been better said before.
Can we climb out of all this and meet
And what then?
In the sunshine, we'd be smiling
Not inanely. We'd meet – And go for a walk maybe.

And I do, anyway
Not very far with kids
Nothing dramatic
But worth it.

Plenty are worse off
Count your blessings,

You've had it easy, and
Too much time to brood.

Some of us work
Don't talk about work
Don't moan about the admin.
Oh, go on then.

Come for dinner
Fix a time? Diaries?
Five weeks from now?
We'll look forward to it.

No, really, we will
A sinking feeling?
If we really met . . .
Shall we meet?

It's loneliness maybe;
Within the trappings
And the talk;
What do you think?

Of course, we're all basically alone
Another Cliché
Can we feel it?
And share it?

No, let's run away.
There are films, A play? a drink?
We meant to book a concert
There's plenty happening

'Just needs energy
'More than enough to do
Talking helps, keep a Journal
Change the balance a bit

Alright?

The second takes more of a tongue-in-cheek approach to the same theme:

Lost at Sea

I must pick up my phone today
For a lonely moan on the wire
And I've got to meet some friends and play;
'Give my social life more fire.

For the inner life is a place of strife
And a litany of woe
I need to balance up my act
And run a better show.

The mindless blather here inside
Diverts me from my task
Yet endless wittering to friends
Is driving me well past

. . . Despair; the chattering clatters on
And leaves us lost within
We wonder where we're going wrong
And how we'd ever win

. . . A way to meet 'for real' at last
No longer lost in drivel
To stand outside our own pretence
And see if we can chisel

. . . More deeply into joys and tears
Communion profound
It's fantasy perhaps, I know
But I'm trying to come round

. . . To say I'm tired of pointless chat
and endless wild distraction
I wish we'd drop some of our act
And make a little action.

I'd try to end this rambling now
And come right to the point
But lost in my frustration, how
To make this less disjoint

. . . ed seems a hopeless task.

11. Conclusion

The first duty in life is to be as artificial as possible. What the second duty is no one has yet discovered.

Oscar Wilde, *Phrases and Philosophies for the Use of the Young* (1891)

Ours is the age of substitutes: instead of language, we have jargon; instead of principles, slogans; and instead of genuine ideas, Bright ideas.

Eric Bentley, *The Dramatic Event* (1954)

Since so many families are started by adults who are not mature themselves, parents are often in the position of not having learned the things that they are expected to teach their children, for example, handling their emotions. There is nothing like the raising of a child to show up adult inadequacies.

Virginia Satir, *Peoplemaking* (1972)

Communication begins in the womb and, for some, the misunderstandings may originate there too! In the motherhood of myth, the child and mother are 'at one'; each in a state of bliss; each entirely in tune with the other. The mother feels joy and fulfilment in knowing, and meeting the needs of, the infant inside her; and the child floats in a heavenly *nirvana* with all its needs met; trusting and at peace. It has nothing it needs to ask for and nowhere it needs to go. It has no notion either of a 'self' or of an unknown (m)other. The placental boundary between baby and mother is perhaps our most effective channel of communication, although, like others, it is also a (necessary) barrier. Who needs words when you're as close as this? How much closer could you ever get?

The joys of pregnancy can be real enough. There really are radiant mothers who (sometimes, anyway) sit back into the deep satisfaction of sensing that this is a great moment in their lives; and a great obligation, opportunity and source of fulfilment. But 'perfect' union and communion may well not exist on earth; maybe not for any of us; and certainly not for long! I start to get a sense of me as opposed to you when I begin to discover borders, barriers and boundaries that block, blight and blur the messages which previously flowed so easily between us! A child at peace, with all its needs met, is a child at one with all around it. It is therefore less likely to have much of a sense of 'self' and 'other'. But the child that is misunderstood, mistreated, frightened and frustrated is 'one apart from' rather than 'at one with' all around it.

If you were so at one with me that we inhabited the heart of each other; then there would be no notion of a separate self at all. And so, to a great extent, I only find myself as a result of finding that we don't always get through at all and we don't always want to! Sometimes (often!), one or other, or both, of us wants to get away from, get round, get over or get the better of the other!

This loss of communion, this breakdown, this imperfection in communication cannot really be imperfect or unnatural since it is impossible to envisage any other outcome! The relationship between a particular mother and child might be wonderful in that the mother understands her offspring 'often enough' and is loving and caring and capable (enough). But frustration is inevitable for every child if only because, as it gets older, there will be times when what it wants may not be what it needs. On such occasions frustration may be essential for the good of the child. Sooner or later, we need to realise that we won't get all we want and need however just and fair our demands!

Frustration then, is inevitable, even if our parents manage to meet our needs 'often enough'. Sadly, many parents fail to meet their children's needs often enough to prevent the children from carrying into adulthood a legacy of insecurity, unease, and 'unfinished business' of one sort or another. Moreover, it can take years of hard work if we are to unlearn self-destructive behaviour and attitudes that we may have learnt as children. Furthermore, if our insecurity lies deep and our style of communication is vague, indirect and dishonest then it may be a mammoth task to change some of these deep-seated feelings and neuroses.

In an ideal world, our parents would have provided us with a secure base from which we could venture out into the mystery all around us. Our mother, in the first instance, would have communicated to us in a direct, clear, specific and honest fashion; she would have been sensitive to our needs; she would have loved us unconditionally, without expecting us to perform or put on a show for her, or bottle up inconvenient emotions. She would have wished to meet our needs rather than use us to meet hers. She would have communicated with us, and encouraged us to express ourselves, in a real and genuine way, rather than live a life of pretence that forced us to collude with her own rationalisations and fantasy. She would not have pushed us out into the cold before we were ready to cope with it; nor would she have clung on to us when we wanted and needed to explore. She would have been there for us when we needed to rush back to her for comfort; and she would have gently encouraged and reassured us when we needed to step out once again and stand for a while on our own two feet.

In an ideal world, our mother would have done all this in the knowledge that fulfilling her role successfully, so that we grew up fit, strong, courageous and loving, was more than enough of a reward for her. And so she would not have expected anything in return from us; she would not have demanded that we feel grateful, or expected us to feel guilty *"because of all I've done for you."* She would have taught mainly by example rather than exhortation and, because of our ideal role model, we too would have learned how to communicate openly and honestly and trust others (without being naive in our trust). Most important of all, we would have learned to be at peace with ourselves as we are. We would have found that we wanted to make a successful life for ourselves and others, as a consequence of, rather than a requirement to, feeling okay about ourselves. We would not be needing to achieve and achieve in order to prove that we were okay, since we would be in no need of proof.

Just think what it would be like if you really felt okay about yourself, warts and all. No longer would you need to pretend to yourself that you were better, or worse, than you really are. Consequently, you would not want to pretend to others; or defend yourself against the truth they offered; or get them to collude with your pretences. If other people, too, felt okay about themselves, so that they did not feel the need to pretend; then just think how much more simple a business communication could become. As it is, though, I may well not want you to get through to me, since this might bring to my attention aspects of myself that I don't want to face.

In my insecurity, I may well sense that I could be slaughtered by the truth, even if that was not your intention. And so I may well feel quite unwilling and unable to hear what you say, if I fear that it will undermine the illusions and fantasies that underpin my fragile sense of self-esteem. Similarly, you will be reluctant for me to get through to you in certain respects. You will want me to pretend to be other than I am, and you may well make this a condition of our relationship. And, if I am very reliant upon you (perhaps because you are my father or mother), then I will be quite prepared to sacrifice parts of my own identity in order to preserve our relationship. I may thus lay the foundations for a life-long habit of pretending to be other than I am, in order to be in relationship with other people. My motto will be (to quote the popular song), *"I'm not necessarily the boy/girl you think you see. Whoever you want is exactly whom I'm more than willing to be."*

The more fragile and insecure we are, the more there will be 'no go' areas that are too uncomfortable for either (or any) of us to explore. Instead, without any conscious intent, we will agree to a set of rules to ensure that we cover up, pretend, divert and distract ourselves away from all the unpalatable truths that haunt us. And when there is, say, a whole family of us, we will devise a whole complex system of rules and roles for everyone. This will keep all the family skeletons locked away in the proverbial cupboard, and preserve everyone's self-esteem. At any rate, such a family system will preserve the self-image and fantasies of the key players! It may require that minor players sacrifice their own identity and well-being; for the 'greater good' of the more powerful individuals.

Thus, in order to keep the family system intact, it may be necessary for some individuals to become scapegoats, or play the role of delinquent, 'madwoman', backward child, cold father or whatever. Moreover, appearances may belie the underlying reality, so that, for example, the supposedly weak, martyred, sick, victim of the family may in fact be the one who has the most power, with the most attention and the most rewards. Everyone, though, will have his own reasons for colluding in the family game, with his own payoffs and costs. Everyone, too, for as long as we are playing games, will pay the price of being out of touch with the truth about themselves and others.

If we don't even want to get through to ourselves, but would rather pretend, pose, play games, rationalise and hide, then what chance is there of our being able to get through to each other? Indeed, how can we even face up to any of our rationalisations if we deny that we have any? How can we get through to our games if one of the games involves pretending that we are always for real? How can we uncover what we hide from ourselves, if we hide from the fact that we hide anything at all? How can we stop posing and pretending, if we pretend that we are not posing at all? No wonder then, that uncovering such a tangle can be so tortuous and complex.

Ideally, we would not have had any need to think much about what it is to communicate successfully and to be at peace with ourselves and the world around us. We would not have needed to explore these questions since, with an ideal childhood behind us, we would have already known the answers. We would have felt them in our bones and our being without needing to talk about it. And so our childhood would have been the perfect springboard with which we were able to take a confident leap into the future, rather than (at the opposite extreme) a traumatic nightmare which, at best, takes the rest of the our lives to overcome!

Maybe you had such a 'perfect' childhood yourself? If you did, I am surprised that you have bothered to read this far, since it ought to have become clear by now that there is nothing I can tell you and nothing you need to know about effective communication. Certainly, I would not bother to read about problems of communication unless I experienced such problems myself. For that matter, I doubt that I would bother to write about communication if I thought I had got the whole matter sorted out and had nothing else to learn about it!

Realistically, though, such 'ideal' childhood circumstances do not exist in the real world, and it is hard to imagine that they ever will. We all need to forgive our parents to some extent as a result of the legacy they have left us and, needless to say, some people have far more that needs to be forgiven than others. Some have a very great deal to cope with as a result of what their parents did (or didn't do) to them. But they will cope with it better if they can, somehow or another, find a way of forgiving all of this. (Though to begin with, realistically, we may need to forgive ourselves for being unable to forgive. There is no point in pretending that we have forgiven when we have not!) Along with the forgiveness of others, we might try to forgive ourselves, and thus edge our way towards a more effective and caring way of being in the world.

When damage has been done it may not be possible to undo it. But let us at least try to limit the damage we do to others, and try to recover from at least some of the damage that others have done to us. We can never get over our past traumas altogether any more than a tree can recover entirely from damage inflicted by wind, cold or other deficiencies. Years of stunted growth are recorded in the heart of its trunk as the narrower bands of concentric rings that are its history. Similarly, with ourselves, the pain that has been inflicted upon us is something that we may well have to carry with us for the rest of our lives. Our scars will be evident, to the skilled observer, in some of our attitudes, insecurities, behaviour and styles of communication. Such wounds may have healed in that they no longer seep; but they will not have disappeared altogether. They may no longer weigh us down as they once did. But that which has been learned in a very deep-seated way from childhood, and reinforced for years afterwards, may not be eradicable altogether.

The motherhood and childhood of myth focuses on love, care and understanding. But, being human, we cannot always understand and care in the saintly way of the imagined Gods and paragons in heaven or utopia. We can misunderstand; we can be careless, carefree or overly careful. We can be unaware of the sort of care that is needed. We can be unlovely, unloving and unloved. We can hate!

In fact, love and hatred tend to go hand in hand. Hatred may seem like the antithesis of love; but love is more likely to be absent in an atmosphere of indifference. It is almost impossible to hate someone we care nothing about. It is easy to most hate the person we most love. (S)he who gives, cares and understands the most is the one who has all the more to withhold from us. It is (s)he who can most comprehensively ignore, malign and misunderstand us.

The 'perfect' communication of myth is all about freely giving of ourselves to others. I give you a message; you give in return, and each of us thus reveals a part of who we are and what we are about. But, to repeat, there is another key to real communication which is at least as important as giving and receiving. And that is forgiving.

There is so much that every mother needs to give her child. But she will not be able to give very freely or easily unless she is also able to forgive herself for being the ordinary mortal that we all are. We may like to be godlike in relation to our children; all-knowing, all-seeing, all-capable. But we cannot manage this; and the child does not need such a perfect environment. Indeed, how could it ever survive in the real world if it did not learn, at home, to cope and come to terms with frustration, limitation and imperfection?

In childhood it can be easy for (some of) us to imagine that our parents really are gods. They contain and control the boundaries of our entire world; they have, seemingly, answers to all our questions; solutions to all our problems; insights and skills about which we can only speculate and marvel. But, sooner or later, our 'Gods' fail us! They are too concerned with themselves. They refuse to listen. They misunderstand. They belittle us. They get in our way. They are misinformed, mistaken old fuddy-duddies who ought to be pensioned off right now. In extreme cases, we may decide to 'fire' them as parents altogether, and see them simply as living examples of how not to do anything.

More often, such strong negative reactions exist alongside our strongly positive ones. We love/hate our parents; and they may very well love/hate us. We give each other so much. Equally important, and it needs re-emphasising, we also need to forgive ourselves and each other for what we can't/won't/shouldn't give!

Ideally, we can learn to give thanks and forgiveness for all our parents did and didn't do for us. To the extent that we fail to do so, we will find it difficult to give thanks for, and to forgive, ourselves. Equally, it will be difficult to give to, and forgive, others. To survive in the real world will require us to forgive, forgive and forgive again!

Communion is the (generally mythical) state in which we are at one with each other such that nothing comes between us. In such an idealised state of being, we keep nothing from each other and each of us is entirely known by, and knowing of, the other. There is no separation; there are no barriers; nothing divides us; we are not alone. In such a (supposedly) ideal existence, there would be no need for communication at all! The moment you had a thought, or feeling, I would know it too. I would know you so well that your experience would be my experience. All experience, indeed, would be our experience. You would not need to tell me about it, explain or describe it. I would simply know it directly, without any need for words or signs of any sort.

We may get nearest to this when we communicate with mother or child through the placenta or, if we are identical twins, through looking out on the world with (almost) identical eyes, hearts and minds. But let us not forget, communication only becomes necessary because communion is impossible. Communication then, by its very nature must be seen as a source of frustration and imperfection for as long as we cling on to the wish to be in communion with others. We can only come together from time to time because the underlying reality of our existence is that we are separate. We are not often in communion; and so, instead, we must (try to) communicate!

'Answers' to Exercises in Chapter 5

i.   *"You stupid fool!"* (insulting, labelling)

ii.   *"Just get out of my sight!"* (ordering, possibly threatening)

iii.   *"Just look at the state of you!"* (ridicule)

iv.   *"I'll do what I can to help you but, knowing you, that's going to be an uphill struggle."* (condescension, sarcasm)

v.   *"You never say anything worth listening to, and you are the most insensitive clod that walked the Earth!"* (sweeping allegation, insult, abuse, accusation, condescension)

vi.   *"You only said that in order to get at me."* (mean-spirited interpretation)

vii.   *"I think you ought to know that many people have been laughing at you behind your back recently."* (slaughtering with 'the truth')

viii. *"It's all your fault; and, if you don't change, I'm going to leave!"* (blaming, threatening)

ix.   *"You need to make a much better job of this; the work so far just won't do."* (complaining)

x.   *"You must realise that the way you've been behaving lately is simply awful. You've treated me terribly badly, and I just can't stand it anymore!"* (probable exaggeration and distortion; 'musterbation', 'awfulising', 'terribilisation' and 'can't-stand-it-itis.)

xi.   *"Go and buy yourself a shirt and make sure it is a blue one so that it matches your trousers."* (giving orders, providing 'answers')

xii.   *"I hope you're not about to start another one of your tantrums are you?"* (provocation, condescension)

xiii. *"You're not exactly the biggest stud in town are you?"* (sarcasm, condescension)

xiv. *"Just think about what you've just said. Can't you see how it makes me feel? I'm at my wits end."* (Giving orders, possible manipulative use of hurts and 'powerlessness')

xv.   *"Don't come near me. I don't want you to touch me."* (Possible passive aggression and withdrawal-as-punishment)

xvi. *"You've really been very good to me lately (and God knows it's about time!)"* (Sting-in-the-tail)

xvii. *"It's been good to see you and I hope we meet again soon. You're nothing like as gauche and clumsy as they said you are."* (Hit and run)

xviii. *"Well, it's not really been the way I wanted it to be this evening."* (Vague, indirect)

xix. *"Look, everyone in this room can see that you have made a complete hash of this job. It's about time you faced up to the facts."* (Merciless slaughtering with 'truth', cornering a person)

xx.   *"When I think of the way you have been for all these years; and you expect me to be nice to you now!"* (Possible brooding and revenge seeking)

xxi.   *"Don't come to me now with your apologies; it's too late! The damage is done!"* (Rejection and belittling).

Suggested Reading

Andersen, M. & Savary, L., *Passages: a Guide for Pilgrims of the Mind*, Turnstone, 1973

Argyle, M., *The Psychology of Happiness*, Methuen, 1987

Argyle, M. & Henderson, M., *The Anatomy of Relationships*, Pelican, 1985

Bandler, R., *Using Your Brain – for a Change*, Real People's Press, (U.S.A.) 1985

Bandler, R. & Grindler, J., *Reframing*, Real People's Press, (U.S.A.) 1982

Berne, B., *Games People Play*, Grove Press, 1964

Bloch, S., *What is Psychotherapy?*, OPUS, 1982

Brandes, D & Phillips, H., *The Gamester's Handbook* Vols. I & II, Hutchison

Brandon, D., *Zen in the Art of Helping*, Routledge, 1976

Campbell, S., *The Couple's Journey*, Impact, 1980

Clare. A. & Thompson, S., *Let's Talk about Me*, BBC, 1981

Corey, G., *Manual for Theory and Practice of Group Counselling*, Brooks/Cole, (U.S.A.) 1891 (1985)

Dass, R. & Gorman, P., *How Can I Help?*, Rider, 1985

Dickson, A., *A Woman in Your Own Right: Assertiveness and You*, Quartet

Dryden, W.(ed), *Individual Therapy in Britain*, Harper & Row, 1984

Dryden, W.(ed), *Marital Therapy in Britain*, Harper & Row, 1985

Dyer, Wayne W., *Your Erroneous Zones*, Sphere, 1979

Ernst, S. & Goodison, L., *In Our Own Hands: a Book of Self-Help Therapy*, Women's Press, 1981

Gordon, T., *Parent Effectiveness Training*, Plume, 1975

Gough, T., *Couples Arguing*, Darton, Longman & Todd, 1987

Ferrucci, P., *What We May Be*, Turnstone (Thorsons), 1982

Hopson, B. & Scally, M., *Lifeskills Teaching*, McGraw Hill, 1981

Howard, A., *Finding a Way: a Realist's Introduction to Self-Help Therapy*, Gateway, 1985

Howard, A., *Anatomy of Errors*, Gateway, 1989

Krupar, K., *Communication Games*, The Free Press (U.S.A.) 1973

Lasch, C., *The Culture of Narcissism*, Abacus 1980

Lazarus, A., *Marital Myths*, Impact, (U.S.A.)1985

Levine, S., *Who Dies?*, Gateway, 1988

McFadden, C., *The Serial*, Pan 1978

Minuchin, S., *Families and Family Therapy*, Tavistock, 1974

Nelson-Jones, R., *Human Relationship Skills*, Cassell, 1986

Nelson-Jones, R., *The Theory and Practice of Counselling Psychology*, Holt, Rinehart & Winston, (U.S.A.)1982

Rainwater, J., *You're in Charge*, Turnstone (Thorsons), 1981

Satir, V., *Conjoint Family Therapy*, Souvenir, 1978

Satir, V., *Peoplemaking*, Souvenir, 1983

Scott, B., *Negotiating*, Paradigm, 1988

Sheehy, G., *Passages: Predictable Crises of Adult Life*, Corgi, 1977

Shepard, M., *Do-it-Yourself Psychotherapy*, Optima, 1976

Skynner, R. & Cleese, J., *Families and How to Survive Them*, Methuen, 1983

Skynner, R., *One Flesh: Separate Persons*, Constable, 1976

Smail, D., *Taking Care: an Alternative to Therapy*, Dent, 1987

Tweedie, J., *In The Name of Love*, Granada, 1980

Walrond-Skinner, S.(ed), *Developments in Family Therapy*, Routledge, 1981

Useful Addresses:

British Association for Counselling: 37a Sheep Street, Rugby, Warwickshire. CV21 3BX Tel. 0788 78328/9

BAC responds to the increasing demand for information and advice concerning both counselling and counsellors. Contact the Rugby office for information and advice about the counselling support available in your area.

MIND (National Association for Mental Health). Central Office: 22, Harley Street, London W1N 2ED

- Provides advice and information about mental health; including a very useful list of pamphlets and other publications.
- Campaigns for improved standards and forms of mental health care.
- Provides a legal casework service to consumers of mental health services and their families.
- Encourages and demonstrates good practice in the development of local mental health services.
- Provides education and training for mental health workers, volunteers, consumers and members of the public.

Regional resource centres:

Northern MIND: 158 Durham Road, Gateshead, Tyne and Wear. NE8 4EL

North West MIND: 21 Ribblesdale Place, Preston, Lancashire. PR1 3NA

Trent and Yorkshire MIND: First Floor Suite, White Buildings, Fitzallen Square, Sheffield, South Yorkshire. S1 2AY

Wales MIND: 23 St. Mary Street, Cardiff. CF1 2AA

West Midlands MIND: Princess Chambers (3rd Floor), 52/54 Lichfield Street, Wolverhampton. WV1 1DG

MIND also has 190 affiliated local associations,

RELATE: National Marriage Guidance: Herbert Gray College, Little Church Street, Rugby. CV21 3AP. See telephone directory for local branch.

Samaritans: Confidential telephone support for people in distress. See telephone directory for local branch.

Courses:

A variety of agencies provide general interest courses for the general public on Communication Skills. Ask at your local public library for Local Education Authority, Workers' Educational Association, and University Continuing Education Department brochures. Other privately run institutes and agencies offer similar courses, of varying quality. Again, your local public library is likely to be the best place to look. Alternatively, the British Association for Counselling and MIND will each be happy to deal with enquiries for information about courses on offer in your area, provided they are in the form of a letter with a stamped addressed envelope. (Addresses above).

Subject Index

Other books by ALEX HOWARD

FINDING A WAY:
A Realist's Introduction to Self-Help Therapy

A teach-yourself course in self-discovery and in relating to others –
going through the vital areas of living where we often have learned
to accept second best. So we say: "I don't want to commit myself" or
"I can't make any difference". Can we learn to relax, to be better listeners, to be more assertive, to avoid useless worry and self-torture,
to cooperate, to take responsibility, to be more effective parents?

Though none of these skills in human relationship is easy to master, a practical programme is presented, with questions for self-as-
sessment at every stage.

"This exceptionally helpful and down-to-earth book is a revealing, teach-yourself course in removing those masks we hide behind
... providing many practical guidelines and a deeper spiritual understanding of who we really are ... I strongly recommend this valuable
book." (*Editor, Science of Thought Review*)

"If it were a text in our schools, it would change society." (*Marriage
Guidance Journal*)

224p   ISBN 0–946551–13–18   paperback £5.95

ANATOMY OF ERRORS:
A self-help course in Problem Solving

The good (and not-so-good) reasons we have for making the same
old mistakes over and over again.

Life is never problem-free. But the work of problem solving only begins when we realise that problems are self-created. Alex helps us identify where we're going right or wrong by providing key statements
which pinpoint critical errors. This is an unthreatening and common-
sense approach to making new strategies for succeeding in life.

"Howard commends the need to share problems appropriately,
as well as the need for intelligent self-confrontation. He also looks at
the distinction between true and false spirituality ... One feature I
particularly like is Howard's critical sense, as when applied to unba-
lanced modern self-assertive-morality. We must not only assert our
will, but also, he argues, be sensitive to others' needs and deficits. I
would recommend this book warmly to anyone seeking a first read
on self-help psychology." (*Colin Feltham, Counselling Magazine*)

224p   ISBN 0–946551–44–6   paperback £6.95

Some other GATEWAY BOOK titles that might interest you!

EARTH'S EMBRACE
The Shadow of the New Age Movement
Alan Bleakley

Life is a balance of the light and the dark. If we over-emphasise well being, transformation and growth, our shadow side erupts unpredictably. Drawing on the psychology of archetypes (ways of seeing), Alan calls for a psycho-ecology that appreciates both the upfront, daylight side and the shadowy, underworld side in inner growth.

240pp, 30 illus.   ISBN 0–946551–40–5   paperback £6.95

THE FRUITS OF THE MOON TREE
The Medicine Wheel and Transpersonal Psychology
Alan Bleakley

This book is about becoming. It takes us on a journey to discover the masculine and feminine within, buried by modern 'education'. The author eclectically connects Jungian psychology with ancient traditions viewed through the teachings of the Medicine Wheel. It has a strong alchemical flavour with themes such as transformation symbols, the symbolism of plants and animals, and the world of the imaginal, the Dreamtime.

320pp, 120 illus.   ISBN 0–946551–10–3   paperback £7.95

SOMETHING IS HAPPENING
Spiritual Awareness and Depth Psychology in the New Age
Winifred Rushforth

A profound book that has already achieved the status of a classic, it shows how the spiritual and psychological ways of understanding are one; both bound up with the healing process that must take place before we can become mature and whole human beings. Winifred Rushforth pioneered therapeutic and creative groupwork in Scotland where she was well known for her religious broadcasts. "I feel like passing on this book as a gem to my friends. It makes me feel very friendly to Prince Charles when I read that he was so deeply moved by *Something is Happening*, that a month before she died, he visited her to have an intimate discussion."

(*Damarisk Parker Rhodes in The Friend*)

160pp   ISBN 0–946551–05–7   paperback £4.95

MEN AND FRIENDSHIP
Stuart Miller

Most men have had a close male friend, yet we're taught to keep a distance and be independent, to our eventual detriment. An open and very feeling book about sharing and sensitivity, about the New Man beyond the hand-shake and the hype. Based on hundreds of interviews with men, and on the author's own loneliness after a mid-life divorce. For men of all persuasions and lifestyles.

224pp   ISBN 0–946551–02–2   paperback £4.95

SCIENCE OF THE GODS
Reconciling Mystery and Matter
David Ash and Peter Hewitt

About the nature of matter and energy and a deeper purpose of our exis-tence. This book merges physics and metaphysics in a study of the power of the vortex, first researched in the 19thC by Lord Kelvin. New and credible light is cast on traditional beliefs about life after death, miracles, telepathy and clairvoyance and the powers which lie behind them. A book for free-thinkers who seek a new understanding of life and the universe!

192pp, 25 illus.   ISBN 0–946551–62–6   Hardcover £9.95

LIVING WATER
Viktor Schauberger & the Secrets of Natural Energy
Olof Alexandersson

The story of a pioneering/Austrian naturalist, inventor and iconoclast who developed a new understanding of natural energy, energy systems and landscape design to overcome environmental destruction. He developed ingenious inventions in forestry, farming, water-purification and propul-sion systems. This book has revolutionary implications and its time has now come.

160pp, 53 illus.   ISBN 0–946551–57–X   paperback £5.95

THE CROP CIRCLE ENIGMA
Grounding the Phenomenon in Science, Culture and Metaphysics
Ed. by Ralph Noyes

Mysteriously swirled crop circles, appearing in geometrical arrangements and as pictograms, have become an international mystery and controversy. This book, for a wide range of disciplines, brings the whole question into focus, including reports of unusual sounds and light effects, with surprising suggestions about their causes.

192pp, 68 col 48 b & w illus.   ISBN 0–946551–66–9   Hardcover £14.95

THE GOLDEN THREAD
Words of Hope for a Changing World
Calligraphy and illustration by Dorothy Boux

A heart-warming book, bringing reconciliation in a divided world. In gathering together this anthology, written in calligraphy and delightfully illustrated on every page with watercolour paintings, Dorothy has drawn on the teachings of many religions and philosophies all leading toward one and the same goal.

128pp, 4 colour throughout   ISBN 0–946551–65–0   Hardcover £12.95

THE NEW AGE IN A NUTSHELL
Lorna St Aubyn

A very accessible introduction to New Age ideas, the merging point of many traditions and perspectives, ancient and modern, and a coherent philosophy for life today. Themes include: astrological ages, reincarnation, karma, healing, earth energies and leylines, guidance, ecology, forgiveness, death, education, family, jobs, authority and sexuality.

96pp, illus.   ISBN 0–946551–58–8   paperback £4.95

JOURNEY THROUGH THE CHAKRAS
Exercises for Healing and Internal Balancing
Klausbernd Vollmar

A new approach to working with the chakras as a path to greater self-aware-ness. It combines insights of humanistic psychology with links to other he-aling systems and astrology. The first part is an introduction to yoga and the chakras, the second is made up of yoga exercises, visualisation techniques and meditations.

176pp, illus.   ISBN 0–946551–42–1   paperback £4.95

MAXIMUM IMMUNITY
Michael A Weiner Ph D

This is the first lay-person's book to explain the immune system clearly and understandable. Diseases resulting from immune deficiency include cancer, rheumatoid arthritis, AIDS, diabetes, rheumatic fever, influenza and various allergies. The book includes a programme to monitor and im-prove the health of your immune system.

336pp   ISBN 0–946551–34–0   paperback £6.95

WHO DIES?
Conscious Living and Conscious Dying
Stephen Levine

This is about participating fully in life as the perfect preparation for whatever may come next, be it sorrow or joy, loss or gain, death or a new wonderment at life. Refreshingly written, Stephen has worked with and writes for dying and bereaved people, showing how living and dying are intimately connected.

332pp   ISBN 0–946551–43–6   paperback £7.95

HEALING INTO LIFE AND DEATH
Stephen Levine

In working with dying people to help them finish business and open their hearts, Stephen found himself healing bodies as well as minds. Here he shares his vision of healing, dealing with choice and application of treatments, pain and grief, forgiveness and teaching others. A compassionate, gentle and timeless guide for anyone seeking any level of healing.

314pp   ISBN 0–946551–48–0   paperback £7.95

LOVING MEDICINE
Patients' Experience of the Holistic Treatment of Cancer
Dr Rosy Thomson

This is a collection of experiences and techniques pioneered at the Bristol Cancer Help Centre. These stories show how physical disease, pain and the depression accompanying cancer and its diagnosis can be overcome. Many case-histories and personal stories, showing how patients have chosen their future, found inner peace, aliveness and fulfilment in the midst of their predicament.

224pp   ISBN 0–946551–49–4   paperback £5.95

CANCER AS A TURNING POINT
A Handbook for People with Cancer, their Families, and Health Professionals.
Lawrence Le Shan Ph D

Most cancer sufferers have an unrealised dream, which, with other healing methods, can change everything. This book is about the use of psychological change and self-healing to help a compromised immune system. Full of advice and wisdom and many case histories, this book is the culmination of a pioneer's work in the holistic treatment of cancer.

224pp   ISBN 0–946551–59–6   paperback £6.95

OPEN THE WINDOW
Practical Ideas for the Lonely and Depressed

Joan Gibson

Loneliness is one of the main causes of depression and can come at any age:
yet it is a state of mind which can be overcome. This book helps you cope,
and discusses procrastination, the panic attack, making friends and using
time more constructively.

   "Only someone who has known depression could write such a personal,
warm book."

(Therapy Weekly)

128pp   ISBN 0–946551–17–0   paperback £4.95

Please write for a complete catalogue to:
GATEWAY BOOKS, The Hollies, Wellow, Bath, BA2 8QJ